Agile Testing

Manfred Baumgartner • Martin Klonk •
Christian Mastnak • Helmut Pichler •
Richard Seidl • Siegfried Tanczos

Agile Testing

The Agile Way to Quality

Manfred Baumgartner
Nagarro GmbH
Vienna, Austria

Martin Klonk
Sixsentix Austria
Vienna, Austria

Christian Mastnak
Nagarro GmbH
Vienna, Austria

Helmut Pichler
Nagarro GmbH
Vienna, Austria

Richard Seidl
Essen, Germany

Siegfried Tanczos
Nagarro GmbH
Vienna, Austria

ISBN 978-3-030-73208-0   ISBN 978-3-030-73209-7   (eBook)
https://doi.org/10.1007/978-3-030-73209-7

Translated from German edition: Agile Testing: Der agile Weg zur Qualität by Carl Hanser Verlag,
© Carl Hanser Verlag München 2018. All Rights Reserved.

This Springer imprint is published by the registered company Springer Nature Switzerland AG.
The registered company address is: Gewerbestrasse 11, 6330 Cham, Switzerland

Foreword

In the winter of 2001, in a remote ski hut in the state of Utah, a conspiratorial clique of well-known software developers called for a revolution in the software world. They created the Agile Manifesto. With this manifesto, the group defined what they were already doing with extreme programming. However, with their written formulation, they succeeded in gaining worldwide attention for their cause. The development experts gathered in this ski hut were fed up with rigid process rules, nonsensical bureaucratic guidelines, and unworldly approaches of the software engineering discipline at the time. They realized that monotonous development, "done by the book", was outdated in the new fast-paced times. They wanted to free themselves from the shackles of project bureaucracy in order to develop software together with the users, as needed. The previously cumbersome, phase-oriented, document-driven software development was to be replaced by flexible, human-driven development with small, manageable steps. Agile software development should be the approach of the new century.

Agile development is not focusing on the project, but the product. As software development became more and more an expedition into the unknown, the product needed to be created little by little in small increments. Instead of writing long declarations of intent or requirement documents about things that one could not know at the time, one should rather program something that can elicit quick feedback from a future user. It should not take months or even years to find out that the project is on the wrong track, or that the project team is overwhelmed by the task at hand. This should be uncovered within a few weeks.

Thus, the basic principle of agile development is incremental delivery. A software system is to be completed piece by piece. This gives the user representative in the team a new opportunity to participate in every step of the development. After each new delivery, they can compare the delivered intermediate product with his ideas. Testing is thus built into the process. The software is continuously tested right from the start. Whether a tester was also to take part in the agile process was left open at first. The authors of the Agile Manifesto spoke out against strict division of labor. The division into analysts, designers, developers, testers, and managers seemed too artificial for them, and was feared to cause too much loss due to friction. Of course, the project team should have all these skills, but the roles within the team should be interchangeable. The development team should be responsible for everything. It was only through the contributions of Lisa Crispin and Janet Gregory that the role of a dedicated tester in the team emerged. They campaigned to ensure that someone in the team would take care of quality issues.

Software development requires both creativity and discipline. Toward the end of the last century, proponents of order and discipline had the upper hand, and sometimes thwarted the creativity of the developers with rigid processes and quality assurance measures. But when something is overdone, it will be reversed in a pendulum swing: too much discipline had been imposed onto traditional development projects. The reaction to it is the agile movement, which was designed to bring the spontaneity and creativity back into software development. This is most certainly to be welcomed, but again this aspect must not be overdone. The creativity of users and developers should remain grounded—and an experienced, impartial tester can support that.

Each development team should have at least one dedicated tester to represent the interests of quality. They ensure that the resulting code and product remains clean and meets the agreed quality or acceptance criteria. In the urge to move faster, non-functional quality requirements may fall behind the functional requirement. It is a tester's job to help the team to maintain a balance between productivity and quality. The tester is the good spirit, so to speak, that keeps the team from making progress at the expense of quality. In each release, not only should functionality be added but quality should also be increased. The code should be regularly cleaned or refactored, documented, and freed of all defects. It is the tester's job to enable the whole team and to ensure that this happens.

Of course, agile project organization also has consequences for testing and quality assurance. The people responsible for quality assurance are no longer in a remote office, from where they monitor the projects, check the project results between the phases, and test the product in the last phase, as was often the case in traditional projects. They are now firmly integrated in development teams, where they constantly verify and validate the newest results. It is their responsibility to point out deficiencies in the architecture and code and to detect any errors in the behavior of the system. The tester's role is developing into an agile quality coach, supporting the team in all quality-related matters. They point out problems and help the team to enhance the quality of their software. Contrary to what some said at the beginning of the Agile Manifesto ("Testers are no longer necessary in agile projects"), their role is more important than ever. Without their contribution, technical debt grows and, sooner or later, brings the project to a standstill.

This book describes agile testing in ten chapters. Chapter 1 describes the cultural change that agile development has brought about. With the Agile Manifesto, the course was set for a reorganization of the IT project landscape. Development should no longer be done rigidly according to the phase concept, but flexibly and in small iterations. An executable sub-product should be presented after each iteration. In this way, solutions are explored, and problems are identified early. The role of quality assurance is changing. Instead of acting as an external authority on the projects, testers are embedded in the project so that they can immediately carry out their tests on-site as participants in the development process. Of course, business organizations have to adapt their management structures accordingly: Instead of waiting on the side for a final result, the business users are asked to actively participate in the project and to control the development via their requirements, i.e., "Stories." On the development side, they work with developers to analyze and specify the desired functionality. On the test side, they work with testers to ensure that the product meets their expectations.

Ultimately, everyone—developers, testers, and users—must adjust to achieve the common goal. Many traditional roles, such as project manager and test manager, are vanishing. Still there are new roles emerging, such as Scrum Masters and Team Tester or Agile Quality Coach. Project management in the traditional sense no longer takes place on a team level. Each team manages itself. The IT world is changing, and, with it, the way people develop software is transforming.

In Chap. 2, which addresses agile process models, the authors focus on the role of quality assurance in agile development projects. They are not afraid to objectively consider the various conflicting goals, for example, between quality and adherence to delivery dates, between quality and budget, and between quality and functionality. The reconciliation of these conflicting goals is a challenge for agile testing.

Contrary to the still common opinion that not much testing is required in agile projects, a lot of testing is in fact necessary. Test-Driven Development (TDD) should not only apply to the unit test, but also to the integration test and system test, according to the motto: first the test cases, then the code. In this case, it means: first the test specification, then the implementation. Test automation plays a crucial role here. Only when a test is automated can the required quality be achieved at the required speed. The whole team should participate in the automation process, as a tester alone will not be able to do it. In addition to the test, audits are also required at certain times during the development of the software product. The aim of the audits is to reveal weaknesses and shortcomings in the software. A good time for this is after every sprint in a Scrum project. The priorities for the next sprint can be set based on the results of the audits. These short audits, or snapshots of the product quality, can be executed by external QA experts in collaboration with the team. The purpose is to help the team identify risks in good time.

In addition to the Scrum process, the second chapter also deals with Kanban and the lean software development process (Lean Software). With the inclusion of examples from the authors' project experience, the reader gets several tips on how to incorporate quality assurance into these processes.

Chapter 3 deals with the agile test organization and the positioning of testing in an agile team. There are quite varying views on this topic. The authors explore which test fits what purpose with the help of the four test quadrants by Crispin and Gregory. On the one hand, the question is asked whether the test is business- or technology-oriented, and on the other hand, whether it relates to the product or the team. Four test types can be derived from this:

1. Unit and component test = technology-oriented/team-supporting
2. Functional test = business-oriented/team-supporting
3. Exploratory test = business-oriented/critique the product
4. Non-functional test = technology-oriented/critique the product

For the explanation of these test approaches, examples from test practice are provided, which show which type of test serves which purpose.

At the end of the chapter, the authors discuss the agile expansion model by Scott Ambler and emphasize how important it is to be able to expand the test process at will. There are core activities that must take place, and marginal activities that are added depending on the stage of expansion. Thus, there are not one but many possible organizational forms depending on the type of product and the project conditions.

The environment in which the project takes place and the product characteristics such as size, complexity, and quality are essential for the selection of the suitable organizational form. In any case, we must not lose sight of the main goal, i.e., the support of the developers. The aim of all test approaches is to uncover problems as quickly and as thoroughly as possible, and to notify the developers in a non-intrusive way. If several agile projects run side by side, the authors recommend setting up a test competence center. The task of this instance is to support the teams in all matters of quality assurance, for example which methods, techniques, and tools they should use. At the end of the chapter, two test organization case studies are presented, one from the telecommunications sector and one from the health sector. In both cases, the test organization is based on the project structure and the respective quality goals.

Chapter 4 raises the question regarding whether an agile tester should be a generalist or a specialist. The answer is, as so often in the literature on agile development, both. It depends on the situation. There are situations, such as at the beginning of an iteration, when the tester might negotiate with the user or product owner about acceptance criteria, in which the tester needs both technical and general knowledge. There are other situations in which testers must deal with automated test tools where the tester needs special technical knowledge. An agile tester must be able to take on many roles, but still the most important thing is that the tester fits into the team as a team player, no matter what role he or she has to take on at the moment. Soft skills are an imperative requirement. In any case, testers are the advocates of quality and they must ensure that the quality is preserved, even when time is running out. For this, they must participate in all discussions about product quality, while simultaneously checking and testing the software. They should uncover problems in good time and ensure that they are resolved as early as possible. Of course, testers cannot do this alone; they need the other team members to contribute. That is why testers must act as a kind of quality coach and help their teammates to identify and solve problems. After all, the quality of the software is a responsibility for the team as a whole.

In the context of the role of the tester in an agile team, the chapter addresses the experience profile of employees. What do the career models look like in the agile world? The fact is that there are no longer fixed roles in agile development. The roles change depending on the situation, including that of the tester. Employees with exclusive experience in traditional development methods can no longer retreat to traditional roles; they need to adapt. This will not be easy for every employee. The authors suggest a training program which prepares for the role of an agile tester. In the program, they emphasize positive experiences and conclude with a confident note that flexible employees, old or young, can grow into the role of an agile tester.

In Chap. 5, the authors turn to the methods and techniques of agile testing. In doing so, they emphasize the differences from conventional, phase-oriented testing. The process starts with the test planning, whereby the plan is much more non-binding than in traditional projects. It should remain flexible and be easy to update. Agile testing is much more intertwined with the development and can no longer be viewed separately as a sub-project in the project. There should be at least one tester in each development team and fully integrated there. Testers should only be accountable to the team. There may be a project manager outside of the team, who serves as a reference for the testers in several teams, but he or she must not have any influence on the work within the team. At most, a project manager has an advisory role. The previous planning, organization, and control of a separate test team under the leadership of a team manager is no longer necessary. It does not fit the agile philosophy of teamwork.

As for the test methods, the methods that best suit the agile approach are emphasized—risk-based testing, value-driven testing, exploratory testing, session-based testing and development-driven by acceptance testing. Conventional test techniques, such as equivalence class partitioning, boundary value analysis, condition analysis, and decision tables or trees, are still applicable, albeit in a different context. They should be already built into the test tools. The importance of test reuse and test repetition is emphasized. All techniques must meet these criteria. The integration test is a never-ending story, and the acceptance test is repeated over and over. The cyclical nature of an agile project creates a redefinition of the test exit criteria. The test never ends—as long as the product continues to grow. At some point the development is declared finished and the product goes into maintenance.

In Chap. 6, the authors describe which documents the testers still must create in an agile project. This includes a testable requirement specification from the user stories, a test design, user documentation, and test reports. The test cases do not count as documentation, but as test ware. A concern of agile development is to reduce the documentation to a minimum. In the past, documentation was, in fact, exaggerated. In an agile development project, only that which is absolutely necessary is documented. It remains to be seen whether a test strategy or test design is necessary. Test cases are essential, but they are part of the software product as well as the code. Therefore, they are not considered documentation.

The most important document is the requirements specification that emerges from user stories. It serves as the basis for the test, the so-called test oracle. The test cases are derived from it and are tested against it. It also contains the acceptance criteria. The only test reports that are really required are test coverage report and defect report. The test coverage report shows what was tested and what was not. The testers need this document as proof that the testing has been done sufficiently. The user needs it to gain trust in the product. The defect report records which deviations have occurred and how they are being handled. These two reports are the best indicators of the state of the test.

Testers are predestined to write the user manual because they know the system best and know how to use it. Someone has to write the manual, and the testers are the right candidates for it. They ensure that this document is updated after each release. Otherwise, the book follows the agile principle of restricting the documentation to the essentials. The main aspect is that there is always a solid requirement specification and comprehensible user documentation. A structured, semi-formal specification of requirements forms the basis for the test and no user wants to do without user instructions.

Chapter 7 explains the important topic of "Test automation." Test automation is particularly important in agile development, as it is the main instrument for project acceleration and necessary to support state-of-the-art DevOps approaches. Only through automation can the test effort be reduced to an acceptable level while maintaining product quality during continuous integration. The authors differentiate in this case between unit test, component integration test, and system test. The unit test is shown in detail using the example of JUnit. It shows how developers must work in a test-driven manner, how to build up test cases, and how to measures the test coverage. The component integration test is explained using the Apache Maven integration server. It is important to simulate the interfaces of the integrated components to the components that are not yet available using placeholders. The system test is described by a technical test with FitNesse. The most important thing here is the writing of the test cases in test scripts, which can be expanded and repeated as required. The authors also emphasize how important it is to be able to manage the test ware—test cases, test scripts, test data, etc. —conveniently and securely so that the test runs as smoothly as possible. Tools are also needed for this.

Chapter 8 adds examples from test tool practice, extending test automation with test management functionality. At first, the Broadcom Rally tool is described, which supports the agile life cycle from the management of stories to error management. The agile tester can plan and control this tool in his test. An alternative to Broadcom Rally is Polarion QA/ALM, which is particularly suitable for recording and prioritizing test cases and for tracking errors. Other test planning and tracking tools include the Bug Genie tools, which particularly support test effort estimation; Atlassian JIRA, which offers extensive error analysis, and the Microsoft Test Manager.

For testers in an agile project, the ongoing integration test is crucial. They must integrate the last components as quickly as possible with the components of the last release and confirm that they work together smoothly. To do this, he or she must conduct the testing not only via the user interface, but also via the internal system interfaces. With Tricentis Tosca, external as well as internal interfaces can be generated, updated, and validated. The test messages are conveniently compiled using the drag-and-drop technique. The authors describe how these tools are used and where their limits lie based on their own project experience.

Chapter 9 is dedicated to the topic of training and its meaning. The authors emphasize the role of employee training in getting started in agile development. Training is essential for success in using the new methods, and this applies particularly to the testers. Testers in an agile team need to know exactly what to focus on, and they can only learn that through appropriate training. There are many interpretations of agile approaches; nevertheless, the quality of the product must be ensured, and this requires professional testers who are trained to work in an agile team. Training programs focused on the needs of agile testing are discussed in this chapter.

In summary, this book covers the essential aspects of agile testing and offers a valuable guideline for testing in an agile environment. The reader gets many suggestions on how to proceed in agile projects. He or she learns how to prepare, conduct, and approve the agile testing. As a book written by test practitioners, it helps testers find their way in an often confusing agile world. It gives them clear, well-founded instructions for implementing agile principles in test practice. It belongs in the library of every organization that runs agile projects.

Harry M. Sneed

Preface

The first German edition of *Agile Testing: The Agile Way to Quality* was published in 2013, followed by the second edition in 2018. Since then, we have been asked again and again by our international contacts and colleagues whether there would be an English translation. Thanks to the support of Nagarro, we were able to realize this project, and we hope that it will be well appreciated by the agile community. As mentioned, this book is a translation of the second edition with some necessary updates and not a completely revised new edition. But the next edition is already included as a Theme in our backlog. Until then, we wish you a great time reading this first English edition!

When the "Manifesto for Agile Software Development" was signed in 2001 by a group of software engineers in Utah, USA, it probably initiated the most significant change in software development since the introduction of object orientation in the mid-1980s. The "Agile Manifesto," quasi the Ten Commandments of the agile world, can certainly be regarded as an expression of a countermovement to the strongly regulating process and planning models that spread from the end of the 1980s onwards, such as PRINCE, the V-Model, or even ISO9001. These models tried to counteract the previously chaotic and arbitrary development processes by planning and structuring the processes and documenting them. The Agile Manifesto consciously positions itself in relation to these aspects and gives its central four agile values—interaction, cooperation with the customer, reacting to changes, and finally functioning software—a higher relevance for a successful software development.

The way the Agile Manifesto is formulated in values and principles was one reason why the triumph of agile software development in the years since the publication of the Agile Manifesto has been marked by many dogmas, not to say religious wars. We, the authors of this book, are seeing this not for the first time. In the decades of our professional experience, we have often been confronted with new solutions for the "software problem": structured programming, object-oriented programming, CASE (Computer-Aided Software Engineering), RUP (Rational Unified Process), V-Model, ISO9001, SOA (Service-Oriented Architecture)—a long list of salvation promises, always accompanied by self-proclaimed gurus; some even call themselves evangelists. And many of these innovations were based on very similar patterns: While they presented themselves as *the* solution or were sold by their promoters as *the* saving idea, previous approaches were dismissed as wrong or outdated. There were also many believers who followed radical ideas, often without reflecting on them and almost without will, because the number of dissatisfied people was and still is large. In this case, the preachers and counselors, who use every hype to make profits, have an easy game—which is a big risk for good ideas.

The last thought was also a central motivation for this book. We, the authors, have always been unhappy with the way people have tried to dogmatically implement new approaches in software development. In most cases the baby was thrown out along with the bath water. In contrast, we see the changes as an opportunity for a process of continuous improvement and optimization. However, we have been confronted in agile projects in recent years with the fact that everything we have acquired and developed as testers in terms of methods, techniques, self-image, or standards (like the test processes according to ISTQB) should no longer apply. This may also be due to the fact that in the past it was mainly the software developers who pushed the agile community. This fact is one of the reasons why the tasks and role of the software tester in agile methods and projects are often not defined or only vaguely defined. Differently interpreted terminologies also contribute to this. For example, when in Scrum we talk about an interdisciplinary development team, some people think that the team only consists of developers (in terms of programmers) who do everything. Others believe that in Test-Driven Development with the development of an automated unit Test Set, the test tasks in development are sufficiently fulfilled and the rest is the responsibility of the user in the User Acceptance Test. So where are the test phases and test levels we are used to? Where and how do we find ourselves as testers in agile projects? The agile approach obviously raises more questions for us testers than it provides answers to previous problems.

These are exactly the challenges we want to tackle with our book, because the book was written by testers for testers. In each chapter we provide answers to the key questions we have come across in our projects. The book deals with general or almost cultural change processes, with questions regarding the approach and organization in software testing, with the use of methods, techniques, and tools, especially test automation, and with the redefined role of the tester in agile projects. A broad spectrum that is certainly not final and comprehensive within the scope of this book, but nevertheless we hope to cover it with ideas and suggestions for the reader.

To make the described aspects even more tangible, the specific topics of this book are accompanied by the description of experiences from concrete software development projects of various companies.

The examples should demonstrate that different approaches can lead to effective solutions that meet the specific challenges of agile projects.

With this in mind, we wish the reader every success in implementing the contents presented here in his or her own projects and at the same time invite him or her to visit us on our Internet platform www.agile-testing.eu.

Practical Examples

The practical example of EMIL in this book comes from a company in the healthcare industry that can look back on 25 years of successful product and software development. However, as the company has grown, new customer requirements and stricter legal regulations have increased, as has the need to optimize development and test processes and make them more efficient. The idea of switching from the traditional to the agile development process has already come up here and there in the company. The software development project EMIL was the starting point for this initiative. The project's goal was the re-implementation of an analysis software that has been successfully used worldwide for ten years and which has been developed by various developers. Particularly from a technical and architectural point of view, the new requirements could no longer be implemented without problems; over the years, many functions were added as "temporary balconies"—but were never removed or integrated. It was estimated that a rough time frame for the re-implementation of all functions of the existing software was about two and a half years. The lack of experience in the target technology and the regulatory requirements that the healthcare industry brings along were identified as the biggest challenges on the way to agile development. The positive and negative experiences, the problems encountered, and the attempts to solve them, from the first year and a half of the project, can be found in this book and are marked accordingly in the corresponding chapters.

Another practical example is provided by OTTO. As an online retailer, OTTO operates in a very agile market environment and uses innovative technologies to ensure a positive shopping experience on otto.de and in the stores. As part of the Otto Group, OTTO is one of the most successful e-commerce companies in Europe and Germany's largest online retailer for fashion and lifestyle in the B2C sector. Over 90% of total sales are generated online. In the practical examples, Ms. Diana Kruse talks about her experiences in her transition from a tester and test manager to Quality Specialist and Quality Coach, visualized by graphics of her colleague Torsten Mangner.

Vienna, Austria   Manfred Baumgartner
Vienna, Austria   Martin Klonk
Vienna, Austria   Christian Mastnak
Vienna, Austria   Helmut Pichler
Essen, Germany   Richard Seidl
Vienna, Austria   Siegfried Tanczos

Acknowledgments

We thank the companies Nagarro GmbH and Otto (GmbH & Co KG) for their contribution to the work on this book.

We would also like to thank our colleagues for their diligent support, and our reviewers, who kept us grounded with critical remarks and made a valuable contribution to this book: Sonja Baumgartner (Graphics), Stefan Gwihs, Diana Kruse and Torsten Mangner (practical examples and graphics Otto.de), Anett Prochnow, Petra Scherzer, Michael Schlimbach, Silvia Seidl, and Harry Sneed. Also, our sincere thanks to our editor, who fixed the countless errors in copy-editing that we had overlooked.

Contents

About the Authors

Manfred Baumgartner Manfred Baumgartner has more than 30 years of experience in software development, especially in software quality assurance and software testing. After studying computer science at the Vienna University of Technology he worked as a software engineer for a large software company in the banking sector and later as quality manager for a CRM solution provider. Since 2001 he has built up and expanded the QA consulting and training offerings of Nagarro GmbH, one of the leading service providers in the field of software testing. He is member of the board of the Association for Software Quality and Further Education (ASQF) and the Association for Software Quality Management Austria (STEV) as well as a member of the Austrian Testing Board (ATB). He contributes his extensive experience in both classic and agile software development as a sought-after speaker at internationally renowned conferences and as author and co-author of relevant technical books: *The System Test - From Requirements to proven Quality* (2006, 2008, 2011), *Software in Numbers* (2010), *Test Automation Foundation* (2012, 2015, 2021), and *Agile Testing: The Agile Way to Quality* (2013, 2017).

Martin Klonk Martin Klonk is a Senior Test Expert at Sixsentix Austria GmbH. Trained as an industrial engineer at the Technical University of Berlin (and the Université Libre de Bruxelles), he started his career in 1996 as a Software Test Specialist at SQS Software Quality Systems in Cologne and Munich. Later he moved to SQS, ANECON, and Nagarro Austria in Vienna. Martin Klonk has worked in a wide variety of industries and has been actively involved in almost all areas of software testing. As a member of the Austrian Testing Board of the ISTQB he regularly contributes to curricula and their German translation and also conducts training courses. Since he managed to implement successful testing strategies in an agile project in 2007, Martin Klonk has been a strong advocate of agile practices in testing and has led several agile projects as a testing specialist. He is a certified tester, project manager, and scrum master.

Christian Mastnak Christian Mastnak works as principal software testing consultant at Nagarro with over 15 years of QA experience. He leads Nagarro's global "Agile Testing Practice" and implements innovative solutions for international customers in a variety of industries. Pursuing a very hands-on approach in all his projects, he enjoys switching between different QA roles—from Test Manager to Agile Quality Coach, from Test Automation Architect to Test Consultant. These roles allow him to pursue his passion for continuous improvement of QA processes and methodologies. Christian Mastnak has shared his expertise as a popular trainer and speaker at international conferences including 'EuroSTAR' and 'Agile Testing' in Munich and the 'Software Quality Days' in Vienna.

Helmut Pichler Helmut Pichler is responsible for the trainings at Nagarro GmbH and works as a consultant for test and quality management in both domains, traditional and agile. He has actively witnessed the "growth" of agile at conferences and in the community from the beginning and is one of the first trainers of the former Certified Agile Tester (now PAQ) training program developed by iSQI. Helmut Pichler has been President of the Austrian Testing Board, the regional representation of the ISTQB in Austria, for more than 15 years and is an active member of the international testing community, working with experts from Austria and in close cooperation with the Swiss and German Testing Boards, contributing to the updating and further development of international testing standards.

Richard Seidl Richard Seidl is an agile quality coach and software test expert. He has seen and tested a lot of software in his diverse professional career: the good, the bad, and the ugly. The big and the small, the old and the new one. He now combines his experiences into an integrated approach—development and testing processes can only be successful if the most diverse forces, as well as strengths and weaknesses, are balanced. Just as an ecosystem can only exist harmoniously with all aspects in all its quality, the processes in the testing environment must be viewed as a network of different key players. Agile and quality then becomes an attitude that we can practically live for instead of just working it off. He has published various specialist books and articles as an author and co-author, including "The System Test - From Requirements to proven Quality" (2006, 2008, 2011), *The Integration Testing - From Design and Architecture to Component and System Integration* (2012) and "Test Automation Foundation" (2012, 2015, 2021).

Siegfried Tanczos Siegfried Tanczos has been working at Nagarro GmbH since 2004 and has also been a team leader and manager in the software test organization for many years. In addition to his management role, Siegfried Tanczos has been involved in several software testing projects since the beginning of his employment at Nagarro. He has gained a wide range of experience in software testing during his professional career in the banking world, and has been working as a software tester since 1998. Through his work at Nagarro in various customer projects and business units, Siegfried Tanczos has been able to gain extensive experience in dealing with classic and agile process models.

Agile: A Cultural Change

In order to better understand the cultural change toward agile software development and to understand "Agile Testing" not only as a buzzword, it is important to take a look into the past. Much of what we perceive today as common knowledge has its justification in the methodical and technical progress of software technology in the last 30 years. Experience is an essential element of innovation and improvement. For example, the average age of the signatories of the Agile Manifesto in 2001 was about 47 years, and back then it wasn't just about doing everything differently; it was about doing it better. This is often overlooked when "agile" is used to simply get rid of unpleasant things or to hide one's own weaknesses. The honest approach to developing software in a cooperative, benefit-oriented, and efficient, economic way is the core of the agile idea.

1.1   The Journey to Agile Development

The transition to agile development in the practice of IT projects has been ongoing for a long time, since the spread of object-oriented programming in the late 1980s and early 1990s. The object-oriented approach changed the way software is developed. The primary goals of object orientation were

- Increased productivity through reuse
- Reduction in the amount of code through inheritance and association
- Facilitation of code changes with smaller, exchangeable code blocks
- Limitation of the effect of errors by encapsulation of the code modules (Meyer, 1997)

These objectives were fully justified, as the old procedural systems were getting bigger and bigger and bursting at the seams. The amount of code threatened to grow

M. Baumgartner et al., *Agile Testing*, https://doi.org/10.1007/978-3-030-73209-7_1

immeasurably. Therefore, a way had to be found to reduce the amount of code for the same functionality. The answer was object orientation. New programming languages such as C++, C#, and Java emerged. The developers began to switch to the new programming technology (Graham, 1995).

However, this technological improvement also had a price—the increase in complexity. By decomposing the code into small, reusable blocks, the number of relationships, i.e., dependencies between code blocks, increased. In procedural software, the complexity lay in the individual blocks, whose flow logic was increasingly nested. In object-oriented software, complexity was outsourced to the architecture. This made it difficult to maintain an overview of the entire system and to plan a suitable architecture in advance. The code had to be revised several times until an acceptable solution was found. Until then the code was often in a messy state.

There were two answers to this challenge. One was modeling. During the 1990s, different modeling languages were proposed: OMT, SOMA, OOD, etc. In the end, one of them prevailed: UML. By representing the software architecture in a model, it should be possible to find the optimal structure and to gain and keep the overview. The developers would—as expected—create the "suitable" model and then implement it in the concrete code (Rumbaugh, Blaha, Premerlani, Eddy, & Lorensen, 1991).

Software engineering changed from procedural to object-oriented modeling with use cases. Modeling was much more detailed and was supported by new tools like Rational Rose (Jacobson, 1992). However, modeling proved to be very tedious, even with the best tool support. The developer needed quite a lot of time to work out the model in every detail. In the meantime, the requirements had changed and the assumptions on which the model was based were no longer valid. The modeler had to start from scratch, and the customer was getting more and more impatient.

Another answer to the challenge of increasing complexity was "Extreme Programming" (Beck, 1999). Since the appropriate model for the software was not predictable, the developers began to translate the requirements directly into the code in close communication with the user and in short iterations (Beck, 2000).

This approach carries the risk of getting lost in a dead end due to constant change requests in many details but has the advantage that the customer soon sees what is coming. If the code blocks are designed flexibly, they can be reused if a different path needs to be taken. Another advantage of the Extreme Programming was that the user could be taken along on the journey. The user could follow the results of the coding—the real user interfaces, lists, messages, and database content—which he or she could not do in the case of abstract modeling. Thus, in practice, Extreme Programming prevailed, and modeling remained in the academic corner (Fig. 1.1).

The "Test-Driven Development" turned out to be a useful consequence of the Extreme Programming (Beck, 2003). When entering unknown territory, one must protect oneself. The safeguard in code development is the test framework. The developers first build a test framework and then fill it with small blocks of code (Janzen & Kaufmann, 2005). Each component is tested immediately to see if it

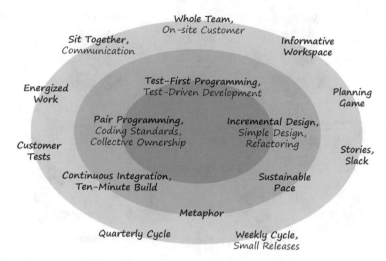

Fig. 1.1 XP practices

works. The developers make their way through the code area and always ensure its status by testing. In this way they finally reach a satisfactory, tested intermediate state which they can demonstrate to the user.

There are only intermediate states in software development, since software, by definition, is never completely finished. Test-Driven Development has proven to be a very solid approach even outside Extreme Programming. This has also been confirmed by several scientific studies, and unit testing and continuous integration have become standard in software development.

It goes without saying that Extreme Programming and Test-Driven Development contradicted the prevailing management methods. The management of software projects requires predictable, pre-dispositioned development where it is possible to determine what will be delivered, when, and at what cost. Systematic Software Engineering should ensure this (see Fig. 1.2).

The 1990s were also the decade of process models, quality management, and independent testing, in short, the decade of software engineering. Software engineering was intended to bring order to software development and maintenance through clearly defined processes with a strict division of labor. Free, unrestricted development was abolished. Many measures were taken by management to finally bring software development under control. The V-Model is representative of these attempts to structure software development (Höhn & Höppner, 2008). Unfortunately, most of these measures were in stark contradiction to the new "extreme" development technology.

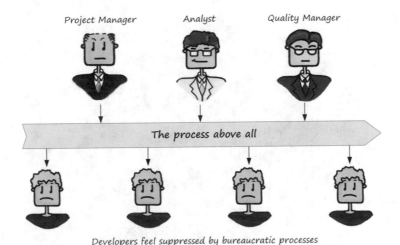

Fig. 1.2 Software engineering creates order in a chaotic software world

1.2   The Reasons for Agile Development

One of the most important reasons for agile development is user proximity. In classical, non-agile development, the gap between developers and users has widened. In the 1970s, this gap was not so wide. When Harry Sneed, who was kind enough to write a foreword to this book, began his career as a programmer, the developer shuttled back and forth between the customers in the engineering department, his/her desk, and the data center every day. The developer discussed the task with the user almost daily, wrote the program, and tried it out in the data center, usually in the evening. Being close to the customer was the most important thing.

This way of working changed in the 1980s and 1990s. In the traditional test world, which was created by Gelperin and Hetzel in the mid-1980s, there is a fundamental distrust toward the developer. It is assumed that the developers—on their own initiative—will produce faulty and poor-quality software (Hetzel, 1988). Moreover, they do not recognize their own errors, and if they do, they are declared as inevitable characteristics of the software: "It's a feature, not a bug." They do not let anyone talk about the quality of their architecture and code. In their eyes, everything is always fine. There is no need to improve it.

With this image of the developer in mind, the call for a separate test organization was raised. For larger projects, there should be a separate test group that supervises several projects. In any case, the test group had to be independent of the developers. This was the prerequisite for the testers to be able to work effectively. A system should be created in which the testers control the work of the developers. The developers produce the bugs and the testers find them. A bug reporting and tracking system should support the communication between the two groups.

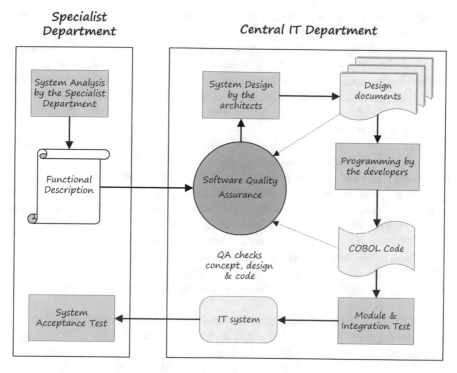

Fig. 1.3 The Software Engineering Model Bertelsmann

This division of labor between developers and testers has been propagated and practiced worldwide. New terms such as "Quality Engineering" and "Quality Management" were created and it was deemed that every larger organization should have a quality manager. This was required by the ISO 9000 standards. And where there is management, there is also bureaucracy. A software quality bureaucracy was established, based on standards and regulations, to guide developers to work correctly (ISO 9000, 2005).

The development process at Bertelsmann AG—the Bertelsmann Software Engineering Model—was a typical example. According to this model, the specialist department should first create a complete functional description of the topic. This was accepted by the quality assurance and development departments and an estimate of the effort required was prepared (Bender, et al., 1983) (see Fig. 1.3).

Based on this cost estimate, an agreement was reached with the specialist department, with a fixed price, a fixed date, and a fixed result. The requirements were then frozen and initially implemented in a system design. This was presented to the customer, who rarely understood it or, more precisely, could have understood it. Most of the time, the users just nodded their heads and said it was okay. The system design was followed by implementation and testing, whereby the testing was always a bottleneck. The finished system was presented to the user many months, sometimes even years, later. The reaction of the user was often that he or she would not have expected it this way. At Bertelsmann, this well-intentioned but cumbersome process eventually led to the reorganization of IT and the distribution of developers among the departments. Other German companies had also adopted the Bertelsmann Model, but the result was usually the same as at Bertelsmann: disappointed users. The conclusion is that the separation of developers and users has never worked well.

A classic example of a bureaucratic development process is the V-Model or the V-Modell-XT (Rausch & Broy, 2006). This model was primarily designed for software development in the German authorities. It prescribes every step in the process. The demands are collected and defined in a requirements specification. Based on the specifications, a project is put out to tender and offers are gathered. The cheapest or best offer is selected, and the winner of the tender then draws up a functional specification and presents it to the client. If the client understands something about it, the client has the opportunity to make corrections. The system is then implemented and tested. Many months later, the more or less tested final product is handed over to the client for acceptance. It often turns out that the product in the form in which it is delivered cannot be used or cannot be used to the expected extent, and thus the maintenance or evolution process begins. Changes are made in and around the software until it finally meets the user's expectations. This can take years.

In 2009 Tom DeMarco literally wrote the death sentence for such rigid, bureaucratic development processes. He stated that software engineering is an approach "whose time has come and gone" (DeMarco, 2009). From the very beginning, software engineering was aligned to large projects such as those of the United States Department of Defense, which required a strict division of roles. Looking back, we must ask ourselves whether the approach has ever worked for smaller projects. In fact, there was something seriously wrong from the beginning: the long time span between the award of the development contract and the delivery of the final product. During this time, requirements and customer expectations had changed too much. This was already the case in the 1980s and is even more the case now in our fast-moving world. Ergo, proximity to the customer, the principal, must be maintained and development cycles must be shortened.

What applies to the collaboration between developers and users also applies to the collaboration between developers and testers. Here too, the gap had widened over time. When the testing discipline emerged in the late 1970s, developers usually tested their software themselves. At that time, the outsourcing of testing was a revolutionary event. In recent years it has become a matter of course. However, the criticism here is the same as for software development. The time span between the handover to the tester and the first error messages is simply too long. When the first error messages arrive, the developer has already forgotten how they were created. This is the reason why testers and developers should work together on a piece of software and why testers must test the finished component immediately after its creation. Afterwards, the developer can discuss the problems with the tester immediately and fix them until the next component delivery. This fast feedback is the key to agile testing. It must be done quickly, otherwise the agile test will fail (Fig. 1.4).

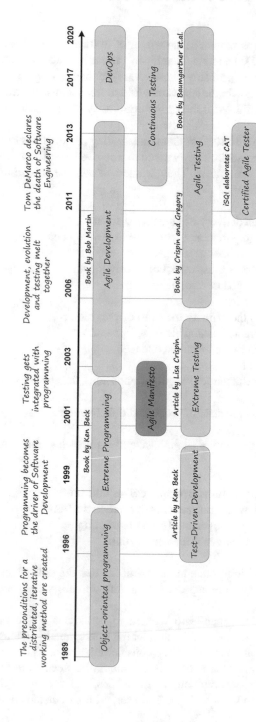

Fig. 1.4 The history of agile development

1.3   The Significance of the Agile Manifesto for Software Testing

The Agile Manifesto was written in the winter of 2001 at a ski lodge in the state of Utah (Beck, et al., 2001). The term "manifesto" already indicates something revolutionary and was therefore probably chosen very deliberately by the authors. They wanted to start a revolution in the software world to free themselves from the tyranny of processes, and they did. With their revolution, they have succeeded in changing this world profoundly.

The motives of the authors, all of them outstanding personalities of the American programmer scene, were noble: They wanted to improve the software world for users and developers at the same time. They wanted to achieve this through "Twelve Principles of Agile Software" :

- Early and continuous delivery of valuable software.
- Welcome changing requirements, even late in development.
- Deliver working software at short intervals.
- Business and developers must work constantly together.
- Trust in highly motivated development teams.
- Face-to-face conversation.
- Working software is the primary measure of progress.
- Agile processes promote sustainable development.
- Continuous attention to technical excellence.
- Simplicity is essential.
- Flexible, mature architectures, requirements, and designs emerge from self-organizing teams.
- Regular reflection on the state of work and effectiveness.

In the manifesto, the authors emphasize the following four "revolutionary" values:

- **Individuals and interactions over processes and tools**
- **Working software over comprehensive documentation**
- **Customer collaboration over contract negotiation**
- **Responding to change over following a plan**

The authors also explicitly state in the manifesto that the aspects on the right side also have their value, but the aspects on the left side are valued higher by them (Beck, et al., 2001).

The 17 authors of the manifesto wanted to break out of the protectorate of software bureaucrats—administrative project managers, quality managers, auditors, process fetishists, and all those who they consider unnecessary people who monitor and prevent software projects. Programmers should be freed from the shackles of what they see as nonsensical regulations, guidelines, and standards. They should be released to do their own work with the end user, without outside control.

This may sound very promising from a developer's point of view. Programmers have always complained about obstructions by management and quality assurance. Developers always try to pursue their creative urge unhindered and hate nothing more than attempts to stop them. This conflict between creativity on the one hand and discipline on the other has always been a problem in software development. Harry Sneed has pointed this out in an article about the Data Processing Handbook 1976 entitled "Organization of Software Manufacturing and Maintenance" (Sneed, 1976). More creativity is required when designing and developing a software product. More discipline is emphasized in maintenance and further development. The fathers of agile development emphasized creativity. The date on which the manifesto was published is significant—the year 2001, which followed a decade of attempts to bring order to development projects through phase concepts, process models, quality guidelines, process ideologies, independent testing, and a range of other regulatory and standardization measures. From the beginning, these measures were unpopular among the developers themselves, and they often offered passive resistance to what they deemed to be a restrictive system. They announced their revolution with the Agile Manifesto.

It goes without saying that this new movement was mainly directed against previous management methods. These include quality assurance by external technocrats and the separation of development and testing. According to the original ideology of agile development, developers should take care of the quality of their software themselves and testers, if at all, should only support them. Unfortunately, this attitude has long prevailed in many agile projects. A change of power has taken place. It should come as no surprise that the word "manager" has now become a non-word. There is the user representative, the product owner, and the scrum master, but no managers—neither project nor product managers. In an agile project the team manages itself (Schwaber, 2007).

For testers and quality assurance experts, this revolution initially also meant a loss of roles and power. The tasks and the role of the software tester in agile methods and projects are often not or not clearly defined. But Martin Fowler already pointed out in his essay "The New Methodology" that there are many other people involved in the software development process besides the software developer, including testers (Fowler, 2000). These are also part of the interdisciplinary team, such as programmers, architects, and analysts. However, all those people involved must think in an interdisciplinary way and increasingly take on tasks that go beyond their central responsibilities. This rethinking is also a challenge for the testers. In agile teams, the developer can sometimes take on testing tasks and the tester will—depending on the demands and the development skills—also take over development tasks. However, it would be a mistake to assume that this is so simple: a trained developer cannot become a good tester by pushing a button, nor are testers automatically equipped with the appropriate programming experience. It would also be fatal not to have excellent representation of all software engineering disciplines in the team. Agile methods require the highest level of expertise and experience:

- Analysts who clearly understand user requirements and can grasp them as a whole
- Experienced architects who design architecture that does not lead to chaos through constant change
- Programmers who write code in such a way that the same applies to it as to the architecture, and who consequently define unit tests that do more than just test the existence of classes and their methods
- Professional testers who adapt their test approaches and test methods to the specific and constantly changing tasks and who increase the degree of automation in system testing during development

1.4   Agile Requires a Cultural Change Among the Users

The revolution triggered by the Agile Manifesto is not limited to software development projects. It also has an impact on the user organizations where the projects take place. These impacts were expected. If the way projects are carried out is fundamentally changed, the conditions under which the projects take place must also change. In this case, the project processes can no longer be defined in advance. Each project, like water, must find its own way to its goal. The goal may change as the project progresses. An agile project can be compared to an expedition to a foreign world without maps. The expedition team has to explore its own way.

Traditional methods of project planning and control are outdated in an agile world (Mainusch, 2012). At the start of an agile project, nobody can predict how much it will cost or by when the goal will be reached. We can specify a time limit and an effort/costs limit, but not what will be implemented by then. The client just gets what can be achieved with the productivity of the team in time for the money. The available time and cost determine the scope of functionality and the quality that the project can deliver with its productivity. What is implemented in terms of content only emerges in the course of the project along the constantly changing requirements and priorities.

According to the traditional approach, functionality and quality are specified, and it is up to the project manager to calculate how much time and effort is needed to achieve the specified goal. Based on his calculation, an agreement is made with the user, and this agreement remains binding. Contracts between the client and the contractor are also concluded based on these calculations, which sometimes include penalties for the contractor if the contractor does not comply with the agreement. If the required functionality is not achieved within the agreed time by the agreed resources, first the quality is reduced, and if this is not sufficient, the unfulfilled functionality is moved to the so-called maintenance phase. According to the Standish Group's regular Chaos Reports, very few IT projects achieve their specified functionality within the planned time and effort (Standish Group, 2013). Nevertheless, IT users are under the illusion that they can plan their IT projects. The Agile Manifesto does away with this. The cooperation between client and contractor takes precedence over contracts and fixed agreements. According to the Agile Manifesto, we are supposed to jointly explore and work toward our goals, and, considering new findings, we are free to change these goals at any time. In doing so, we adapt our goals to what can be achieved.

In this respect, the agile movement does have an influence on the organization. The management can no longer set fixed goals with fixed costs and a fixed deadline. The management itself must be flexible. The goals are no longer formulated in terms of a requirements specification, but as value/benefit created for the organization. The functionality and quality that can be achieved is left to the agile development team—which also includes the users. The management can only set a time and cost limit, but these limits can also be adjusted if it makes economic sense. The management only has a trend-setting function. There are no longer any directives on how projects should be carried out. Management's influence on this is limited by the agile approach (Gloger, 2013).

What applies to management also applies to operational quality assurance. The quality assurance department, under the direction of the quality manager, was responsible for ensuring the quality of the software delivered by the projects. This has led to the separation of testing from development. The dual approach with one development track and one parallel test track has been propagated for more than 20 years.

With the introduction of agile development, central departments for quality assurance and quality management have been questioned or are simply no longer needed. A large part of the responsibility for quality is transferred to the agile teams and to the employees of the specialist departments involved. This applies both to the definition of quality requirements and their review and to the procedure for how they are to be achieved.

The testers of the central test teams work directly in the agile project teams. Although the role of a test manager no longer exists, the previous test or quality assurance department becomes a resource pool and support organization for the various agile projects in an organization (Golze, 2008).

If we look at it that way, the quality managers and test managers are the big losers of this turnaround. Unless they understand how to redefine their role.

In every revolution there are winners and losers. The other losers here are the systems analysts who have written the requirements specifications so far. They are no longer needed, at least not in the role of a link between the user and the developer. In the agile world, they can only act as user representatives and formulate stories. However, to do this, they need much deeper business expertise than most analysts have had in the past. To act as true end-user representatives, they need to adopt their view and to have the same level of knowledge about the subject.

The clear winners of the agile revolution are the developers and potentially also the end users if they seize the opportunity and actively participate in the design of future application systems, especially in the role of a product owner (Fig. 1.5).

Fig. 1.5 The user as a central role in the agile project: product owner

1.5   Consequences of Agile Development for Software Quality Assurance

Of course, the rise of agile software development has many impacts on software testing, for example spatial and time-related consequences.

1.5.1   Spatial Consequences

The testers were mostly separated from the developers. In the past, the testers worked on a separate floor of a high-rise building or in another building and visited the developers from time to time. This was a result of the philosophy that quality assurance must be independent to be effective. Quality assurance even had the right to delay or stop a release. This often ended up in trench warfare, with the head of the QA group getting into a fight with the head of development. The developers wanted to release their software as early as possible, and the quality assurance people felt that the software was not mature enough. Decisions were often escalated to senior management. The conflict was incorporated and was also intended according to the principle of "Checks and Balances"(Evans, 1984).

For the analysis of the requirements documents and draft documents as well as for the inspection of the code, quality assurance received the relevant documents via the official channels and had a certain amount of time to review them. The auditors wrote their reports and submitted them to the development department. They then met to discuss the results of the audit. For testing the software, the development department had to deliver its compiled and unit-tested component to a test library, from where it was taken over by the quality assurance department for integration and system testing. The testers performed their prepared test runs and reported the errors found to the developers. The developers fixed the errors and returned the component.

This was repeated back and forth until the quality assurance department decided that the software had been sufficiently tested, or until management decided to release the software despite quality defects (Sneed, 1983).

Since the developers and testers were separated, a typical "us and them" mentality began to emerge. The developers considered the testers to be overly pedantic troublemakers, while the testers considered the developers to be incapable of doing their job properly and as employees whom they needed to train and educate. This understanding of roles, combined with the physical separation, often came at the price of the project. Instead of concentrating on content, the "opponents" became entangled in unnecessary disputes over formalities. The confrontation was further intensified by the spatial separation.

When the developers and testers physically sit together, the fronts begin to blur. The fathers of agile development assumed that everything would get better when the organizational walls were broken down. Physical proximity and the common goal defuse the inevitable conflicts (Gloger & Häusling, 2011). This aspect must be considered today when thinking about development and testing activities in different outsourcing strategies or in agile teams distributed around the world. The communication possibilities have improved dramatically since the publication of the agile principles, but still "business and developers must work constantly together" and "face-to-face conversation" are not automatically fulfilled by the installation of a video communication software.

1.5.2   Time-Related Consequences

In terms of time, agile development has further consequences for quality assurance. The time in which it could check the documents and test the system no longer exists. Traditionally, quality inspectors spent several days checking and evaluating a requirements document or system design. If they now check user stories at all, they do so only the day they are being told (as in the case of Scrum in sprint planning). Otherwise it is too late: the story is implemented immediately. Previously, the testing process took several weeks, if not months, for traditional quality assurance. The system remained in testing until most of the bugs were fixed—and that could take weeks or months depending on the size of the system. The developer would wait to fix the bugs and the user would wait until he or she could finally see the system.

In the case of agile development, there are no weeks or months to test a system. The system is built piece by piece, and each piece is tested within a few days. If a release cycle is to last a maximum of four weeks, there is a maximum of a few days for final testing of a release. The technology of "Continuous Integration" offers the possibility and necessity of "Continuous Testing" (Duvall, Glover, & Matyas, 2007). Each component is tested as soon as it is developed. Testing begins on the day the first component is produced.

This is a significant change compared to the traditional way of working. In this approach, testers had months to develop a test plan, specify test cases, and write test scripts. In agile development, the preparation time has shrunk to a few days—the short time until the first component is delivered. As a result, testers must learn to plan and execute in parallel. While testing one component, they plan to test the next component. They must complete several tasks simultaneously.

No one can claim that agile development will make life easier for testers. They have little time to complete their tasks and must constantly consider which task they prefer to carry out next. There is no test manager who plans and assigns the test work for them. The testers must manage themselves and schedule their time on their own. This may be a big challenge for some testers, but they must accept the challenge to keep up with the team. The agile test is designed for quick reactions. The developers step in a certain direction, and the testers have to follow this. In this respect, agile testing is not for ponderous, inflexible people. The emphasis is on the here and now.

Time is the decisive factor in agile development. Testers must therefore ensure that the quality is as high as possible under the given constraints of time. The shortened time changes the working conditions and often comes at the expense of quality. The result is technical debt, which we will talk about later. It will probably be the case that it is more important to build the right product incompletely than the wrong product correctly. In the end, however, this will be judged by the user. There are follow-up releases where the quality can be improved. Maintenance takes place in the development team. The most important thing is that the user gets a reasonably functional product as soon as possible (Martin, 2002).

Project EMIL: Cultural Change—What Agile Means

The conversion of a development and testing process that has "grown historically" over the last 20 years will not work overnight. Many information flows, processes, and methods have been introduced and are not easy to change. Within a project, the transition to an agile approach can be controlled. The most important thing is acceptance or at least tolerance by the management. The change process is more difficult at the interfaces between the project and the rest of the company. The EMIL project was not intended to change all processes in the company, but rather to start a pilot project. To allow the project team to fully concentrate on its work, the interfaces with the other departments were handled by the scrum master and the product owner. For example, the product owner transferred the project progress into a milestone plan to provide an external group of stakeholders with information they need for their work. This did not burden the project team. In addition, classic project status reports were written and made available to management. Here again, the project team was not involved.

At the same time, the scrum master and the product owner presented the know-how and experience in the company to dispel the prejudices and myths of the agile approach. One of these myths is development speed. For example, some managers expect faster developments through the agile approach. But

(continued)

this is not the case. One more reason for team members to point out what the project has defined as "agile" and what is essential for application developments in the healthcare industry: agile does not mean "faster"; agile means "higher quality."

Agile Process Models and Their View on Quality Assurance

Centralized quality assurance groups or departments are practically not envisaged in the agile world. But quality assurance is as important in agile process models as it is in conventional and long-established software development models. However, the approach to quality assurance itself is a little different: more important is customer satisfaction and thus customer benefit, which requires that the structure of the project teams, the roles of the individual project members, and the working methods and techniques in the entire software development process are designed accordingly.

The early involvement of the customer in the development process is intended to ensure that the customer's requirements are implemented as desired. It is also important in this case that the customer does not evaluate or accept the delivered software only at the end of a software development project, but continuously during the acceptance of individual and short implementation cycles. In terms of close coordination between the customer and the project team, this basic rule is largely responsible for ensuring that change requests from the customer, as well as clarifications from the customer, can be processed and implemented promptly.

To achieve high quality of the software to be delivered, test automation is very important in an agile environment—especially in the area of regression tests. The software developed in short cycles must be checked by automated regression test cases and after several iterations the error-free implementation of customer requirements must be confirmed.

Quality assurance in agile projects also means that the entire team, which is responsible for the implementation of customer requirements, sets the course for a successful project through close coordination, collaboration, and communication. If everyone involved has the same understanding of the requirements and the problems and solutions that arise, the project will finish successfully.

In agile process models, audits are also used to reflect the project progress and experience—both positive and negative—and subsequently define improvement measures for the subsequent implementation cycles. These learning cycles are crucial for the continuous improvement of operational implementation, collaboration, and communication, but above all, for the quality of the software packages to be delivered.

2.1   Challenges in Quality Assurance

- The experience of the authors in projects in the field of software testing shows that the challenges in quality assurance with traditional process models are recurring and often the same—depending on the maturity level of the project and/or company organization.
- The test, as an integral part of a successful project, often needs a lot of strength, effort, and persuasion. Setting up a functioning software test in an organization and in projects does not happen overnight. For this, many framework conditions and influencing factors need to be considered and measures need to be taken that have little chance of success without adequate support from the organization and management. This principle also applies when introducing agile process models—especially when changing from traditional models that have been in use for a long time to agile methods. It is important to do a lot of persuading to be able to carry out the transformation process quickly and at a high level of quality.

2.1.1   Quality and Deadline

Which software tester is not familiar with this challenge? Ensure quality, even if the time until the planned roll-out is already very short. In addition to general difficulties that may arise in the pre-project phase, such as budget questions, resource provision, and technical issues, the integration of the software test is often forgotten or not even considered. A full integration of the test is a key success factor in the entire software development process in traditional process models, and this applies particularly to agile projects.

Quality and deadlines are very much related to the term "time to market". The time between product development and product launch on the market is becoming an increasingly important factor in these fast-moving times. The credo is to quickly establish new products on the market that are of interest to end customers. This also includes the idea of keeping the time between the product idea, product development, and product delivery short. Above all this stands the "competitive advantage," which can only be achieved for those who are the first to cross the finish line. Achieving good prices on the market is only possible for those who are the first to launch their idea or product. Many industries at present are shaped by this "time to market" view.

For this reason, it is important not only to consider the required functions and advantages of the customer when introducing a product, but also to ensure a high quality of the product in general. In the age of new media, errors in products and software quickly become known to a broad public.

In traditional process models in software development, it often happens that the product quality is reduced by shortening the planned time frame for test execution when deadlines are threatened. Agile methods follow the approach of constantly paying attention to quality and checking it with suitable measures and methods and securing it in a sustainable way. Continuous Integration, test automation, team structure, and the know-how of the team members are just a small extract. The quality assurance approach is implicitly linked to agile methods. Software quality in agile projects is primarily based on the defined process elements that are the basis for successful projects and products.

2.1.2 Quality and Budget

Software development projects—like product developments in other industries—are always faced with the challenge of meeting the requirements of the product with the budget provided. The provision of budget can become an administrative hurdle, especially in large organizational units and companies. When the decision is finally made regarding how much budget is available for which product measure, various general conditions may have already changed in such a way that the original acceptance of the required budget is no longer valid and the budget decision process has to be reopened. Weeks and months can pass before a final budget decision is made.

Priorities are inevitably set for budget questions for the realization of a project. Typically, the following questions are asked: Which strategic measures are implemented during which project? Which product or project secures us a good position in the market and brings the necessary turnover, which an organization needs for economic success? These are just a few decision questions, but experience has shown that the relevant budget funds are made available for "important projects" to be equipped for implementation and, above all, for quality assurance.

One thing is clear in any case: testing software costs money, as does not testing software. Costs are always associated with a certain amount of pain. And the (cost) pain is worse when customers are confronted with poor quality and a lot of money has to be spent to improve software that has already been delivered, thus restoring customer satisfaction. However, in addition to the cost of these repairs, imminent or existing damage to the organization's image is a far greater loss.

But what can we do if the quality of a software leaves much to be desired, or if there is generally no or too little budget for quality assurance measures?

It will be inevitable to make the lack of quality and the related causes visible, on the one hand to derive concrete countermeasures from it and, on the other, to receive a budget for the implementation of improvement measures. If a product is characterized by a lack of quality, there are ultimately only two solutions:

1. Investment in quality improvement and, thus, quality assurance for suitable sustainability
2. Living with the shortcomings in quality and taking selective measures to avert major damage

In agile approaches, however, a sometimes only roughly specified budget framework is not yet matched by a finally specified product. This arises in the course of the project. The budget is used to design the software application according to the current business requirements. Therefore, there is no fixed budget for the implementation of a predefined quality assurance plan or a detailed test concept. The budget for quality assurance and testing is part of the project budget, but like the conventional approaches, the quality assurers, mostly testers, have to stand up for "their" part of the budget and, sometimes, also fight for it in an agile environment.

2.1.3   The Importance of Software Testing

It is undeniable that software must be tested—in whatever form, with whichever means and whatever tools. The year 2000 and the associated necessary software adaptations or new developments gave software testing an important status, as the risk was simply too great to have software that did not work from one day to the next and thus the everyday needs of people, such as withdrawing cash from an ATM, would no longer be fulfilled. For this reason, a great deal has been invested in testing across all sectors and areas. And in retrospect, it must be stated that this investment has also been worthwhile.

The topic of software testing itself has become "socially acceptable"—and in a professional manner. While at the beginning it was mainly internal employees and testers who were responsible for quality assurance, there are now many companies whose focus is on testing software. Different approaches, strategies, and methods, supported by the use of commercial or open-source tools, show that testing has generally become more important.

The need for testing in general is also noticeable in the fact that the number of appropriately trained and certified testers has increased significantly in recent years and the "qualified tester" is increasingly required for tenders for projects. In addition to methodical know-how, special technical skills—especially in the area of non-functional testing—and experience as an "agile tester" are in high demand.

Even if the trend toward "more software testing" is noticeable, there is still a lot of potential to further "professionalize" the software test and to spread the associated perspectives on higher software quality. In the past, the testers were often seen as a control instance for the developers, and a gap between development and testing was created. An important part of professionalization in software testing is to close this gap. As a tester, you inevitably come across software errors, and pointing them out, ensuring that they are corrected, and eventually showing error rates is part of the business. The basic idea of software testing, however, is not to make software development bad, but to work together to improve quality and ensure customer satisfaction.

A study initiated in 2011 by ANECON Software Design und Beratung GmbH and carried out in cooperation with the universities of Bremen and Bremerhaven, the Cologne University of Applied Sciences, the German Testing Board (GTB), and the Swiss Testing Board (STB) provides information about quality assurance in the software sector.

This study, entitled "Software test in practice", showed that over a third of the respondents already used quality assurance measures in the preliminary study of the project (Haberl, Spillner, Vosseberg, & Winter, 2011). The repetition of the survey in 2016 confirmed this trend (Vosseberg, Spillner, & Winter, 2016).

In the area of agile approaches, too, the surveys from previous years have shown that a lot has happened and that agile has come to the fore. It is also stated that Scrum is the most commonly used approach in an agile environment.

"The awareness of the early integration of quality assurance, the influence of agile procedure models in testing and the possibility of outsourcing the test execution was also of great interest to us. With the results of this study, we can make an important contribution to the entire IT industry and, thanks to the high level of participation, the statements derived from the answers are secured well." This was the statement by Manfred Baumgartner, former member of the ANECON management board.

Tilo Linz, former chairman of the German Testing Board, was also pleased with the high level of training: "It goes without saying for professional testers to work methodically in all test levels. Thanks to the globally established ISTQB Certified Tester certification, the tester's level of training is also very high. However, the test qualification options for developers still hold great potential. This is because even at unit test level and especially in test-driven development, the knowledge and mastery of basic test methods is crucial for the effectiveness of the tests."

The survey results also showed that quality assurance measures increased in the early phases. However, there is still focus on the late phases in software development. A trend toward the early application of quality assurance measures can be seen above all where high-quality requirements exist (Automotive, banking, aerospace).

All in all, software testing and software testers have proven to be extremely important for software development. However, it must be noted that this has been accomplished within the given framework of traditional procedures. Now it is important to maintain this status in an agile environment. But this is not always easy, since most agile techniques, methods, and process models have been developed in a rather developer-dominated manner. In addition, there were and still are agile projects that believe that test-driven development (by the developer) and the involvement of user representatives adequately cover the test tasks. However, this is a dangerous mistake. It would be fatal to forego professional test techniques and well-trained test personnel, and thus great potential for efficiency and effectiveness.

Special training courses, such as the ISTQB Certified Tester Foundation Level Agile Extension, are a reaction to the "threat" on the one hand, and an opportunity for professional testing on the other, resulting from the trend toward agile projects. These training courses focus on the transformation of useful testing techniques into the new framework and the integration of testers into agile teams, thus ensuring the value of software testing.

2.1.4   Technical Debt

Too often, due to lack of time and budget, the situation arises wherein errors that are already found or errors that could not be found due to insufficient testing time are not corrected in a timely manner. Known errors are documented neatly and cleanly, and are perhaps also analyzed for errors, but the actual correction is no longer carried out because other implementations are given higher priority or the changes are so far-reaching (e.g., design changes) that they can no longer be considered in the current project or the next release. Workarounds are defined to avoid the mistakes and, if possible, to satisfy the customer in this way. Once a workaround is found and it manifests itself as "the solution" (albeit the wrong one), the workaround quickly becomes the standard. This does not make software maintenance any easier—nor the test.

In many project situations, we find such solutions (workarounds) that are only partially documented or are not documented at all. As an "old hand"—as the saying goes—one is the hero, because one knows what works in which way. And all of this comes from memory and years of experience. So far so good. But how do you set up an effective software test at this stage? Errors that are not found on time become a cost trap. If the error correction is downgraded again and again due to the implementation of new and important functions, a so-called Technical Debt arises over time. In this environment, it becomes tedious to develop good-quality software, to test it, and to guarantee high customer satisfaction.

As long as the environment does not change, i.e., the composition of the project team remains largely constant, this system state can still be managed somehow; over time, however, it becomes more and more complex and opaque. When the environment changes and essential key players drop out for whatever reason, the limits of what is possible are quickly exceeded. It then needs detailed work, analysis, and workshops with knowledge carriers to define a system state that allows further work and improvements. For this purpose, it is helpful if an error management system is set up and managed from the start, to be able to derive information about the quality level of the system and develop measures accordingly.

"Technical Debt" is the term for defective software that can arise due to the causes described above. The emergence and handling of this Technical Debt and the impact on the team are dealt with in more detail in Chap. 4 of this book.

2.1.5   Test Automation

In agile projects, the approach to test automation is different from the traditional process models. Whereas in the traditional procedure, test automation is seen as a supporting tool in the test approach, automated regression tests are a "must have" in the agile environment to be able to complete the test tasks in the short intervals of the development cycles on time and at a high level of quality. Using test automation in a traditional project environment is often associated with a lot of persuasion work, which begins with the tool selection and burdens the project budget if an automation tool is not yet available in the organization. Test automation is therefore often the first victim of the budgetary stringency. Test automation has to pay off, according to the justified requirement of many decision makers. The use of a test automation tool is often only associated with the fact that the test costs can be reduced. However, the purchase of an automation tool alone does not provide amortization. A concept for the use of the tool and the provision of the necessary resources, and of personnel with the appropriate knowledge and experience, is just as important a component as, for example, the selection of the suitable tool.

The topic of test automation is addressed in detail in Chap. 7. At this point, however, it should be mentioned that, according to the study "Software test in practice," the form and use of test automation are different. In the unit test, the tests are automated to 70% and higher. Around a quarter of the respondents even stated that they had automated the unit test at 100%. In integration testing, the coverage by test automation is already decreasing and the acceptance test is the least automated. Almost 40% of those surveyed conduct the acceptance test completely manually.

Surprisingly, the result was that in agile projects, test execution in the unit test is only automated to 43% completion. It would have been expected that almost all unit tests would be fully automated. As anticipated, test automation decreases with increasing test level. Professor Mario Winter from Cologne University of Applied Sciences emphasizes that "agile testing always also means test automation, since the considerably shorter release cycles only work under the condition that as many tests as possible are automated."

2.1.6 Hierarchical Mindset

"You are just a tester." This and similar statements have surely come up for testers during their career. There are organizations and companies in which the test and the tester per se are still only seen as a necessary evil. However, as can be seen in the previously cited study, "Software test in practice," this picture has changed very positively in recent decades. Not only has the work of the testers become more professional and respected, but also the knowledge of what qualities and skills the testers must demonstrate in order to perform the daily test work has had a positive effect.

Agile process models are a guarantee that the view regarding the test will be different and is already changing. The team spirit and the merging of roles and functions bring about a positive change. The work is no longer thought of so strictly in terms of roles; the team and the team spirit are the success factors in addition to pronounced technical but also personal skills.

2.2 Importance of the Team

A manager recently stated in a project how impressively and reliably the scrum team works together in a certain development environment. This was not the case some time ago. At the beginning of the introduction of the agile approach in this scrum team, many points were still very unclear, and productivity suffered greatly. In addition to the lack of productivity (too little functionality in the sprint cycles), the poor quality of the software deliveries was also the order of the day. As a tester, one of the authors of this book was faced with these challenges every day. In the course of the joint work, however, it soon became apparent that the team was taking shape over time, that cooperation was clearly improving, and, above all, that trust prevailed. Many small measures taken by the team were decisive in establishing a homogeneous team in the end. And the best thing was that working together on the challenges was fun.

This example illustrates what teams are capable of. The self-organization of the team and the ongoing improvement measures have shown what is possible with team spirit, suitable roles, and personalities in a team. The first sprints seemed to be ill-fated. The initiated change process and the lack of success weighed heavily on the team members.

A well-functioning team ensures that the work results fit, and that the quality of the delivered software is correspondingly high. Therefore, when introducing agile procedures, it is important to ensure that the teams achieve rapid success to remain motivated. A lack of success quickly causes negative energy and frustration.

Of course, an essential success factor for a well-functioning team is that the individual team members are integrated and that difficulties can be addressed openly. To solve problems in the team or with individual members of the team, the best way is to let the team overcome the conflicts and obstacles by itself. Management often feels compelled to intervene and make decisions without knowing details. This is not the approach of agile methods. Leave the decision to the team and success will come soon. And with this success, a high-quality software as well.

Project EMIL: Mindset: The Team Is Born

The project team consisted of five developers and two testers. Two of the developers had already contributed to the development of the existing analysis software, one of these two developers being the project manager and chief developer. The three other developers were partly new to the company or previously used in other projects. A tester already had experience with the existing analysis software.

All team members had in common that no expert knowledge about the new technology was available to anyone, and that the planned agile procedure was only known from the books. Up until this project, every developer had a subject matter (e.g., a printing module or an analysis) as a task area and worked on expanding or changing it on request or according to his own ideas. As a result, only those developers could find their way in these areas.

For the newly assembled team, the challenge was not only to familiarize themselves with the new technology, but also to develop more cooperatively and comprehensively and to develop joint artifacts that everyone could further

(continued)

develop if necessary—a joint responsibility for the complete product. This affects not only the source code, but also the way in which unit tests and acceptance tests are formulated and described, how code reviews are carried out, and the granularity in which design and source documentation is written. This led to a lot of discussions right at the beginning, which were always focused on being constructive and necessary to establish a common approach. Only then was teamwork possible.

Falling back into old patterns is a risk for testers and developers. This often happened in a somewhat hidden form and meant that the scrum master and the other team members had to be attentive. These are a few of the indicators that have been noticed in the project and have been corrected:

- Testers wait until shortly before the end of the sprint for "the version" of the test and will then still find many errors: the test must start with the first build. If there is not enough time for the test and/or more regression tests are necessary, more automation needs to be done. Tasks from test automation can/must also be performed by the developers: the team is responsible for quality.
- Developers cannot deliver an executable version during the sprint: the changes and enhancements to the software should be planned in the sprint so that they take place in small stages and each version (e.g., Nightly Builds, Continuous Integration) remains executable.
- Testers complain about constant changes to functions that have already been implemented: the learning curve is steep, especially at the beginning, and many of the effects on the existing architecture are not yet known. This means that repercussions for the existing one are pre-programmed and welcome, since the software as a whole must be consistent and must not be "littered with balconies," just so that we do not have to change anything that already exists.
- Developers want to release the design in the sprint at first, and then implement it and eventually provide the test team with a version for the test: there is a mini waterfall inside which has little to do with the agile thought. The same danger exists at the sprint level (a sprint conception, a sprint implementation, a sprint test).

The team needs time to internalize the agile mindset. Thus, these "Relapses" were not demonized, but clarified in the team during the retrospectives. On the other hand, we can see how certain situations got the team members on the right track, for example the moment when a developer experienced the benefits of his unit tests for the first time and then liked to create them. Or if the tester contributes to fewer errors in the software by participating in the code review. It is not for nothing that agile practices are "best practices," but sometimes you have to experience them yourself.

2.3   Audits for Quality Assurance in Agile Projects

There are many approaches to quality assurance. In the agile world, in addition to the ongoing test activities integrated into the development process, audits are increasingly used. Meetings and structures that serve to improve the work process, the cooperation, and the quality of daily work in a sustainable manner.

2.3.1 Scrum

Most of the projects that follow the agile approach are handled in Scrum. This insight can also be found in the study "Software test in practice." However, project experience with several customer projects has also shown that the ways and means of implementing and using Scrum vary widely. Scrum is often used to keep up with the flow of modern development. However, it soon becomes clear that the mere idea of introducing Scrum is not enough to carry out product development on time, transparently, and at a high level of quality. The team that is the key success factor in Scrum must function well and must be well positioned. Good positioning in this context means that not only the technical skills but above all the social skills and interaction with each other are correspondingly well developed. The introduction of Scrum in large organizations is not just about introducing Scrum as such, but also about enabling self-determined and, most importantly, creative work. The smooth communication between the teams and within the individual Scrum teams is also the focus of the general introduction of Scrum (Fig. 2.1).

The quality assurance process in Scrum begins in the planning phase. It is about making sure that the planning steps defined in Scrum are followed to achieve the vision. For this, a strategic planning process is specified which, according to Boris Gloger, consists of ten planning steps (Gloger, 2013):

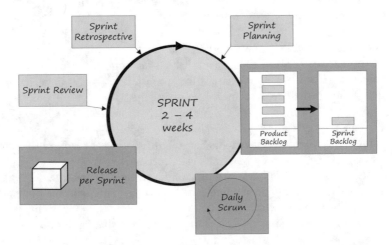

Fig. 2.1 The quality assurance process in Scrum

1. Creating a vision
2. Writing the first stories
3. Creating a product backlog and setting up the sprint goals
4. Writing the backlog items that implement the vision
5. Prioritizing the backlog items based on business value and sprint cycles
6. Estimation of the backlog items in order of prioritization
7. Re-prioritization
8. Estimation of capacity of the Scrum team—velocity
9. Development of the release plan and incorporation of planning buffers
10. Introducing the release plan into Sprint Planning 1

To keep the ongoing work of the team flowing, the daily meeting ("Daily Scrum") is held, which is a very important factor for the productivity of a team and the quality of product development. The main purpose is to make the progress of the current sprint target transparent by discussing and documenting

- The completed tasks
- The tasks planned until the next meeting
- The obstacles that prevent progress

jointly within the team ("Daily Scrum with Task Board"). Daily Scrum is also governed by a set of rules stating that it is held at the same time and place each day, and that all team members are present. This meeting is not—as is often the case with traditional approaches—a long project meeting, sometimes lasting several hours. Daily Scrum is about treating the three questions mentioned above very effectively in a very short time (approx. 15 min).

This daily meeting during the individual sprint cycles ensures that the work and progress as well as the problems that arise during the operational work are made transparent, and that timely measures are taken so that the progress of the project is not jeopardized. However, it requires each team member to actively participate in this meeting.

When all tasks of a story are finished, it is time for the home straight; the team checks the finished story against the "Definition of Done." If this milestone is also successfully completed, the story can be registered immediately upon completion for acceptance by the product owner, who will review the acceptance criteria as part of the acceptance process.

2.3.1.1 Sprint Review Meeting

The Sprint Review Meeting is an audit in which the team presents its results. Every sprint has a goal, and whether this goal has been achieved is made transparent in the Sprint Review Meeting. Transparency and customer involvement are cornerstones of the agile approach. The periodic presentation of the new functionality allows stakeholders to quickly determine whether the project is on the right track. Is what was promised for the current sprint delivered and in a form that brings the customer the desired benefits? Is the status the one from which work can continue?

Scrum also means that "usable software" is delivered at the end of a sprint—thus, software that can be used without post-processing. The software has the defined functionality, has been tested, and can ultimately be delivered in this form.

The composition of a Sprint Review Meeting can be as follows:

- Scrum master
- Product owner
- Team members
- Management
- Customer
- Representatives and/or users of the business departments
- Internal and external suppliers

The product owner presents to the participants of the Sprint Review Meeting what the task of the completed sprint cycle was. The team presents the results by detailing the executable software to those present. The aim is not to bring the results of the sprint closer to the meeting participants in the form of presentations, reports, or the like. Rather, being able to present the executability of the software is the top priority of the Sprint Review Meeting.

In addition to proving that the delivered code is in a deliverable state, the review meeting is also used to determine actions that will result from this audit. In addition to new functionalities, adjustments to the product backlog may also result. This is especially the case if the team was not able to deliver all planned elements of the backlog and therefore a new prioritization of the elements must be made. A change in the prioritization of the items can also be the result of a review meeting, as it is recognized that certain functions have a different relevance than previously assumed.

If new functionalities are required or if there are changes in the prioritization of items, the team can be reorganized or restructured. Possible reasons for this may be that these adjustments require the use of other developers with specialized knowledge, or that the team generally determines that knowledge is needed that is not yet covered.

Overview of essential rules for the Sprint Review Meeting:

- Duration of the meeting: depending on the duration of the sprint: approximately 1.5 to a maximum of 4 hours.
- Presence of the product owner and the team at the review meeting is mandatory. However, there may also be representatives from management, the specialist departments, the customer, as well as internal and external suppliers.
- Presentation and demonstration of the executable software.
- Presentation of the results in the form of PowerPoint presentations or the like is *not* allowed.

2.3.1.2 Sprint Retrospective

In contrast to the Sprint Review Meeting, the Sprint Retrospective focuses not on the presentation of results (from a functional point of view), but on the "continuous improvement process." The insights gained in the daily work are analyzed and measures are derived from them, so that a sustainable improvement of the project work is achieved.

How do you guarantee a successful retrospective? According to Boris Gloger's definition in his book *Scrum: Developing Products Reliably and Quickly* (Gloger, 2013), this requires six steps:

1. Create security
   In order to address upcoming topics in the retrospective openly and without anxiety, it is necessary to create a climate of appreciative cooperation. There should be a pleasant atmosphere, and the room for this meeting should be chosen so that undisturbed work is possible.
2. Gather facts
   The participants receive moderation cards and write on these cards those events and information from the last iteration that are considered significant for them. These notes are pinned to a pinboard. In addition, a few sentences are used when pinning the cards to explain why this event or information is important and significant. In this way a short story is told, and the topic is made clearer and easier to understand for the other participants. Thus, the team gradually builds up a picture of the last iteration.
3. Find working processes
   At this point, positive findings are asked for to identify well-functioning pro-cesses. Again, participants are asked to write the results on cards and pin them to the pinboard.
4. Find non-working processes
   The question here is: What can and should be improved? The focus is on the improvement process and not on finger pointing.
5. Initiate changes
   There are two main questions at this point: Who is in control of the situation? and Who can do something? These questions result in two types of measures:
   - Issues that can be changed and improved by the team itself
   - Issues that need to be addressed outside the team (customer, management, etc.)
6. Decide on the importance
   Experience shows that many topics are listed, and it is usually not possible to cover them all. A decision must be made on what to work on in concrete terms. At this stage, the team members prioritize the importance and benefits of the topics to be implemented. This means that they prioritize which points should be implemented by the team and which points by the organization to achieve a sustainable improvement (Fig. 2.2).

Fig. 2.2 The Sprint Retrospective

Once the above questions have been answered and the next issues to be addressed have been prioritized, they are discussed when planning the next sprint, and it is determined which measures the team should implement in the next sprint. During the Sprint Planning the effort for the implementation of these points is estimated and the next steps are discussed with the product owner. The effort required may also mean that certain functionalities cannot be implemented in the next sprint. This closes the circle, and the cycle starts all over again.

Roman Pichler, author of the book *Scrum—Applying Agile Project Management Successfully* (Pichler, 2007), also describes the typical mistakes of a retrospective, which we would like to mention at this point:

- **Self-destruction:** personal attacks, making accusations, or even losing respect for each other. This must be avoided absolutely in the context of a retrospective. The scrum master must react immediately when these situations occur and initiate a de-escalation. Personal attacks can finally lead to the trusting cooperation in daily work suffering severely.
- **Sitting out**: Finding and discussing potential for improvement can be quite difficult for a team. Various activities but also moderation techniques can help. As a scrum master you can improve the situation by pointing out possibilities for advancement and thus acting as a role model. Creating an atmosphere of trust is also very helpful.
- **Babbling:** Talking a lot does not mean that a lot is said or achieved. In the retrospective, it is important to point out concrete and realistic improvement measures. It is therefore important to concentrate on the essentials and to generate measures for implementation in one of the next sprints.

Project EMIL: A Retrospective

What had happened?

A year and a half ago, the project team ventured a change from the traditional to the agile approach and gradually discarded the old patterns. The lone fighters have become a real team that develops the product with very high quality. The result is an agile process that is ideal for the project and the team in this company. Although it is not error-free and partly not designed according to the "doctrine," it fulfills its purpose: an efficient team develops an application with great benefits and high quality for the customer—and has a lot of fun on top of that.

What went well?

- It was possible to define a goal that the team—developers and testers—worked toward together.
- An understanding of each other's tasks and the planned content of the application was created for everyone.
- The team has become highly networked and integrated. The testers support the developers with unit tests and code reviews. The developers support the testers with test automation and with technical understanding of the architecture.
- An atmosphere has also been created in which errors are seen as an opportunity to do things better and in which everyone is allowed to make changes and provide feedback on the application and the process.

What went badly?

- The implementation of the test automation started too late. This deficit was gradually reduced but is still noticeable. Due to insufficient regression testing, some errors were discovered later than they should have been.
- The patterns were underestimated. It is often easier to do things the way we have always done them than to do them differently. Thus, through carelessness, old patterns have crept in again and again, which has led to conflicts.
- Objections and feedback were sometimes not sufficiently considered. Thus, justified criticism was rejected and not discussed, which led to frustration within the team. It was particularly challenging when indications of risks, which later led to real problems, were ignored.

What should be changed specifically?

- Team members should be given even more opportunities to express change requests—especially in the process and procedures—so that the team

(continued)

cannot rest on the status quo and will continue to strive to become better and better.

- Test methods should be sharpened at all levels of testing. Both developers and testers should use implicitly structured test methods when designing their tests in order to write better test cases.
- The tools should be simplified to allow the team to concentrate more on the actual work. For example, automatisms and other plug-ins in the tools should make documentation work easier and more efficient.
- Pass on experience: other projects in the company should also benefit from the team's experience. The first product developments in the company have already taken the path to an agile approach. The existing team can and must provide support here.

2.3.2 Kanban

David J. Anderson describes this process model in his book (Anderson, Kanban: Successful Evolutionary Change for Your Technology Business, 2010) and he is also considered the founder of Kanban in software development. Kanban originates from the Toyota production process with the goal of reducing inventory and achieving a steady flow in production. This approach was applied to the software development process and the following core practices emerged:

- Make work visible (via Kanban Board).
- Limit the WIP (Work in Progress— determined for each production step, depending on what makes sense for the rapid processing of the work).
- Manage the flow (i.e., avoid getting work stuck in certain areas and making others wait an unreasonably long time before they can contribute).
- Make process rules explicit (most teams create small sets of rules and stick them on the wall next to the board).
- Implement feedback mechanisms (in the workflow itself, between workflows and from within the organization - > the test has an important role here).
- Make collaborative improvements (based on models—not retrospectively, but permanently, if something gets stuck).

Kanban or Scrum? This question often arises when introducing agile approaches. Which variant is used depends on the circumstances under which the team has to fulfill its requirements and tasks. In the end, the team decides which model is the right one.

A major difference between Scrum and Kanban is that Scrum is a model in the classical sense—with tasks, result types, and roles, i.e., very standardized. Kanban, on the other hand, is primarily about controlling and visualizing work processes.

Table 2.1 Scrum versus Kanban

	Scrum	Kanban
Team	• Three fixed predefined roles • Cross-functional team • Commitment	• No specifications • Specialists allowed • Commitment optional
Tasks	• Prioritized • Must be small	• Prioritization optional • Size does not matter
Estimates	• Necessary in the planning	• Optional
Release cycles	• Timeboxed iterations	• Optional—either with a fixed period or event-based
Changes	• Fixed selection in a sprint	• Selection is made dynamically based on capacity
Limitation	• Velocity per sprint limits the WIP indirectly	• WIP is fixed per status
Meetings	• Strict specification	• Undefined

Both process models are tools that are used to execute tasks well and work more effectively. To choose the right tool, it is advisable not to evaluate the tools but to understand them.

Below is a small selection of the differences between the two models (Table 2.1):

There is no general statement about which of the two processes is the better one. We will not be able to avoid considering the team's requirements, the concrete tasks, and the organizational conditions in detail in order to select the appropriate process. Furthermore, both methods can complement each other (so-called SCRUMBAN).

2.3.2.1 Kaizen: Continuous Improvement

An essential point in Kanban's approach is Kaizen. This word comes from the Japanese and means "Change for the better" (continuous improvement or the continuous improvement process). Like the audits—as usual with Scrum—Kanban pursues the approach of continuously looking at the experiences gained and continuously identifying improvement measures and implementing them promptly. Retrospective meetings, as they are defined and lived in Scrum, do not take place in Kanban in this form; respectively these considerations are perceived differently. In Kanban, these meetings take place irregularly and they also allow the participation of people outside the team, and thus also representatives from other organizational units and from the management.

In short, problems are addressed as soon as they become apparent. And the Kanban methodology ensures that they become obvious. The problems and challenges in the workflow and division of labor literally catch the eye on the Kanban Board. Hence, the audit in Kanban is a permanent one—it focuses on the work process and the rapid completion of work items.

2.4   Continuous Integration

The term *Continuous Integration* is a term from software development and a very
important one in the agile world. Continuous Integration is an XP (Extreme Programming) practice and provides the basis for delivering high-quality software.

In projects that follow traditional development models, the code status is often
made available for testing at longer intervals. Agile methods take the approach of
continuously testing the software to detect errors very quickly and correct them
immediately.

Experience from various software projects shows that the late handover of the
software to the test teams poses many problems. It often happens that the software is
not sufficiently tested in advance by the development department. The software
handed over to the test team frequently has teething troubles. Therefore, a lot of
unnecessary time passes until the software has reached a status that allows a smooth
test to be performed. This results in higher costs in the test phase, increased
personnel costs, delays in delivering the software to the customer, and quality
defects in the operation of the software.

Continuous integration is one way to remedy this. The ongoing (continuous)
integration of software versions through development and the permanent unit test of
the checked-in software makes it possible to detect and eliminate errors at an early
stage and to ensure the software quality in the long term. By developing and testing
only a small part of the software code per iteration, errors and malfunctions of the
software can be detected more easily. The automated build process and automated
testing are the cornerstones of this approach. A high degree of automated testing is
recommended, thus enabling a high coverage of regression testing.

The use of version control is essential to continuously integrate the software
changes of all developers. It should be noted that every developer integrates his
changes into the common code base as often as possible. Each integration must pass
defined tests before the changes are integrated. The respective test cycle before
integration must be kept short to allow for frequent integration. The tests should be
performed in a production-like environment. An automated distribution helps to
easily transfer the software packages and versions to the test environment as well as
to the production environment after approval.

2.5   Lean Software Development

Scrum, Extreme Programming (XP), and Kanban are the most widely used methods
in agile software development. Regarding the aspect of quality assurance, we would
also like to take a closer look at "Lean Software Development," as this approach is
very interesting and quite successful.

Lean Software Development was developed in 2003 by Mary and Tom
Poppendieck (Poppendieck & Poppendieck, 2003). However, "Lean Thinking"
originated in Japan after the Second World War. To keep pace with other countries
in the economy—especially in the field of mass production—it was necessary to

handle the available material efficiently. Lean production processes and resource-saving use of materials was the approach to get the best out of the financially strained situation. This approach was developed and used in automotive production at Toyota.

Mass production in the USA was—in the eyes of Toyota—typical assembly line work. In monotonous work, parts were produced that were added to the inventory when they were not needed. "Waste" was the perception and ultimately the trigger for change.

Lean Software Development has seven principles that form the framework for general access to this idea:

1. Eliminate waste
   Increasing productivity and efficiency is the central point of Lean Software Development. Anything that does not add value to the customer is considered waste. First, however, the waste must be recognized. This includes features that are not used or documentation that is not read, errors that have occurred, incomplete work, and much more
2. Amplify learning
   The longer projects last, the more you learn. In Lean Software Development, this learning is in the foreground and, as with agile approaches, is achieved through feedback loops: requirements are not fully analyzed, but screen masks, for example, are designed, discussed, and agreed with the customer. Learning does not mean that only the project team or the developers learn; the customer learns as well. This ensures not only customer satisfaction, but also high software quality.
3. Decide as late as possible
   Decisions should only be made if all the information necessary for making the right decision is available. However, this does not mean that we have to keep waiting. The technical analysis, development, design, etc. will be further elaborated. Thinking in options is a tool for decision making. As long as not all information necessary for the right decision is available, different options remain open. However, it is important to recognize the right time to make a decision. The time when we would otherwise block an important alternative is the right time to decide.
4. Deliver as fast as possible
   Software should be delivered as early as possible. However, this approach requires appropriate measures and tools, such as prioritizing tasks that tell developers what to do next. As with the agile process models, these tasks are presented transparently and discussed in regular meetings.
5. Empower the team
   The team is given responsibility and sets its own goals. However, goals alone are not enough for a good team to be built. Visible progress and togetherness in the team are just some of the factors necessary for well-functioning teams. It also requires a leadership personality, who averts disturbances from the outside and provides the right direction or figures it out together with the team.

6. Build integrity in (Build quality in)
   There are two types of integrity in Lean Software Development:
   - Internal (conceptual) integrity: refers to architecture, design, features, etc.
   - External (perceived) integrity: design of the user interface, usability, etc.
     However, integrity is only achieved if there is an ongoing—i.e., recurring—critical questioning as to whether the design still fits, whether the user interface meets the requirements, etc. Another means of achieving and ensuring integrity is test automation, which is the standard for agile methods.
7. See the whole
   There are many influencing factors in a project, ranging from the budget, to the interests of the client and the customer, to the time component. "To look at the big picture" implies dealing with all these factors and considering them the right way. To achieve this goal, the "measurement" serves as support. "Measurement" refers to measuring and controlling the project and the course of the project with simple means. A few metrics are often enough to see how the project is doing. The representation of the error rate and the error correction progress is one of these simple methods.

Lean Versus Agile

Lean and agile have many common goals:

- Improve software quality.
- Improve the productivity of the software development process.
- Implement changes in requirements as quickly as possible.
- Customer satisfaction.

While agile methods rely primarily on communication, Lean tries to achieve customer satisfaction by eliminating waste. Which method is the right one depends strongly on various factors, and cannot be adopted 1:1 for all projects.

Organization of the Software Test in Agile Projects

At the "Agile Testing Days" conference in November 2012, Scott W. Ambler presented his comprehensive process model "Disciplined Agile Development," which is intended to provide agile teams with an easily adaptable project procedure similar to the Rational Unified Process (Ambler & Lines, 2012). He claims that agile teams should face the reality in large, complex environments, and leave the definition of tasks and roles to process experts. Scott comes from an environment where one must get the work of several thousand employees under control.

The reaction of the other thought leaders in agile testing, above all Markus Gärtner and Gojko Adzic, did not take long: They asserted that if Scott was to be believed, they would have to live in a fantasy world, a world of dwarves, sorcerers, and unicorns. From then on, kitschy and suggestive pictures of unicorns graced the presentations of a whole host of speakers who defiantly resisted Scott's accusation of being out of touch with reality. Their daily experience was not marked by the needs that he described so vividly. And yet, they were very successful with it.

Now, who was right? Reality teaches that both—as much as it may bother some of us—are right. There is no *one* right approach. Rather, it depends on the reality *in which* we are working. Accordingly, each of us must orientate oneself.

This is no comforting realization for a book that clearly and unequivocally teaches its readers about agile testing. But here we are, at the heart of agile paradigms: The environment and the mission of software projects is usually so complex that it is difficult to plan everything in advance according to a predefined scheme, and a project team is more like a research team than a production team in a factory building. Thus, if we want to successfully design tests in an agile project, we must take a closer look at our situation and subsequently choose the thinking model that best fits this situation.

In this chapter, a few approaches will be examined, all of which have been proven to offer useful models of thought for agile project teams and are successful—in their specific project environments. This chapter will also show where the limits of these approaches lie so that the reader can find and decide on the right approach according to their project reality. A few case studies will be briefly presented, to illustrate what an agile test organization can look like.

3.1 Positioning of Test in Agile Projects

3.1.1 The Fundamental Test Process According to ISTQB

Many self-proclaimed agile projects are embedded in a less agile environment, or not as strictly agile as they might think. Therefore, we take the liberty of naming an approach right at the beginning that does not correspond to agile thinking at all: the fundamental testing process of the International Software Testing Qualifications Board (ISTQB).

There are two very simple reasons why it is quoted at the beginning of this book. First, testing itself is the same activity, regardless of whether it is agile or not, and secondly, it enables the transition from a traditional thinking test approach to a consistently agile testing approach.

The fundamental testing process of the ISTQB (Spillner & Linz, 2019) generically describes the basic main activities needed in each test:

- Test planning and control (a management process that accompanies the other four processes)
- Test analysis and test design (analyzing the test basis and deriving high-level test cases based on it)
- Test implementation and test execution (creating low-level test cases from the high-level test cases using suitable test data and subsequently executing and logging them)
- Evaluating exit criteria and reporting (evaluating, summarizing, and preparing test results for specific target groups)
- Test closure activities (handover, archiving, lessons learned)

In this structured form, however, these main activities are a hindrance for agile projects, since the implicit underlying roles are not found there, and the steps usually run in parallel. The boundaries of when the main activity begins and when it ends become blurred in agile projects. Nevertheless, for each main activity of the fundamental test process, it can explain where this activity is usually found in agile projects and what we must pay attention to.

3.1.1.1 Test Planning, Monitoring, and Control

In traditional projects these activities include:

- Definition of test objectives
- Definition of the test activities that are necessary to achieve the scope of tasks and test goals

- Checking the current test progress against the plan (including any possible deviations from the plan)
- Describing the test status
- If necessary, the initiation of corrective measures

These tasks are also relevant for agile teams, but depending on the agile approach they are performed by the entire team. Management tasks in the team are not easy to implement right from the start, and we have already seen quite efficient teams that would never have been able to perform these tasks even jointly. It is therefore quite common for a (often informal) test coordinator to emerge in the team, who at least ensures that test planning and control are appropriately carried out by the team.

The chosen agile process model naturally plays a decisive role in this field of activity. In Kanban teams, the determination of the test activities is made possible via a suitable board with the processes shown there. Planning and control are also well covered by the methodological principles such as the pull principle, WIP limit, and expedite/intangible tasks (Epping, 2011). In some cases, there are also explicit test coordinators who control the other testers. Scrum teams cover a lot of this via the backlog and the planning meeting. The main thing, in this case, is a good effort estimation by the team as well as tight and well-coordinated communication in the Daily Stand-Up Meetings (Gloger, 2013). Sometimes the scrum master is not suited for this, because they can underestimate test issues which include complex, coordinative tasks. Here, a primus inter pares in the team proves itself for the test expertise, i.e., someone from the team who stands out through special test competence and thus significantly controls the test. XP projects, on the other hand, can rely on a rich set of very helpful working principles, which means that the test control focuses more on coaching to comply with these principles in everyday life. To do this, XP projects must create their guidelines to organize and ultimately plan the test. The four test quadrants of Crispin and Gregory (Crispin & Gregory, 2009) (see Sect. 3.1.2) can provide orientation in this case.

It is particularly crucial that the measurement and the associated control are reduced to the essentials in agile projects, and that they are constantly adapted to the needs during the project. Each metric must prove itself, iteration by iteration, through the resulting successful control measures, otherwise it may disappear again. This happens almost every day in Kanban. Much of what is monitored using metrics in traditional projects takes on everyday communication in agile projects. The control loop of measuring, evaluating deviations, taking countermeasures, and evaluating effectiveness, which is also often referred to as the Deming-cycle (Deming, 1982), is informal in agile projects and must be supported by suitably promoted and practiced communication within the team (Fig. 3.1).

The environment of the project and its size is, of course, a very limiting factor in detaching from the traditional planning and control approach. Some teams are formally relying on a V-Model, e.g., in the public sector, in the health care sector, or some safety-critical industries. Externally, clear plans must be submitted, and control measures made visible that would be without added value for the agile team itself. In addition, some tasks are so complex that several iterations are required to

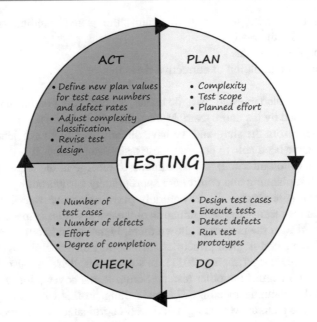

Fig. 3.1 Deming-cycle for testing

achieve anything like a preliminary project. The "Disciplined Agile Development" approach, which offers a suitable procedural model framework, is particularly suitable here (Ambler & Lines, 2012). There are now several extremely successful teams that work in a traditional style to the outside and are consistently agile on the inside. Their success is probably due to the fact that they consequently follow both approaches—clearly independent and separated from each other.

However, in every agile project the fundamental questions of meaning remain to be clarified: What do we want to achieve with the test, and what quality level are we aiming for? Although agile procedures—if they are followed consequently—take on early testing on their own, many other strategic questions of the test remain open to be dealt with, and have to be renegotiated or answered before the start of the project. Above all, scrum teams must decide what the ratio of test experts to the rest of the team should be. This is possibly a ratio that changes considerably during the project and thus may lead to unwanted team changes. The Definition of Done is usually not clear from the outset and requires strategic thinking by a test expert again and again before the project begins.

A common mistake in agile projects—even if they have test experts in the team—is that the testers are not involved in all important communications in time. This can mean that bad planning on both sides, i.e., during analysis/development as well as testing, is inevitable. In agile projects, the team spirit is not a pleasant luxury, but a principle of survival. Good communication must compensate for sophisticated test planning and control, and that can only be done with team discipline. Everyday decisions must be discussed with everyone involved, right from the start.

3.1.1.2 Test Analysis and Test Design
In traditional projects these activities include:

- Review of the test basis, such as requirements, software integrity level, risk analysis report, technical architecture, design, and interface specification
- Assessment of the testability of test basis and test objects
- Identification of required test data to support the definition of test conditions and test cases
- Identification and prioritization of the test conditions based on the test object analysis, the specification, the behavior, and the structure of the software
- Draft (design) and prioritization of high-level test cases
- Design of the test environment and identification of the required infrastructure and tools
- Generation of (or ensuring of) traceability between the test base and test cases in both directions

Every test case requires an examination of what and how a feature should be tested. This also applies to the explorative test approaches, which are often used in agile projects—wherein this activity only takes place during the test execution itself: The tester responds to the test results and designs further tests based on them.

What is special about agile projects is often the lack of a comprehensive test basis that can be analyzed and evaluated before the test. In agile projects, the test designs are often an essential part of the requirements and the result of well-structured communication processes with the department. Traceability is no longer a core concern in agile projects, although great care is always taken to ensure that test designs are defined as closely as possible to requirements (e.g., more detailed acceptance criteria in user stories).

Testers in agile projects need to understand that they are part of the analysis. Exploratory tests are often used to determine or sharpen requirements for the next releases. Deviations from such tests are a reason to consider changes and/or additions to the requirements for future iterations. Many testers in traditional projects, simply given their role, take on the mediating role between the development team and the end user or business department. In agile projects, however, this is carried out systematically.

Another part of the test cases often becomes part of the development because—as with ATDD (Acceptance Test-Driven Development) approaches—it is written right at the start as an automated test script that is maintained by the development team with every change (Gärtner, 2012). In this case, the test expert in the team has the task to carefully select these tests and to coach the other team members during the test analysis and the test design in a suitable (and not consuming) way. A resilient, lean, but entirely meaningful regression test portfolio, which automatically runs with every build, is an essential success factor for many agile projects.

Incidentally, in more complex project environments in which many teams work on a complex overall system or multi-system, we have found that testers also become technical coordinators as they have to invest a great deal in maintaining their test environment across the entire organization.

3.1.1.3 Test Implementation and Test Execution

In traditional projects these activities include:

- Definition, implementation, and prioritization of low-level test cases (including the definition of test data)
- Creation and prioritization of the test workflow, creation of test data, test scenarios, and often preparation of the test framework and development of scripts for test automation
- Creation of test suites based on the test workflow to make the test execution as efficient as possible
- Checking whether the test environment was set up correctly and ensuring the correct configurations
- Checking and updating the traceability between test basis and test cases in both directions
- Execution of test procedures (manual or automated) in compliance with the test plan (sequence, test suites, etc.)
- Logging of test results and documentation of the exact version of the respective test object and the test tools and test equipment used
- Comparison of the actual results with the predicted results
- Analysis and documentation of failures or incidents found
- Retesting (confirmation testing) and regression test

This main activity is in principle the same for traditional projects and agile projects. The central questions for agile projects are automation and specialization.

Because of the frequent changes and early testing, test automation is no longer an optional accessory. On the other hand, test automation finds difficult conditions in agile projects, i.e., short lead times and frequent changes. Most teams respond to this by relying on easily automatable areas for test automation and otherwise paying more attention to quality rather than quantity, or area coverage when selecting test cases. Additionally, it is a good idea in many teams to adapt the test scripts for automation during development. Depending on the context (distributed teams, customer-supplier relationship), the latter cannot always be implemented. The short lead times from the test idea to the test execution are intercepted very effectively by the fact that more extensive test scripts are only realized a sprint later and are then available for the regression test.

Specialization becomes a challenge for agile teams because of their size and universal orientation. It will be difficult to keep a security tester or load and performance testing expert on the team all the time. These tests require a high level of specialization; for example, a security tester that has not been involved in the community for half a year loses contact with the relevant topics. A team cannot consistently "nourish" these specialists. As a result, many organizations are starting to have certain tests done by a test competence center that either "lends" specialists to projects or takes on test orders for project teams. Nonfunctional tests (load and performance, technical security, maintainability, usability, portability) are usually areas in the test that are outsourced to test center experts. The four test quadrants of Crispin and Gregory (Crispin & Gregory, 2009) offer a good approach to identify the relevant areas for specialists—namely the fourth quadrant.

Defect management within an agile team is reduced to the bare minimum. For defects found outside of sprint development, accounts must be kept very carefully, and all open tickets are integrated into the next planning meeting. Accordingly, sophisticated error management or defect management systems are often interesting at the organizational level, but not so much at the team level. The team itself helps in case of major errors by including them in the product backlog of Scrum, for example as a separate task, and thus reliably tracking them.

3.1.1.4 Evaluating Exit Criteria and Reporting

In traditional projects these activities include:

- Evaluation of the test protocols regarding the end criteria defined in the test concept
- The decision as to whether more tests should be conducted, or the final criteria should be adjusted
- Preparation of the final test report for the stakeholders

If we come from traditional project environments, we must dramatically change our minds regarding this main activity: Reports are only used consistently where it is necessary. Every report must prove useful, otherwise it will be deleted and possibly reintroduced later. Useful, in this context, means that the team can optimize its work based on the reports. The control of the work and measurement of the work progress is simplified on task boards or using a backlog with only a few exceptions.

In traditional project environments, for example, elaborate error statistics are kept that provide information regarding which errors were found and when, and how good the correction rate is and whether it keeps pace with the error detection rate. In agile projects, the statements of these reports are more of a topic of conversation in the various team meetings. As long as there is trust between the team and stakeholders, these statistics will not be kept. (If the trust appears to have withered, such reports become a necessity again until the trust has been restored.) However, defects that cannot be fixed immediately must be documented and managed. Otherwise, they will be easily overlooked. Agile teams must therefore be careful about where the limit is. A very common mistake among developer-controlled teams is to always treat defects during the unit test, i.e., to fix them immediately, and to pin the defect correction to the task board or to include it in the backlog only in exceptional cases. Issue Tracking Tools are now so easy to use that tool-based defect management no longer violates the principle of simplicity.

Incidentally, the same could be said for the usual test progress statistics as for the defect statistics. As long as the test can be handled and managed well in everyday conversations or team meetings, extensive test status reports can also be omitted. But here, too, caution is advised: What makes sense at the beginning of a project does not have to remain the same for the entire project. For "hot" release phases (e.g., in Hardening Iterations in case of Scrum), it can be considered extremely important to measure and display the test progress over time, based on the test case status.

And here is the *unicorn* again: In which universe do we live? There are project environments where detailed reporting is mandatory or at least appropriate. The test must take this into account from the start. Only within the team do we still have a certain freedom of choice. For other stakeholders or the project management office of a multi-project program, detailed test status reports may have to be delivered or acceptance reports may need to be drawn up. This may have clear consequences for the team: There must be at least one test coordinator who will take care of the outside reports, and the team will be forced to make certain recordings (mostly tool-based). In such cases, it is advisable to make a clear distinction between the needs of stakeholders outside the team and the needs of the team itself. Even in this case, some teams make the mistake of making external requirements their own without questioning them. This often leads to confusion in retrospectives and creates unnecessary tension in the team. External reporting requirements must be negotiated and are just as much part of the "scope of delivery" as the code or the user documentation.

Finally, it should be pointed out that the immediate test evaluation, i.e., the question regarding whether the test is sufficient, or whether testing needs to be done further, has to be handled in the same way in agile projects as in traditional ones. Here, experienced testers can contribute their expertise well and coach their teammates. Some techniques, such as session-based explorative testing (Bach, 2000), have deliberately incorporated test evaluation into their methodology: At the end of the Exploratory Testing session, the tester must briefly and meaningfully present their observations and test results to an expert or the test team before a test mission for another test session is developed.

3.1.1.5 Test Closure Activities

In traditional projects these activities include:

- Checking which of the planned work results have been delivered
- Closing the error reports/deviation reports or creating change requests for further errors/deviations
- Documentation of the acceptance of the system
- Documentation and archiving of test equipment, test environment, and infrastructure for later reuse
- Transfer of the test tools to the maintenance organization
- Analysis and documentation of "lessons learned" to derive necessary changes for later projects
- Using the information collected to improve test readiness

"After the test" is "Before the test'" This also applies to traditional projects, but in agile projects the test cycles are much tighter and more frequent, so that a real completion of a test in agile projects is hardly imaginable. However, most agile projects do not go live immediately after a sprint or build. Even in Kanban-controlled projects, not every single feature is immediately deployed in production. In addition to the training and commissioning measures, there are other tasks or iterations according to which an orderly deployment in production is due. The Scrum Community has coined the term "Hardening Sprint" (or "Session") for these moments. We have seen many Scrum-driven projects go live only every 3 to 6 months.

It is therefore also worthwhile in agile projects to schedule a test completion from time to time, in which open test activities are completed. Handover to the maintenance organization may well be necessary for large organizations, as may training measures. Test experts in the team should incorporate these moments into the overall strategy of the project from the outset and list all the measures to be taken, in case of a Hardening Sprint.

Many of the final activities in traditional projects are, however, practiced in a different form and much earlier and more frequently in case of agile projects, for example acceptance of the features that are due at the end of the sprint by the product owner, and the retrospective, which, also in Kanban-controlled projects, can take place in the daily Stand-Up meeting.

Acceptance in agile teams is usually defined by the so-called *Definition of Done*. Although this is a term from the Scrum environment, it is now generally used in agile teams. The Definition of Done could be all acceptance conditions of a user story run without errors. Based on these criteria, the fulfillment of a backlog entry at the end of a sprint is measured in Scrum. However, our experience has shown that many agile teams have a hard time following this if there is no experienced tester among them. The criteria are often too abstract or partially exaggerated, which is why they cannot be verified and are therefore worthless. For this reason, testers should regularly review the Definition of Done and check whether it is meaningful and applicable.

In Scrum, we have a retrospective ceremony, while in Kanban, optimization options are discussed almost daily, just as soon as they are noticed. XP also has principles that make us constantly think about improvements. So-called lessons learned considerations should therefore also be actively used by testers, since agile projects often provide space and possibilities for this. In contrast to traditional projects, optimizations are not only understood in one direction: Measures can be perceived as optimization for a while, and at some point they may turn out to be an impediment. Changing measures back and forth is therefore not necessarily an expression of chaos. But one must be careful: It could also be a sign of disorientation in the team!

3.1.2 Which Test for What Purpose: The Four Test Quadrants of Agile Testing

Janet Gregory and Lisa Crispin have given fundamental thought to which tests are needed in agile projects and who should ideally conduct them. Test experts like to use the V-Model to determine which reviews or tests have to be done by whom and when—even if their project does not work according to the V-Model. This may still work for some Kanban teams to some extent since Kanban is open for this. However, in most agile teams, the integration levels are very close to each other and are hardly separated from one another in terms of personnel. Since both Gregory and Crispin come from an XP environment, they looked for a consistently different approach and found the most effective model to date, which has already proven itself many times in practice (Crispin & Gregory, 2009). They called it the "four test quadrants" because they divided the test into four significant groups based on considerations by Brian Marick (Marick, 2003) using two dimensions (Fig. 3.2).

The first dimension poses the question of whether people will think more in terms of *technology-oriented* or *business-oriented* when creating test cases. It would be interesting to know whether a plausibility check, for example, runs stably in all variants and always returns a processable result or a deliberately provoked exception (more technology-oriented), or whether the same plausibility check is suitable for checking a travel request for completeness, and subsequently forwarding it to the correct person in charge (more business-oriented). This dimension should not be confused with the distinction between unit test and system test or functional and

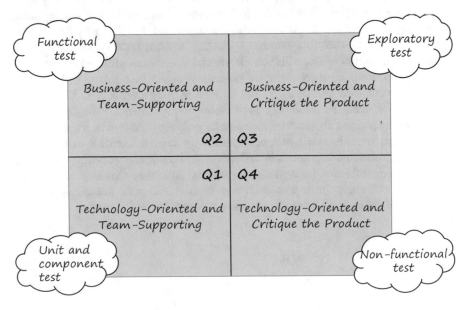

Fig. 3.2 The four test quadrants of agile testing (according to Crispin & Gregory)

nonfunctional tests. Technology-oriented versus business-oriented deliberately simplifies these distinctions to make them easier to handle in agile teams. Otherwise, there may be a fruitless discussion about who in the team is testing, for example, the usability or the authorization concept and who is not. We can also avoid the system testers having to wait until everything has been integrated into a complete system to carry out their system tests.

The second dimension deals with the question of whether we simply want to verify what the development team had planned—Marick calls this *supporting the team* —or whether we want to check if the team has thought of everything necessary—Marick calls this *critique the product*. For example, it may be that the team did a good job of implementing the feature for purchasing a ticket from a vending station (team-supporting tests), but that response times for it might become too long when clicking back and forth and some decisions made by the buyer are lost (critique product tests). The team and the department only thought of the latter when the implemented feature could be tried out. With critique product tests, we usually want to further product analysis and make the best use of the principle of frequent iterations. The team-supporting tests, on the other hand, are supposed to ensure the basic functions, especially with many code revisions.

Four quadrants can now be derived from these two dimensions. This makes it possible to differentiate between four types of test and to derive different test strategies for them:

1. Quadrant: Unit tests and component tests
2. Quadrant: Functional tests, examples, story tests, prototypes, simulations
3. Quadrant: Exploratory Testing, scenarios, usability testing, user acceptance testing, alpha/beta testing
4. Quadrant: Load tests and performance testing, security testing, "*illity"- testing

As we can easily see, the four test quadrants show groups of tests with similar goals. Whether we conduct an "Alpha test" or prefer to speak of "Running through scenarios" is more related to the individual way of working in a team. The test goal of both forms of tests is the same. This division into four quadrants has proven to be extremely useful in the practice of agile teams to design and control all necessary test activities in agile projects.

3.1.2.1 First Quadrant: Technology-Oriented and Team-Supporting

Tests that are, on the one hand, technically oriented and, on the other, work in a team-supporting manner were usually the first tests conducted after the software had been developed. In agile teams, these test cases are often written before the actual code is created. This approach is called Test-Driven Development, also abbreviated as TDD (Beck, 2003).

This makes it clear how these tests are designed to support teams: They only test what the developer or the whole team has set out to do. Anyone who has already extensively carried out relatively late tests, such as beta tests or acceptance tests in traditional projects, knows that this challenge is not being mastered by many development teams. It is not uncommon for elementary arithmetic errors to occur in fully integrated systems. In agile projects, the risk of such situations increases because part of the work is revised or integrated daily and delivered after a few weeks. Coupled with an intuitive, iterative approach to the functionalities to be implemented (i.e., we deliberately think only until the next step[1]), this can result in a dangerous cocktail for code quality and stability.

Agile process models such as XP (Beck, 2000) or Lean Software Development (Poppendieck & Poppendieck, 2006) have therefore attached great importance to the highest quality right from the start: Only when software has to run against a set of test cases during development (often referred to as "test harness") can it survive frequent changes and revisions and reduce costly coordination processes in later test phases. Kent Beck gave the following example from a production chain:

> If one machine produces cans and the next machine fills and seals these cans, this production line works for a while. At some point, there is a defect in the second machine. The workers keep the first machine running and stack the cans in the hall so that no time is lost. Unfortunately, a little inaccuracy creeps into the first machine after a while, making the can radius too large. The workers only notice this when the second machine has started up again and, after the third storage pallet, for example, cannot fill the cans because the radius is too large. We can now adjust the first machine in a few simple steps, but we have to throw away a number of pallets of pre-made cans.

Translating this example back into testing: The development of code might be the first machine, the integration into an overall system the second. If we do not check the results right away, waste can be produced quickly. Therefore, extensive and early testing is a core discipline in agile projects. In the meantime, test-driven development has become established in many agile teams. In the development environment, the developers first write a test in the same programming language as the feature, and then implement the actual feature and immediately test what has been created with the test cases. One can use these tests again and again later to ensure that the old functions still work correctly after extensions or changes. There is hardly a programming language nowadays that does not provide a unit test framework (e.g., JUnit) that can comfortably execute tests implemented in few lines and report the results back to the developer.

In practice, we often experience the following pattern: An agile team knows the principle of test-driven development very well and is convinced that it will apply TDD. However, later tests on the overall system raise doubts about the code quality due to the errors. It turns out that every developer was more or less free to decide what and how much to test. Sometimes they don't even have to write test cases—at least no one within the team checks that they have. This discrepancy between claim and reality has a simple reason: TDD is a fairly complex procedure, which on the one hand might pull some developers out of their creative stream of ideas, and on the

---

[1] Architectural considerations and overall visions are of course also developed in agile projects, but during a sprint, teams usually try to focus on the sprint goal only.

other, creates significantly more effort than it appears at first glance. Many teams therefore enter into test-driven development very motivated, but then abandon it piece by piece after the first difficulties, such as tight deadlines or complications in implementing certain solutions/architectures. Once a lot of code has been written without extensive test cases, it will be difficult to catch up with the technical debt.

However, we also observed that in organizations that have multiple agile teams working side by side, the teams that continuously develop on a test-driven basis are more successful. This is shown by the fact that for those teams, on-time releases, high customer satisfaction, and low turnaround in the team become the rule. The rationale could also be reversed: The better the team is in general, the better they just manage to keep TDD. However, the recognition that TDD is now enjoying among experts in IT suggests that TDD is an important success factor, rather than the other way around.

The exact process flow of a test-driven development is provided here using a simple example:

1. Test creation
   Write a test case that checks whether the addition is calculated correctly—usually as a test class with one method per test case. In the test case, several significant examples of an addition can be tried out.

   If necessary, run the test together with other "older" tests. If it is written correctly, it will run through, but will return an error (red marking in the test case list) as the addition feature is not implemented yet.
2. Feature implementation
   Then write the actual feature that calculates the addition.
3. Test execution
   Run the tests again. If the program has been developed correctly, the tests no longer deliver an error (green marking in the test case list). If not, repeat steps 2 and 3 until the test is executed successfully.
4. Refactoring
   Optimize the code and the test case (refactoring). Perhaps "old" functions have now become unnecessary or you have taken detours when coding, which you can now remove once you have found the solution. The test can also be adapted in the same way: Perhaps tests have become unnecessary because they are now being tested in others or the function has changed.

   Do a retest after every change to make sure the functionality is still the same despite refactoring. Refactoring is intended to simplify code and tests without changing functionality or test coverage.

Anyone who does this ensures that the code is kept as simple as possible and has not lost any function even after multiple revisions and still delivers correct results. Interestingly, one will quickly notice when certain code is difficult or impossible to reach through tests. This is usually an indication of unnecessary parts that have already been implemented in anticipation of supposed future requirements.

Taking the TDD principle one step further, the principle of Continuous Integration has been established in agile teams: Code is integrated into the subsystem or sometimes even the entire system as soon as it has been implemented and the unit tests described above have successfully run. There are now mature build tools that automatically run a set of unit tests each time a developer checks in and only accept the build if the test is successful. In an attenuated form, such integration tests take place once a day or at least after 2 to 3 days. This includes the next levels of integration in the tests and ensures high quality early in the implementation cycle.

There are teams that manage to map entire business processes in the overall system in such integration tests, but the runtime of such extensive tests might exceed the developer's patience: Anyone who has to wait 15 to 30 min or even longer after a check-in to see whether their code is accepted will soon turn away from the principle of Continuous Integration.

Tests in this quadrant should therefore be suitable for automated and repeatable testing, if possible, within the framework of a unit or component test, which is usually carried out in the local development environment, or in an integration test, which is usually run during check-in. One should make sure:

- That the unit or component functionality is complete and works correctly
- That the units or components can be integrated into an overall system and they still work correctly
- That the classes are correctly built, meet the architectural requirements, and are programmed to be sufficiently robust (failsafe)
- That they have been implemented to be as simple as possible, and that they optimally handle resources such as CPU, memory, and bandwidth
- That only the bare minimum has been implemented, for which there can also be reasonable tests

It is advisable to ensure that these tests cover instructions and, if possible, branches (see Spillner & Linz, 2019). Most development environments now offer convenient monitors to make code coverage visible through tests.

The automation of these tests should be an absolute must in agile projects—except perhaps for peripheral areas that are difficult to automate. The additional effort for this, through TDD or Continuous Integration, is usually highly justifiable and pays off later due to significantly lower error rates and improved maintainability.

3.1.2.2 Second Quadrant: Business-Oriented and Team-Supporting

If we could choose, all the necessary tests would run immediately after a development step and report back to the developer whether everything still works as expected. Of course, this is only possible with a small portion of the tests, because even if everything ran automatically, the test run would only be finished after hours or days.

However, another aspect forces us to separate tests: Developers often see solutions from an implementation or architecture point of view and can quickly lose sight of what is important for the end user. For unit tests and component tests, this view could also be obstructive, because certain technically oriented tests are often only feasible in an integrated system, and intermediate steps and aspects of robustness, maintainability, and compliant architecture would be ignored. The change of perspective is also very important to completely cover the test activities within the team.

This leads us to the second quadrant of testing: It is still the aim of the test to determine what the team has immediately devised and planned, but this time from a business perspective. In most cases, several components will have to work together to obtain results that can be used by business. For example, we will not only check the input of invoice data into an accounting system but also start the end-of-day processing to view the printed invoice.

In traditional projects, this was usually the motivation to first integrate up to the system test and then switch to a black box view for testing (Spillner & Linz, 2019). Agile teams do not have to wait that long because they can integrate quickly and repeatedly and communicate closely between developers and testers. The tester can be the same person as the developer (although we do not recommend this), or a colleague, or sometimes a dedicated test expert in the team. The business-oriented test in our example above (accounting) can already be carried out for certain simpler types of invoicing because in the nightly build both the registration system and the end-of-day processing have already been checked in with some of the functionalities and by means of unit/component test are executable to run integrated. This function-oriented integration strategy requires efficient and close communication within the team and an architecture that can be run with partial functionality. Agile teams like to talk about functional tests or story tests. Others simply speak of examples, referring to the examples that are already used in the analysis (a typical element of the 'Specification by Example' approach).

Another approach in this quadrant is deliberately built "Potemkin villages" in the software, i.e., prototypes or already integrated but still half-finished routines, which allow new processes to be played through once. It is typical for embedded system components to integrate them into a prototype system and run exemplary simulations.

In both cases, however, there must be an instance in the team that pays attention to a suitable development order so that such early, business-oriented tests are possible. Therefore, it has now become established in agile teams that there should be at least one test expert in the team who brings these requirements into the team meetings and actively fetches the information about which sensibly testable parts are already finished from their colleagues. It has also been shown that it makes sense that someone deliberately maintains a business view throughout the entire time and thus keeps communication with experts and end users going (usually represented by the product owner in Scrum). Sometimes this almost means acting as an interpreter between the developer and the user.

There is a danger of getting lost very early on and, at some point, no longer being able to make a clear distinction between what one has set out to do with the task at hand and how it should be at some point in the future. One might also find already existing errors in the implementation, as solutions in the application do not prove to be useful. Although these thoughts are all important, they require a completely different test strategy. In the second test quadrant, one has to be very conscious of the tests that determine the functions as the team specifically intended (team support).

To clarify what this means, let us assume that a customer is dissatisfied with a (still) very cumbersome functionality because user data has to be copied manually from one application to the other. Many teams are now tempted to quickly provide an additional interface for the functionality, with which they unknowingly take too much on their plate. Assuming now that the interface function is an extremely complex matter that needs to be well thought out and tested, it is better to complete only what is absolutely necessary—albeit somewhat spartan—and to ensure it through high-quality tests. If the developers in our example then finally take care of the additional interface only in the following sprint, they can rely on effective regression tests and accordingly feel safer changing the code again. This is exactly the mission and advantage of "team-supporting" tests.

Tests that involve supporting the team should always be conducted repetitively and regularly, regardless of whether they are technically or business-oriented. They should simply ensure that the functionality and the nonfunctional aspects such as robustness and maintainability are retained after revisions.

However, business-oriented tests are usually inclining toward automation, although they are sometimes unwieldy because they might pursue an end-to-end view and are not so easy to map in a unit test framework (like JUnit). In terms of test data and test setup times (resetting a test environment, loading basic data, etc.), they are also significantly more demanding than unit and integration tests and are rarely included in the test runs for a daily build or Continuous Integration.

In the course of the last few years, however, very interesting solutions have been developed which allow the principle of unit tests to be extended to business-oriented tests: wiki-based test case editors (such as FitNesse), in which test cases can be described from a business point of view and then connect to technical test routines (so-called Fixtures). The principle in this case: Developers also adapt the affected test routines with the code, just as the unit tests in the TDD "grow" with the code. This means that regression tests can be started again relatively quickly even after a new build and new technical tests can be added based on a wiki. This procedure has established itself under the term Acceptance Test-Driven Development (ATDD). The core idea of ATDD is that the acceptance tests are written before the code is implemented or extended. This can help teams to better adapt their development to the needs of the business-oriented test, for example by first implementing individual business functionality across components and only then gradually completing the components.

It is therefore helpful to have the tests written by business experts (as representatives of the end users) or to derive them directly from the acceptance criteria of user stories. With this goal in mind, the so-called Behavior Driven Development (BDD) has been established as an extension of ATDD, which can best be translated into behavior-driven development. The acceptance criteria described are substantiated by business test cases. These are mostly formulated in semiformal "If-then" sentences and thus the concrete behavior of the application in certain scenarios is described (given-when-then). The test cases are no longer represented in the form of data tables or script tables but are written in normal textual form—possibly supplemented by individual tables for data variants. The advantage is that the BDD test cases can be understood as part of the verbally formulated user story or requirement. Especially the principle of Specification by Example uses this direct possibility to generate automated technical tests from verbal specifications (Adzic, 2011).

The principle of the tests in this test quadrant becomes clear once again: They are team-supporting tests that implement exactly what the team, including its analysts or experts, has planned. What is tested is what has already been defined in the form of user stories or other formulated requirements. Of course, in agile teams, this does not mean page-by-page specifications, but rather concise specifications or specific application examples that structure and promote the team discussion. These tests should run in as automated a manner as possible, or at least be tested regularly in regression. Many technical scenarios can only be automated with great effort, especially when it comes to end-to-end business processes. Therefore, Crispin and Gregory recommend testing both manually and automatically. It is important, however, that these tests are made repeatable. They should therefore be specified in such a form that retains them for future regression and, if possible, allows them to be carried out with the same quality.

3.1.2.3 Third Quadrant: Business-Oriented and Critique the Product

It is hard to imagine that a well-prepared and reviewed set of well-documented test cases covers absolutely everything that needs to be professionally tested in a release. Even in traditional project environments, where this is regarded as the high art of testing, additional "exploratory" tests are usually carried out deliberately by experienced end users at the end as an acceptance test. But why would we do that if we already have the optimal coverage through tests in advance?

With most software, there is an infinite number of possible ways to use it, and it is impossible to cover them all in testing. Experienced end users in the acceptance tests can often find ways to use the software that the implementation team deemed impossible. There are even test methodologists like Whittaker (Whittaker, 2003) who are convinced that software shows its quality weaknesses especially when used in an unusual way.

In the agile world, this test, which addresses the "Impossible," has another important function: It is part of the analysis, i.e., to think beyond what has been considered so far and to generate important requirements for future releases. These tests are therefore called "critique the product." Are the functions that are already implemented suitable for simulating future use in production? It is a point of view that was implied by "Validation" in the traditional V-Model but is often neglected in practice.

Still, such tests are even more demanding than the tests of the first and second test quadrants. In this case, a qualitatively good image of the production in terms of data constellations and system communication is required (possibly simulated via mocking or drivers/stubs). It is not about thinking on "well-walked" paths, but about reacting intuitively to the experience of testing. Test automation is therefore mostly not helpful—it is not possible to script these tests in advance. However, it may very well be the case that the "Best of" tests from this test quadrant will be included in the test portfolio of the first two test quadrants for regression tests in the next iterations. In addition, pre-test or post-test routines, such as the preparation of test data or the target/actual comparison of test results, can be automated in order to be able to concentrate on the actual testing task and gain the necessary flexibility for intuitive or spontaneous test access.

All tests that are close to the end user fall into this category. On the one hand, these are alpha and beta tests or, more generally, typical acceptance tests for end users. On the other hand, there are usually usability tests, which, depending on the area of application, might even have to be carried out on-site with end users, and large-scale, often cross-departmental test scenarios in which many users have to participate.

A typical test method in this test quadrant is Exploratory Testing, wherein tests are performed intuitively, supported by the procedure (Whittaker, 2009). Now every test definition is associated with intuition, but in Exploratory Testing, the tester's intuition is used *during* the test. The tester responds to observations made in the test with further tests. In this way, they can specifically investigate the focus of errors or surprising system behavior and thereby uncover targeted weak points. However, because it is easy to get lost or lose the overview, approaches such as session-based Exploratory Testing (Bach, 2000) have been developed. After each test session, the result is checked by the team or an expert and then a specific test charter is defined for the next test session.

Not only do such methods achieve fair test coverage with relatively manageable effort, but they also expand the tester's experience and offer new approaches for future requirements. Especially when representatives of the end users are involved, who either act as testers themselves or as experts for the test review, a constructive discussion about requirements between the team and the department can take place. One can even extend these tests by simply trying out certain scenarios in an overall system context out of curiosity to see what is already working and where there is still need for additions or corrections.

3.1.2.4 Fourth Quadrant: Technology-Oriented and Critique the Product

There are—in the traditional as well as in the agile project environment—a few special tests, which run significantly differently than the usual developer or business tests. These tests usually need their own test specialists who specialize in the types of errors found: We are talking about load tests and performance tests, security tests, and reliability tests (restart/recovery, etc.). Without specific tool support for testing and test evaluation, these tests can hardly be mastered.

A good system architecture and good development specifications should always take quality features such as reliability, efficiency (load and performance behavior), maintainability, portability, and security into account during development, i.e., the so-called nonfunctional quality features (ISO/IEC 25000, 2005). Accordingly, one can expect that there will already be tests during the development of the code, in which routines and technical precautions have to be checked, which primarily serve these nonfunctional quality features. However, these are routines that the team has deliberately built in, such as high-performance access to data or code structures, which provide reliable access protection.

However, there are effects in the integrated system that are difficult to foresee from a development perspective and must therefore be checked again in a targeted manner. Neither can the developers estimate with certainty whether the routines they provide, for example for performance or security, really work. Long runtimes can arise because the service call between two systems is poorly coordinated or configured. Security problems can also occur because the security precautions in the code are counteracted by the hardware property.

For this reason, these tests, which—usually carried out on completely integrated systems—are aimed at certain technical quality features, are called *technology-oriented* and *critique the product*. Like the third test quadrant, the tests can be used to gain important insights that will become requirements for future iterations.

Reliability is tested, above all, jointly with experts from the operations unit. In this case, it is usually a matter of going through typical fail-over scenarios and paying attention to their usefulness and feasibility. Can the system be restarted in an orderly manner after a failure, and will the data recovery routines also apply? Can suitable capacity be added if the hardware is overloaded? These tests usually also have the advantage that—as with a fire brigade drill—the operations unit can practice their movements once, which later in an "emergency" must go safely and quickly.

Load and performance are relatively easy to test at first glance if we have a suitable load generator and suitable load monitors. Unfortunately, this is usually a more complicated matter because we might test unrealistic situations or cannot get the right data states and amounts (e.g., by forgetting or incorrectly simulating the background load on the machines). The right monitors are also difficult to set up. Even with state-of-the-art tools, we still need extensive access to various test machines, which data center operations are often reluctant to grant to external users.

Security tests are relatively easy for experts to implement when it comes to checking the authorization concept for access and various user roles. However, these tests can usually be predefined exactly by the team and therefore fit in the first or second test quadrant. The aspect of unauthorized access to the software or the system is much more difficult. This requires experts who are constantly up to date on the latest developments and who are very familiar with penetration techniques. Such experts confront the development team or the architecture with interesting weaknesses in their software, which they would not have come across without outside help and without the specific test example.

Overall, the tests in the fourth test quadrant can rarely be carried out by the agile team itself. This usually requires cross-team experts who are consulted on a case-by-case basis. Large organizations set up their own test centers or test laboratories, which act as internal service providers for the agile teams. Others, in turn, have special test experts who selectively perform test orders from different teams and otherwise work like "normal" testers in agile teams.

Even if such tests for reliability, efficiency, and safety are preferably carried out on integrated systems, one should not wait until shortly before going live. Some of the tests can take place in very early phases, for example if we carry out a kind of proof of concept with prototype components for the architectural concept. The remaining tests may have to wait until shortly before the end of the release (e.g., for a Hardening Iteration[2]) but should then only confirm the effectiveness of the implemented measures. In the case of typical production-preventing errors in terms of reliability, efficiency, and safety, there is usually no time to correct the software. Such errors often require a change of third-party components (driver software, frameworks) or an architectural change.

3.1.2.5 The Context

The model that Lisa Crispin and Janet Gregory designed for testing in agile teams clearly addresses the typical XP or scrum team, which has a few specific stakeholders for the technical requirements but can otherwise regulate things relatively independently. The model is also attractive for teams organized with Kanban, but it depends on how the process based on the division of tasks is organized in the respective Kanban team.

This model is always difficult to use when the integration processes from the individual component into the overall system are multi-staged and very complex. Especially in industries such as telecommunications and insurance/banking, we have seen that agile teams can only act to a limited extent independently. Just try, for example, to activate a SIM card for a mobile phone on the customer portal if the area of responsibility of the team is only the billing system. Until such a comprehensive test works, the tester may have spent weeks in the organization with coordination activities only. The billing could be tested separately, but then we would hardly get past the first or maybe even the second test quadrant because it is always only the smallest processes that then require the intervention of a neighboring system.

Limits become clear even if the responsibilities in an organization for the many aspects of software development are organizationally distributed. In general, the local distribution of a team poses a risk since close communication is of great

---

[2]In Scrum, Hardening Iteration means an iteration (sometimes even a second) shortly before a release, in which no new stories are implemented, but only bugs are fixed, or as is commonly heard in agile circles, "The technical debt is settled."

importance in this model. Where this does not work, tests must be planned and assigned sequentially again.

However, these limits are the typical limits that generally apply to agile projects. The more complex the organizational or architectural structure, the more difficult it is to implement communication requirements for agile teams. As in the case of Scott Ambler (see Sect. 3.1.5), a somewhat more tightly organized process framework is then required, which in turn is reminiscent of traditional process models (Ambler & Lines, 2012).

3.1.3 Tips for Software Testing from an Agile Perspective

Agile process models, above all Extreme Programming, or XP for short (Beck, 2000), or even Lean Software Development (Poppendieck & Poppendieck, 2006), tend to reject process and organizational guidelines because teams are supposed to organize themselves. Under these conditions, it seems more sensible to pass on test experience to the teams in the form of tips and recommendations.

Cem Kaner, James Bach, and Bret Pettichord have therefore described their collective experience in software testing as so-called lessons learned (Kaner, Bach, & Pettichord, 2002). These lessons learned reflect general test wisdom, which also applies to traditional project environments. They can therefore be adopted by any team and in daily practice without a specific procedure being necessary.

The lessons that are particularly interesting for test organization are mentioned as examples:

Lesson 157: *Create a service culture*
    Testers should lose the habit of acting as a supervisory authority in the project. This prevents team communication. They should see themselves as a service provider for the other stakeholders in the project (developers, analysts, project managers).

Lesson 167: *Be willing to allocate resources on the project early in development*
    The test must be well prepared and there are, even if it is sometimes hard to imagine, a whole range of measures that testers can take to prepare in a meaningful way without writing a single line of code (align test and measurement methods, review requirements, refine review procedures, align testability requirements with developers, etc.)

Lesson 168: *Contract-driven development is different from market-seeking development*
    Testers need to be able to assess the environment in which they operate. If the development has to provide a firmly agreed delivery, testers will probably have to test mainly against the agreed specifications. If it is about placing the software on the market in an attractive and timely manner, testers will probably have to consider the requirements of a wide variety of customers at the same time.

Lesson 171: *Understand what programmers do (and do not do) before delivering a build*
Try avoiding educating the development team unnecessarily. Either they test in detail before delivery or not. One should know this in advance as a tester and adjust the test accordingly.

Lesson 172: *Be prepared for the build*
A lot must be ensured before the test execution (test data, test environment, etc.). Do not wait until delivery.

Lesson 174: *Use smoke tests to assess a build*
Before a build goes into the test, it should qualify as worthy of testing through a smoke test. Smoke tests should be simple tests that are as automated as possible to ensure basic functionality. Ideally, these tests are already carried out by the developers themselves to prove the testability. This relieves the testers because they do not lose time with "unviable" builds.

Lesson 176: *Adapt your process to the development practice that is actually in use*
Change your test approach rather than the developer's approach. Otherwise, you are just wasting time waiting with your test procedure for an optimized development process.

Lesson 179: *Take advantage of other sources of information*
Even if there are no reliable specifications on which the tests can be based, there are always plenty of alternatives in projects to obtain the required information in other ways (user manuals, protocols from change control boards, marketing presentations about the product, generic error lists on the Internet or in the literature, etc.).

Lesson 182: *Great test planning makes late changes easy*
This point can be misleading: It does not mean an elaborate or sophisticated test concept, but exactly the opposite, a pragmatic and effective approach:

- Rather than developing a large suite of tests in advance of testing, develop tests as you need them. If later changes to the product make these tests obsolete, at least they will have been useful for a while.
- Do not create enormous test documents that have high maintenance costs, such as detailed manual test scripts. Keep your paperwork as lean as possible.
- Do not tie manual or automated tests to specifics of the user interface, other than tests specifically intended for the user interface (UI). Even if you do end-to-end testing, which is necessarily using the user interface, do not tie your test to the details of the UI, because they will change.
- Design automated tests in ways that maximize their maintainability and their portability across platforms.
- Build a set of generic tests that handle situations that recur in application after application. This saves planning time and eases delegation when a new feature is added, or a feature is changed late in the project.
- Build a strong set of smoke tests, to detect basic failures in the software under test quickly (see also lesson 174).
- Seriously consider using Extreme Programming methods to develop automated tests (Beck, 2003). In particular, we recommend building an overall architecture and design for the automated tests and then designing and delivering code iteratively, delivering solutions in an order that minimizes project

risk (the project here is the testing subproject), programming in pairs, and working closely with your stakeholders (other testers, programmers, and the project manager) to determine what needs to be done next. Specifically, it is recommended to use a project-spanning architecture and design for automated testing, create and deliver code iteratively, design automation solutions in the order in which the highest risks are eliminated first, use pair programming, and work closely with test stakeholders such as testers, developers, or the project manager to decide the next steps.

- Develop a model of the users of the product and the benefits they will want to achieve from it. Derive complex tests from this model. Most of these tests will not change rapidly as the project progresses, because they are focused on benefits rather than implementation details.
- Help the programmers develop a large suite of unit tests and other tests of relatively simple functionality. These can be run every time the code is rebuilt before it is sent for testing.

Lesson 186: *Never budget for only two testing cycles*

If you think you can get by with one initial test and one regression test until the release, you are mistaken. It usually takes several iterations until the test runs satisfactorily and the software quality enters the target corridor.

Lesson 190: *There is no right ratio of testers to developers*

This question must always be decided on a case-by-case basis. The circumstances of projects and team skills are just too different.

Lesson 195: *Tests in sessions*

Testers must be able to concentrate during testing and should not be constantly interrupted. Therefore, there should be 60- to 90-min test sessions in which a tester or test team can work in a concentrated manner and only focus on the planned tests.

Lesson 196: *Use activity logs to reveal the interruptions that plague testers' work*

If the test is not effective or efficient, have the tester produce a test log that usually shows how often they have been distracted by other activities or interruptions.

The original list of lessons starts at 1 and ends at 200. Although it is roughly structured, it is not a coherent model of thinking, but contains typical everyday rules that one should keep in mind.

The advantage of these rules is that they can also be used in traditional tests and clearly separate the role of testers from that of developers. Nevertheless, it is clear from time to time that session-based Exploratory Testing and test-driven development are the two core practices that the authors rely on—not without reason.

3.1.4 Scaled Agile with SAFe or LeSS

Scrum, Kanban, XP, or Lean Development have proven to be useful for individual product teams. Agile IT work is now being used so extensively that often ten or more teams have to work on the same products at the same time.

In order to provide an entire organization with good guidelines on how to make agile work constructive even on a large scale, models—also called frameworks—show how agile teams can be organized on a large scale. One of the first was certainly the principle "Scrum of Scrums" (Eckstein, 2011), but since then more comprehensive models have been developed and matured.

We will take a look at the two most popular frameworks at present, namely the Scaled Agile Framework (SAFe® for short) and Large-Scale Scrum (LeSS for short), and explain how testing is anchored in both models.

Testing in both frameworks is clearly the responsibility of each team and *everyone* in the team is responsible for quality. In this respect, both frameworks remain true to the Scrum principles, even if they are deliberately open to other agile process models. But it is still worth taking a closer look.

3.1.4.1 Testing with SAFe

SAFe is based on a suitable organizational structure, so that large projects can be moved in the same direction across many teams. Depending on the size of the programs and projects and the organizational scope, SAFe can be configured in different ways. The latest version, SAFe 5.0, builds on the seven core competencies of a lean organization that are critical to achieving and maintaining a competitive advantage in an increasingly digital age. These are also of corresponding importance in the respective configurations.

Essential SAFe: The basic configuration of the SAFe framework, which provides a minimum of necessary elements to be successful with SAFe.

Core competencies:

- Team Agility and Technical Agility: Agile behavior of the team; solid technical practices such as built-in quality, Behavior-Driven Development (BDD), Agile Testing, Test-Driven Development (TDD)
- Agile Product Delivery: Continuous flow of valuable products, Agile Release Train, DevOps, Continuous Delivery Pipeline, Release on Demand, Design Thinking, and Customer Centricity
- Lean Agile Leadership: Lean agile leadership skills, organizational change by empowering individuals and teams

Large Solution SAFe: The configuration for companies that build large and complex solutions.

Core competencies (additional):

- Enterprise solutions delivery: Solution Train, building and maintaining the largest software applications

Portfolio SAFe: This offers portfolio strategy and investment funding as well as agile portfolio operations and lean governance (Fig. 3.3).

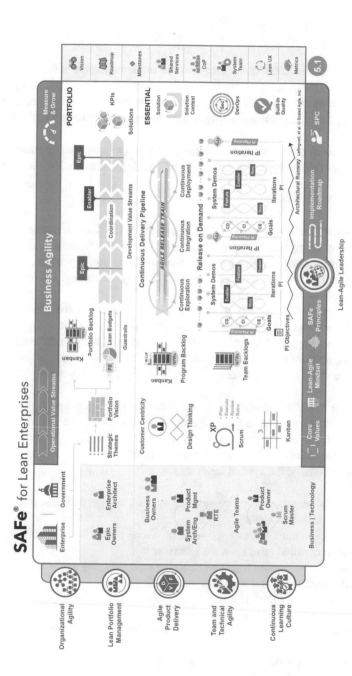

Fig. 3.3 The portfolio configuration of SAFe (source: Scaled Agile, Inc., 2017 © 2011–2017 Scaled Agile, Inc. All rights reserved)

Core competencies (additional):

- Organizational agility: Aligning strategy and execution by applying lean and systems thinking to strategy and investment funding, Agile portfolio operations, and governance
- Lean portfolio management: Charter creation and implementation of the portfolio vision and strategy, lean budgets, portfolio prioritization, and road mapping
- Continuous learning culture: Continually increasing knowledge, competence, and performance by becoming a learning organization, improvement, and innovation

Full SAFe: The most comprehensive configuration that supports the building of large, integrated solutions—typically hundreds of people or more in development and maintenance.

Core competencies: All of the above!

There is a range of useful literature on SAFe (especially the documentation of the Scaled Agile Community (Scaled Agile, Inc., 2017)), so we only want to describe the organization of the software test here. As mentioned at the beginning, quality assurance and thus the test are seen as a special activity of the agile teams and therefore no separate roles for testers are defined in SAFe.

We do know, however, that comprehensive cross-team testing activities must be carried out that clearly exceed the possibilities of individual agile teams. Especially in the area of system integration testing , nonfunctional tests at the system level, test data management, and test environment management the requirements are usually immense and can only be solved across teams—at least if we want to remain efficient.

SAFe defines a so-called System Team for these tasks, which operates at the portfolio level or, in the case of larger projects, at least at the value stream level. Interestingly, this team is also responsible for the infrastructure for the entire development and for the releases, which go very well together.

The *test-related* tasks of the system team are:

- Provide test environments with processes that are as automated as possible.
- Provide technical aids and tools.
- Support planning product increments—a term from SAFe that can be freely associated with individual product-wide releases.
- Provide and carry out system integration tests as automatically as possible.
- Carry out end-to-end tests, and load and performance tests.
- Support test automation across teams.
- Manage comprehensive test data across teams.
- Coordinate and optimize the tests of the individual teams for comprehensive test scenarios.
- Optimize resource-intensive tests or test procedures.
- Carry out reliability and security tests.
- Provide more extensive product demonstrations.

Fig. 3.4 Optimal shared responsibility between agile teams and system team (source: Scaled Agile, Inc., 2017)—

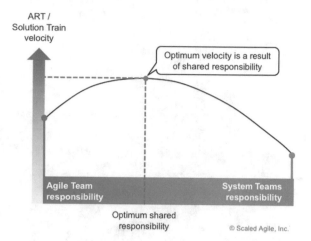

Now a conflict of competence between agile teams and the system team is almost inevitable. There is no definition of where the competence limit lies, but rather a decision support: The system team has the task of working on exactly the optimum of cross-team support. Thus, it should neither patronize the teams and dictate every method, nor stand by and allow ineffective double strategies between the teams.

But how do we find the optimum of responsibility between agile teams and the system team? The key figure here is the velocity of the agile teams being supervised (usually in an agile Release Train, abbreviated as ART). As the responsibility of the System Team increases, the velocity of the ART, i.e., the agile teams together, will increase until it decreases again at some point, as the System Team then takes over things that each Agile Team must better solve on its own. At the portfolio level, we could also use the Value Stream instead of the ART, or at the Large Solutions level the Large Solutions Train. But this does not change the principle of thought (Fig. 3.4).

This is interesting insofar as it is not abstract parameters or interests of the organization that are decisive for the organizational strategy, but rather the benefits for the teams being supervised and ultimately for the end product. Even if we cannot measure the velocity of the entire ART precisely in practice and, above all, we cannot pinpoint the optimum precisely, it is a good principle of thought at hand to negotiate the competencies with each other.

3.1.4.2 Testing with LeSS

Large-Scale Scrum (LeSS), in contrast to SAFe, does not primarily focus on defined organizational structures, but rather on the principles for successful cooperation. The dominant belief here is that the teams can work with and among themselves to find the best organizational form that will make them successful (Fig. 3.5).

Even in the case of LeSS, we will not find explicit instructions on how to organize the test in a team or across teams. Quality assurance starts in the spirit of Scrum with EVERYONE in the team. Thus, everyone is responsible for ensuring that testing takes place to the required and efficient extent.

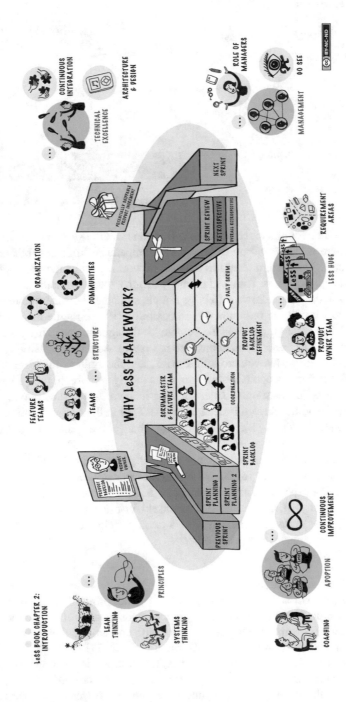

Fig. 3.5 Overview of the Large-Scale Scrum framework (Source: LeSS, 2017)

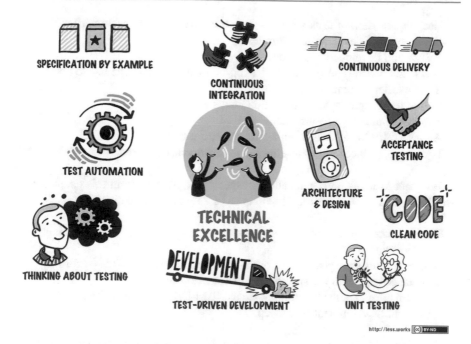

Fig. 3.6 Best practices of technical excellence in the LeSS framework (Source: LeSS, 2017)

However, LeSS provides very interesting guidelines for tests to work well even in large organizations. They are hidden in the LeSS framework under the topic "Technical Excellence". A good number of the skills listed here as essential for the success of agile projects (see also Fig. 3.6) relate to the test:

- Unit testing
- Test-Driven Development
- Thinking About Testing (freely translatable as testing considerations)
- Test automation
- Acceptance testing (includes system test and acceptance test)
- Specification by Example
- Continuous Integration (Fig. 3.6)

Regarding the organization of testing, the section "Thinking about Testing" is particularly clear. In this case, the approaches of the four test quadrants described above and the lessons learned in software testing (see Sects. 3.1.2 and 3.1.3) are the inspiration. The following guidelines are important for LeSS:

- Testing no longer means testing—because it is an important part of the specification.
- Question common assumptions about testing—for example, that testing must be done by independent testers.
- Avoid complex test terms that only confuse others.

- Keep the division of tests simple—there are developer and customer tests!
- Never separate development from test.
- Testers and developers work together.
- Teach and coach (good) testing—testing is not a triviality; one has to learn it.
- Build a tester community.
- Do not form separate test automation teams.
- Test automation as a feature team.
- All tests must be successful, otherwise interrupt and fix the errors.
- The zero-tolerance applies to errors—all errors must be fixed.

We want to focus on organizational aspects of agile testing in this chapter, and here LeSS takes a clear position in all areas of "Technical Excellence":

- Testing takes place in the respective team—never separate testing and development!
- Acceptance tests are also carried out as far as possible in a sprint—regarding user acceptance tests with the specific involvement of the department.
- Tests are created at the beginning—so use Test-Driven Development and Behavior Driven Development (see Chap. 7).

Even test automation should take place within the teams if possible. Unless there is another option, test automation should be carried out by a feature team. Feature teams are a concept from LeSS, among others, according to which various agile teams work on a product and each contributes individual features in a coordinated manner. Test automation would then be regarded as a partial functionality of the product, the sprint increments of which are well coordinated with the work of the other teams.

For all other team-spanning tasks in the test (e.g., system integration test), there is certainly no recommendation for an organizational separation from the agile teams. Here LeSS relies on the so-called Community of Practice (CoP) spanning multiple agile teams, in which experts from the agile teams meet regularly on a topic—in this case, testing. In this CoP we exchange, and evaluate the experience, discuss common procedures, and jointly take up new trends. Organizing methods, keeping them alive and effective, would then be the task of a comprehensive test manager—if there is one.

The test experts in the CoP Test act as test coaches in their own agile teams, so that the knowledge and the team-spanning agreements can be passed on to all other team members. It is also important to mention that in LeSS there are no dedicated test experts who are exclusively coaches and do nothing else. It is just a role that a specially qualified team member takes on.

3.1.5   Scalable Organization of Agile Teams

Scott Ambler, one of the great agile thought leaders, notes that many agile process models have limits in two ways:

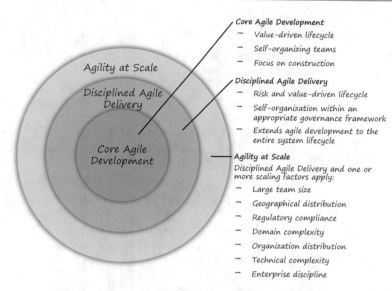

Core Agile Development
- Value-driven lifecycle
- Self-organizing teams
- Focus on construction

Disciplined Agile Delivery
- Risk and value-driven lifecycle
- Self-organization within an appropriate governance framework
- Extends agile development to the entire system lifecycle

Agility at Scale
Disciplined Agile Delivery and one or more scaling factors apply:
- Large team size
- Geographical distribution
- Regulatory compliance
- Domain complexity
- Organization distribution
- Technical complexity
- Enterprise discipline

Fig. 3.7 The three layers of the Agile Scaling Model. Reprint Courtesy of International Business Machines Corporation, © 2009 International Business Machines Corporation

- An overall picture of the software life cycle from the first idea to maintenance is missing.
- The models are difficult to scale or adapt to different project environments.

With his *Agile Scaling Model* he wants to combat these weaknesses (Ambler, 2009) (Fig. 3.7),

The core practices of agile development include well-known procedural models such as XP, Scrum, and Feature Driven Development. They are characterized by three principles:

- Value-oriented life cycles
- Self-organizing teams
- Focus on development/manufacturing

These are being supplemented by life cycle models that focus on disciplined agile delivery. It is now a matter of orienting the software life cycle according to risk and value and developing a governance strategy for the organization that allows and uses self-organization. The life cycle for development and implementation from the agile core practices is completed to a comprehensive software life cycle with conception, elaboration, handover, and maintenance (Ambler & Lines, 2012).

First of all, the life cycle of the software must be supplemented by the phase of conception or start (Inception) at the beginning and the phases of handover to production (Transition) and maintenance (Production). The terms are taken directly from the Rational Unified Process (RUP). The phase Elaboration & Construction from the RUP are represented by the actual iterations, for example a Scrum procedure (Fig. 3.8).

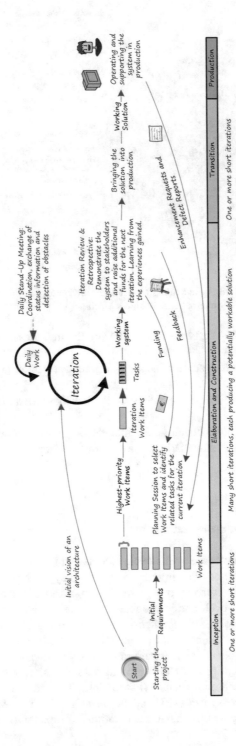

Fig. 3.8 Agile delivery life cycle—as a holistic view of software creation. Reprint Courtesy of International Business Machines Corporation,
© 2009 International Business Machines Corporation

Such a comprehensive process model must have the following four properties so that it also meets the agile requirements:

- **Agile delivery processes are sequential on a large scale and iterative on a small scale.**
  Overall, the projects do not fall into waterfall or V-Models, but—as Scott Ambler puts it—have certain "seasons" in which one or the other is in the foreground. In the inception phase, agile teams will rather develop the project idea and work more prototypically; in the elaboration and construction phase the traditional development process of functionalities and their integration will be in the foreground; and in the transition phase hardening iterations will probably be more popular, in which acceptance tests can also be more extensive. Maintenance is about hot fixing for production and manageable changes in which the regression test is in the foreground.
- **Teams are working on a solution, not just software.**
  It is important that not everything is just software, but always a little—or sometimes a lot—hardware. The term solution is much more robust than just software over the entire software life cycle.
- **The entire software life cycle is always guided by risk and business value.**
  The principle that agile teams generally follow, for example when working through a backlog, must also apply on a large scale. In the early stages, try to avoid the worst risks and first create the solutions that bring the greatest benefit for future use. Especially in an inception phase, the following should be addressed: technology decisions, restructuring of work processes among users that cause the greatest uncertainties, and the fact that the next steps in the development or production should always be based on cost-benefit considerations.
- **Self-organization must remain within the overall corporate governance strategy.**
  It is important that the agile teams have enough freedom to optimize themselves. Nevertheless, we have to draw clear boundaries if an overarching infrastructure (e.g., tools, methods) has advantages or can only be leveraged when used collectively. Agile approaches for self-organization need to be limited if they violate organization-wide beliefs or are not aligned on the goals of an organization (e.g., the implementation of a legal regulation or the achievement of a certain market share). Such organizational conditions are of great relevance, especially for testing. But beware: There is a fine line between joint alignment and smoothing—especially in the test environment (see DeMarco & Lister, 1999).

Nevertheless, it is not wrong to work long term on structures and framework conditions that enable consistently agile teams (as described above). In the meantime, however, one should skillfully and constructively practice compromises. It remains to be seen whether an adapted V-Model or an adapted RUP should serve as a framework for the overall program. The phases delineated by Scott Ambler (Inception, Elaboration & Construction, Transition, Production) can give agile teams a good orientation over time, on what needs to be considered separately and how, for example, testing in the product life cycle has to change.

Of course, it is clear that we are shaking the foundations of self-organization. But as long as we do it carefully, i.e., provide a high-level governance framework, this can support extensive and complex situations.

3.2   Practical Examples

Below are a few examples of how testers organized themselves in agile project environments. In the first example, the subject of an agile team is the test itself, i.e., functioning tests instead of functioning software. As we can see, the variety of solutions is a healthy reaction to the respective boundary conditions.

3.2.1   The Role of the Tester and the Transition to "Quality Specialist" at Otto.de: A Progress Report

Before I started at OTTO in January 2012, there were testers and test managers in a test team. Flanked by the final acceptance tests of those responsible for the business, the traditional way was to test what could or could not be done at the end of a software development cycle.

This procedure was retained for the OTTO legacy Shop until the end of its life cycle. In parallel, however, a new approach started: The entire shop was to be made available to the customer in autumn 2013 using agile methods.

So much in advance: This live event went down in OTTO history as a "non-event." Until then, however, it was a long way to go. Not only was otto.de developed from scratch, new technologies had to be dealt with and the demand for sticky notes grew rapidly, but also the people involved had to rethink the approaches.

I joined the FT2 team as an "agile test manager" (FT = functional team). The team took care of the domains search, navigation, and article detail page including data supply. Like FT1 and FT3, the team consisted of several developers, an agile test manager, and the triad. The triad consisted of the roles of business designer (technical requester), technical designer (technical requester), and project lead.

We followed a model best called "Waterscrum." Every 2 weeks, the business designer brought new stories to the team in Sprint Planning, whose complexity we had estimated in part weeks in advance. The stories committed by the team were developed within 2 weeks. At the end of each story, it was "fully" tested manually. The automation of tests was largely limited to the unit and integration tests that the developers wrote at their discretion. In addition, the acceptance criteria changed frequently during the implementation, which at least in my role led to the rewriting of test cases in the specified test documentation tool. Due to the parallel processing, several stories were often handed over for testing at the end of a sprint. According to the Definition of Done, a story was done as soon as it was accepted by the business designer. This meant that deviations found had to be assessed and corrected if necessary. It is not surprising that stories were often only finished at the beginning of the subsequent print and often only later in case I as test manager was on vacation.

Technical stories (e.g., changing interfaces) without a direct business reference were only checked indirectly when the corresponding business requirement was implemented.

Parallel to the implementation of the individual stories in the functional teams, an overarching team worked on a solution for the release go-live from a QA perspective.

Quite obviously, QA quickly became a bottleneck and was only partially involved in all steps in a software cycle. So, what to do? During the estimation meeting, I was already able to point out the complexity of the tests and thus influence the entire estimate. Furthermore, already during the sprint planning, the typical test cases and edge cases were defined for the story and the acceptance criteria were roughly checked. Finding solutions to the challenges of QA was also a key point in various retrospectives.

A first step was to bring the QA tasks to the common board in more granular form to make transparent which steps were a bottleneck. One problem was the almost simultaneous completion of stories, so I had to test a lot more quickly and in parallel to have everything ready by the end of the sprint. The first thing we tried was working on a maximum of two stories simultaneously. This caused some developers to idle, which in turn led to frustration and underutilized team members.

To counteract this, the team supported the QA approval with varying levels of motivation—in other words, a developer who was not involved in the implementation of the story tested the story. From my QA perspective, this again led to the obvious defects being missed. One possible solution to this is to first make the approvals as a pair so that the individual team members are able to train their test perspective. The enthusiasm in the team for this measure was also varying. An argument that helped both sides was: "Nothing is more annoying than getting something back on the table when you are already deep in the next task."

Another problem was that I often tested things that were not in the acceptance criteria but rather in the body of the story. Thus, we started to work on the quality of the acceptance criteria. Before the stories went into the estimation, there were three of us: requester, developer, and QA. Together we clearly defined the acceptance criteria for all perspectives. As QA, I naturally paid attention to the testability of these criteria. Additionally, developers became so-called story sponsors who contributed to the understanding of the entire team during the estimation meeting and then served as a contact, to relieve the burden on requesters and QA.

During this time, several teams started at least test-driven development, but also behavior-driven development if it was possible. A major challenge in this procedure was to think together about what was to be tested at which level of the test pyramid. The respective discussion was particularly difficult for testers/test managers, whose knowledge related purely to user interface tests. They were often taught: "As a tester, you should have no idea about white box tests, otherwise you cannot carry out true black box tests."

If we design and automate the test cases first and then gradually implement the functionality, these concerns no longer apply. For developers and QA alike, this means that they both have to learn something from the other role.

The cooperation of QA and the developer in the automation of tests has further advantages. First, the manual test effort at the end of a story is reduced. It is often enough to limit ourselves to Exploratory Testing since the most important tests are already automated. Second, only what is necessary is automated and developed. Moreover, the tests are already documented and are continuously executed. Because the test pyramid can be better maintained, the speed of testing a release is significantly higher and the number of false positives/negatives is reduced.

From the perspective of the software products/systems to be managed, we were a big step ahead. But what about the interfaces between the systems and the overall system, and where are the limits of the overall system?

Each team was responsible for one or multiple business domains. These had system/domain interfaces. The first step was to automate test cases for them through a central team. These worked for a few months. But then locators were renamed, functions ceased to exist, or the interfaces changed. We learned from this that we had to find a way that was integrated into our processes.

The solution for us was called CDC Tests (Consumer-Driven Contract). Each team was equipped with its pipelines, which built, tested, and deployed the software. The entire system—with reduced data—integrated directly into the first test environment. So why not run the interface tests from the interface consuming team A in the pipeline of interface provider team B so Team B notices "immediately" if it violates contracts with Team A and can react accordingly? In the case of a real error, correct it immediately or make the interface backward compatible if we intend to make a change and ask Team A to adjust the use of the interface. But what if Team A's system fails and the CDCs fail? We experienced these cases a few times in the beginning. Ninety-nine percent of the solution was to minimize the tests. It is only about getting an expected response from the interface and not processing the response in the system.

In an ideal world, one could assume that the entire system will no longer have a fault if all individual systems and all interfaces between the systems have been tested and the systems are otherwise completely independent of one another.

Since there is no such thing as "ideal" and "error-free" in a software world, there are several possible solutions for checking or repairing the entire system. We are currently using two paths. On the one hand, we check through automated journey tests ,from a customer perspective, that the customer typically continues to have the same positive shopping experience. On the other hand, we have accelerated our go-live process so that any defect correction can be deployed quickly so that a defect is only live for a minimal amount of time.

We implement fast defect correction using various means. There is a shift from the active to the inactive system, on which the previous software version is still located. There is also a fast fix forward that goes live as normal over different stages and the usual tests. We also work with feature toggles that can switch off entire software parts. Incidentally, a fault condition is determined, among other things, by monitoring the systems. It is automatically determined whether, for example, there is an atypically high number of failed login attempts.

Fast live software delivery with consistently excellent quality for the customer works through a high degree of automation of the right tests at the right level, and is possible through the cooperation of various roles involved in the software product. As a colleague says: "... we used to go live 1–2 times a week. Always with an uneasy feeling whether everything is still going well after that, so far, we have had 95 rollouts in production."

My QA colleagues and I have developed further strategies for this. We not only check the software for its functional and nonfunctional requirements, but also integrate ourselves in all stages of the life cycle. We are involved in everything from discovery to implementation and live broadcasting to software monitoring. We influence the optimization of processes in the team, practice (test) pair programming and help the business to ask the right questions. We see ourselves as bridge builders but are also prepared to ask uncomfortable questions.

We are now much more than "agile test managers"; we are quality specialists .

3.2.2 Acceptance Test as a Separate Scrum Project/Scrum Team

At an insurance company, a project that was internally perceived as "catastrophic" came into its final phase. Although the supplier had imposed a Scrum development process, the acceptance of the system by the customer, in this case by an insurance test team, was traditional and therefore organized outside of the scrum team. The quality of the regular deliveries was poor, and the scope of delivery was difficult to understand for the acceptance testers.

Unfortunately, the insurances management held on to the supplier, assuming that the previous deliveries were only incomplete increments, and one could still hope for a successful overall system. Also, the supplier understood very well how to precisely point out weaknesses, such as a lack of technical expertise or sluggish test automation, of the acceptance test team. Unfortunately, the supplier also believed that in the end they could deliver a coherent overall system and was playing for time.

In the meantime, the acceptance test team was exhausted due to resignation or a change of team, and its reputation with the department, the actual user of the software, was in shambles. In these conditions, the last project delivery was due to go live, with an acceptance test in the sense of traditional process models. There were only 4 weeks left for this, with only four of the acceptance testers remaining. Initial projections showed that this team would only be able to cover one third of all features during the time scheduled for the acceptance test.

Now the business department made a brave decision: They provided nine additional employees for the acceptance test for a period of 10 weeks. The new team was to prepare for 6 weeks and then carry out an overall acceptance test in the remaining 4 weeks. Another brave decision was made: The new test team should work according to Scrum!

The first sprints were extremely tense, and it was not certain whether the team of 14 mostly unexperienced testers would be able to deliver. At first, many were not familiar with agile techniques and with the principle of self-organization. In their everyday lives as insurance clerks, their work was clearly regulated and optimized, and it was also clear what the respective goal of the work was. The planning meetings and especially the retrospectives must have reminded the business testers of the group games from their pre-school days. It was difficult to convey that the team was on the right track to reach their goal.

Another circumstance had a very unfavorable effect in this situation: the nonlinear course of test progress. The assumption in the planning meetings was that the productivity of the previous test team would increase slowly and progressively, so that the required velocity would be reached after 6 weeks. Burndown charts in particular, which mercilessly represented the successful tests, measured in test cases per day, soon demotivated the team completely: The productivity of the original four testers was only reached in the third sprint—and that with a total of now 13 testers! The previous testers were almost completely overwhelmed with the training of their colleagues. The new colleagues saw the new application for the first time, were shocked—as is usually the case—at first about the new processes and inputs, and had to prove themselves for the first time in their lives as software testers. On top of that, not all departments and team members were on friendly terms, and had to overcome their long-held prejudices and selfishness.

In this situation, an imperative measure for Scrum projects turned out to be a critical success factor: The role of the product owner was taken on by the department's lead analyst. He specified and prioritized the backlog, consisting of test areas and test cases. At the same time, however, he was able to use his effective network and acceptance in all departments to keep every single tester committed. Without his strong advocacy, they would certainly not have stayed in the acceptance test team.

At the beginning of the final acceptance testing phase, a miracle almost happened: The team's velocity exceeded all expectations. In the four-week acceptance phase, not only were all regression test cases executed, but in many cases additional, in-depth tests were carried out and older, deprecated test cases were corrected with a great deal of expertise. Unfortunately, this also greatly surprised the supplier: No acceptance recommendation could be given after the 4 weeks of testing.

This example shows the patience and perseverance with which we must approach some agile projects. Scrum has proven to be very efficient—also as a working technique for a dedicated test team. The self-organized team has made the transfer of knowledge between the business departments and testers much better than training courses and workshops could ever have done. However, this experience also shows that the training effort for newly formed agile teams should not be underestimated. Especially if the productivity drops at first, we should not demotivate a team, but present it as a "normal" course. It has also been shown that not all previously tried and tested team techniques can simply be transferred to other teams. Whether we like to work with sticky notes on task boards or adopt creative techniques in retrospectives depends on the experience and the habits of each team member.

3.2.3 Test Competence Center for Agile Projects

A few years ago, Scrum was introduced in a large telecommunications company as *the* project procedure. However, the overall context was a complex system from network management to accounting, in which many legacy systems were used in parallel with newer systems. Some systems were developed in-house, others externally developed or bought and adapted as standard software. Accordingly, software projects were set up in a very targeted manner, mostly in connection with special products that they wanted to position on the market—and thus were also spanning many different IT systems.

The first approach was to switch back to the V-Model and thus to traditional sequential approaches for the integration of modified components or subsystems. Another consequence was, unfortunately, that the provision of resources (such as test environments, executable peripheral systems, and test data from production) was still managed on a system-by-system basis. Operations and system administration did not follow the cross-sectional concept of the project organization.

The agile teams showed that the role of a dedicated tester became extremely important. The complex system integration tests alone required concentration and specialization on the test activities that the developers could not and did not want to perform. The tester in the team soon also had another heavy duty: providing resources through operations and system administration. While it was relatively easy to set up a development environment for each of the projects, integration test environments were a challenge in terms of coordination skills and in-house informal networking with key administrators. The dedicated tester taking the role of "troubleshooter" was soon understood and established.

The cost pressure forced the projects to think actively about test automation and to employ many inexperienced and therefore inexpensive resources for simple activities in testing. A single project team would have soon been overwhelmed, as the test automation could not be financed in the limited project environment.

Certainly, a consistently agile path could have been taken, in which test automation and less qualified resources would have found their space in the team. But for that, projects should have been allowed to organize their architecture and access to resources. Ultimately, much of the historically grown infrastructure would have had to be questioned—the resources were lacking, and in the end it would have been very risky for ongoing production processes.

It was therefore decided to set up a dedicated Test Competence Center, which, on the one hand, operated test automation centrally and, on the other, was able to offer test services and resources flexibly to projects. This model was able to work largely because certain system and system integration tests were always the same in several projects. Once we had automated a certain test suite for a project or tested it manually, we could use it again in other projects.

Ultimately, this organization meant a departure from agile principles, but there were reasons to do this in a targeted and well-considered manner.

3.2.4   A Team Using the V-Model in a Health Care Environment

A development team that produced software for components of medical laboratory equipment had decided to become agile. This seemed like a good idea, since the components had architecturally clearly defined interfaces and the software had to be regularly adapted and expanded for new device types and thus had to be iteratively provided as executable software.

The catch was that due to the official regulations, a procedure according to the V-Model is prescribed and suitable verification and validation measures must be demonstrated at every level.

The team nevertheless decided to use Scrum as a procedure and therefore separated the tasks: The work inside the team was consistently agile, with the team also mastering integration tests with the corresponding hardware and neighboring systems. On the outside, however, the tests were structured according to the respective integration levels for which they stood. The documentation was created specifically according to the external requirements and was therefore part of the product to be delivered. Reviews for requirements were also carried out as a backlog item and documented accordingly.

In this respect, all requirements for a sequential integration and the step-by-step test were met, the only difference being that a self-organized team fulfilled all the tasks: on the surface V-Model, inside Scrum.

Project EMIL: Definition of Done

The "Definition of Done" in the EMIL project is strongly influenced by regulatory requirements. The initial proposal came from quality management and was adapted by the team. It has been relatively stable since the third sprint:

- All user stories, defects, and tasks planned for the sprint have been implemented and verified.
- The design documentation is supplemented, adapted, and formally checked.
- The source code is documented according to the defined rules.
- All code changes have been formally checked.
- Unit test suite is supplemented, adapted, and checked.
- Acceptance test is documented.
- A version has been built, and unit and acceptance tests have been successfully carried out.

What at first glance looks like a lot of bureaucracy can be put into perspective very quickly in the sprint, because on the one hand the development and test tools are very well coordinated and thus relieve the team members of a lot of work in documenting and reviewing. On the other hand,

(continued)

the tasks behind it have manifested themselves in the minds of the team members so that they are simply continuously considered. Thus, there is no "rude awakening" in the sprint in the form of "Oh dear, we haven't done a review yet." However, internalizing this attitude took a lot of time.

Usual metrics (e.g., unit test coverage) are not included in the Definition of Done. However, they are used within a sprint.

Role of Testers in Agile Projects

4

With the shift to agile software development, the role and self-image of the tester and test manager have also changed dramatically. While in the past the tester's job was to control what the development team produced, they are now part of the software development team. Understanding this is not easy for everyone and it is also not explicitly defined by Scrum as the most widely used agile approach with its role definitions (Product Owner, Scrum Master, Development Team). For a long time, this terminology even led to companies being under the misapprehension that they could do without testers altogether in the agile approach. In other situations, testers were formally in development teams but did not participate in all the ceremonies, such as sprint planning meetings. In the meantime, however, developers, product owners, and testers have learned what it means to be agile: to share responsibility for the implementation of an application development in an equal interaction of different competencies.

4.1 Generalist Versus Specialist

At conferences or in companies that recruit employees for a project, the question is often asked: What roles or qualifications do we need for projects that are executed in accordance with an agile process model so that a team can become an "agile dream team": generalists or specialists? The short answer, based on our experience from many projects, is always the same: We need both!

Our findings are based on many project assignments and show that what is described below works better the more mature the teams are and have already understood the added value that results from the fact that the testers have a fixed place in the team and their role is undisputed and appreciated.

The requirements for functional and nonfunctional quality features have not changed due to the agile movement. Therefore, there is still a need for both roles. Depending on how agile projects are set up and lived in the organization, only the setting is different. The generalists are more likely to be found in the sprint teams, the specialist more in a team-supporting role outside the team.

Depending on how the team setting is defined, testers cover these tasks either as team members or as supporters outside the team. The role of the tester therefore depends on the size of the project. Our experience confirms the obvious assumption that the role selection is based on the team size:

- In small projects with only one or two testers, generalists bring the greatest benefit to the team.
- For larger projects, having not only generalists but also specialists, for example in test automation, is an advantage.

As generalists we understand testers who can cover a broad spectrum of test activities with varying intensity, but rarely have in-depth knowledge of individual topics. Ideally, these topics are then covered by experts who have specialist know-how, e.g., in setting up and adapting test frameworks for manual or automated tests or in performing nonfunctional tests such as performance, security, recovery, or usability tests.

In projects we often encounter the proven setting:

- Generalists as fixed team members
- Specialists as supporters who work for the team

Specialists can often be found in central regression-automation teams that automate the most important business processes after their completion in the form of end-to-end tests. This is discussed in more detail in Chap. 7, "Agile Test Automation." There are also different roles for agile test specialists in the test literature. Two thought leaders in agile testing, Gregory and Crispin (Crispin & Gregory, 2009), recommend, based on their experience, using the testers in a team with the following priorities:

- Experienced testers in an agile team ensure that the wishes of the business areas are understood. This is because testers put a strong focus on meeting the requirements from the end user's perspective in their test approach.
- Experienced testers in the team are driving test automation forward; They are familiar with the enormous benefits that automation brings, particularly in subsequent phases, in terms of freeing up resources. It is not a given that the testers create the test scripts themselves. Many teams in an agile environment attach great importance to maximum flexibility and prefer automation tools that are very close to development. Therefore, it can make sense for the automation agendas to also be handled by the developers. We cover automation in Chap. 7.
- For tests that require very special skills, such as security tests, load and performance tests, and recovery tests, i.e., mostly nonfunctional tests, test specialists are often consulted by the agile project team.

In one of our project assignments, we experienced the following situation: Two teams in the organization worked independently on the implementation of projects.

- Team 1 installed its own test automation team, which was to automate the finished stories in parallel to the project team, i.e., free of the rapid timing of the sprints. Three experienced test automation engineers were assigned to this support team, who were supposed to extend a regression suite one sprint delayed.
- Team 2 carried out tests in the team itself, whereby two developers were already familiar with open-source automation tools (in this case Selenium) popular in the agile community.
- The test specialists from Team 1 have encapsulated themselves more and more over the years and are no longer communicating as intensively with the development team. They only get the expertise and innovations second-hand, which has led to Team 1 being significantly less efficient than Team 2.
- Team 2, though, has more inhibitions about getting more deeply involved in GUI automation. The disadvantage of using development-oriented automation tools is that these tools often do not support GUI automation as comfortably as commercial test automation tools.
  Even if GUI tests are comparatively less automated (Cohn, 2009), these GUI tests, which usually cover the end-to-end tests, are essential. However, if projects contain hardly any GUI elements, less importance can be attached to the automation of these tests.

Testers who work in agile project environments consistently report the following characteristics:

- In the teams, the tester is increasingly taking care of everything. The following division of tasks has often arisen here: The developers in the team ensure that the stories are implemented, ideally unit-tested and checked in cleanly, while the testers in the team ensure that they are also executable.
  This means that they talk to the system administrators so that a suitable test system is set up and provided and is functional, and that all necessary components and peripheral systems are available in it. They coordinate with the person responsible for deployment/build, when and how, and above all which version is ultimately deployed to the test system, ensure that suitable test data is generated and imported, and often also agree with the business departments to clarify the stories so that the use cases they create are realistic.
  Summary: All of these are tasks that testers have previously performed in traditional projects. It is therefore hardly surprising that teams that do not use dedicated testers often work less efficiently or take considerably longer to "pick up the pace," since they first must learn all of this themselves. In our view, this is a clear argument for "Every team has its dedicated tester experts."
- One of the biggest risks for an agile team is therefore if testers are not consistently and naturally included in all decisions of the team right from the start. If testers only get second-hand information, this not only undermines the agile team idea,

but is bad for productivity—of the entire team. If we want to compare the team setting with well-known films, that could mean: away from "Highlander—There can be only one!" to "Musketeers—All for one and one for all!"

4.2   The Path from the Central Test Center to the Agile Team

If companies want to be successful with their products on the market, it is no longer a secret that one of the most important points is their quality.

No user or customer is willing to invest money in defect-riddled software. Quality has become one of the most important factors, whether products are accepted on the market or fail.

The professionalization of software testing has been massively supported by initiatives such as the International Software Testing and Qualifications Board (ISTQB), where a de facto standard or structured training scheme is developed, offered, and continuously updated at several levels. They have reacted to the success of agile approaches and released a revised ISTQB product portfolio at the beginning of 2016, in which there is now a separate category for agile tester certificates. The success story of the ISTQB continues; the barrier of 650,000 certificates worldwide was recently broken down. Germany, Switzerland, and Austria are among the top ten countries ranking for completed certificates. This clearly shows that for many reputable organizations it is the "state of the art" today to integrate dedicated and certified test experts in the software development process.

Following this trend, over the years some organizations have even institutionalized a quality claim to the extent that they have set up their own test centers in order to have the quality of all products created in the organization checked by dedicated test experts. Before we take a closer look at test centers and agile teams, it is helpful to look at the different scenarios for testers in agile teams.

4.2.1   Tester Involvement in Traditional Teams

There are different approaches to testing within project organizations depending on project types:

- **Tests are conducted directly in the project**
  - **Testers are an integral part of the project organization:** Each project receives testers or test teams specially assigned for this project, who are also organizationally assigned to the project. The project team is staffed solely by employees from the organization. In the traditional world, in addition to the traditional roles such as project manager, architect, business analyst, and risk manager, there are also test managers, testers, and quality officers. The teams handle their projects almost completely self-sufficiently. Testers are committed to a project and are solely responsible for this project. They also handle all types of tests (functional and nonfunctional) independently. Briefly

summarized: All roles and skills are represented in the organization to complete a project.

If one decides within this setting to switch to agile procedures, there are several challenges that are described below, but the change is usually easier because the team is already established and familiar with each other.

- **Testers are a flexible part of the project organization:** Here, too, the project gets explicit testers assigned, but these are organizationally separate, that is, embedded in their own organizational unit (e.g., test management or quality management). These units aim to train and provide qualified testers. These testers serve as a kind of resource pool for the company's projects and are posted to them. At the end of a project, they return to their unit and are available to the organization for other projects, including other departments. This variant is particularly widespread in larger organizations, since targeted support and training of the testers can be better organized and cross-project synergies of the testers can be realized.

- **Tests are done outside the project**
  - **Central test center:** In this case, the organization implements both an organizational and operational separation, i.e., a clear separation of product development and quality assurance including the execution of the tests. There are clear concepts and definitions of how the product development cycle is to be lived, and specifically how the "development unit" or the development team has to hand over their work to the test (QA) team. Everything is clearly regulated and is fixed at the start of the project as part of the overall project management. The main difference to the variants mentioned so far is that responsibility for the overall integration and ensuring all quality features to be fulfilled, especially in the nonfunctional area, is handed over to this central team. In addition, only this team has sufficient high-performance hardware available, for example to set up production-related test systems. It is the same with tool licenses, for example for load and performance test tools.
  This central test center can be operated in two ways:
    - The organization operates its own test center, to which the software to be tested is handed over according to a precisely defined procedure.
    - The organization uses an outsourced test center, which is often also located offshore, to carry out the tests.

In both cases, the organization must have a certain process maturity so that the desired benefit can be achieved. There is already a wide range of literature (Nicklisch, Borchers, Krick, & Rucks, 2008) on outsourcing tests.

The main advantage of a central test center: Well-established, experienced (test) experts work together in highly efficient teams.

Disadvantage: The proof of functionality, i.e., the test, only takes place at the end, and the project implementation is highly structured and therefore very rigid and hardly ever flexible. In addition, there are rarely synergies with the development.

Experience has shown that organizations that are now converting to an agile approach will find it much easier if they have already integrated the testers into the project teams.

4.2.2   Approaches for Tester Integration in Agile Teams

Based on the previously described test center, this approach could also be retained for certain tasks in agile companies, especially when it comes to large, complex systems with many connected third-party systems. The individual teams deliver their subsystems (each individually manufactured and executable), and the final overall integration test takes place in the test center. Furthermore, such test centers can also function successfully as service providers for the individual agile teams, for example for performing nonfunctional tests such as load and performance, security, or recovery tests, or as a service center for providing test data. This will be discussed in more detail later.

4.2.2.1 The Switch from Traditional to Agile

If an organization decides to switch to agile processes, there are several challenges that must be overcome. One of the biggest challenges is changing the mindset in management. The transfer of responsibility and control from the hierarchy to the team is an almost insurmountable hurdle for many organizations.

In addition to the enormous organizational challenges, there are changes for everyone, which are almost exclusively in the soft skill area. Team communication, stress and conflict management, and high transparency (Hellerer, 2013) are just a few that are mentioned here as examples.

In addition to the significant extension of tasks for testers, many teams find the most difficult aspect is the change of individual responsibility of the project manager to collective team responsibility. Setting up the teams requires professional support from experienced experts, for example a scrum master.

> **Hint**
> Rely on experienced professionals when switching to an agile approach. It is important that they are not only experienced in one agile method (e.g., Scrum), but also have sufficient overall experience in the IT environment. The choice of experts, consultants, etc. has become extensive. One can be called a scrum master after a 2-day (!) course, where the basic techniques are barely covered.
>
> In order to be able to accompany a team professionally and efficiently on their way to agility, we need not only thorough knowledge of the methodology, but also a lot of common sense and tact in choosing practices which are most likely to achieve the goal while fulfilling all given conditions.

(continued)

Furthermore, scrum masters as the "engine" of the team need a lot of skill and talent for motivation and mediation.

So be wary of "gurus of method," who might be able to recite the methods back and forth and primarily give "mantra-like" statements from their teachers but can hardly act flexibly according to the "inspect and adapt" principle.

Agile also continues to develop, following the motto "Inspect and adapt." In addition to the adapted view of some "rigid rules" (keyword SCRUM 3.0) (Gloger, 2015), the focus is currently increasingly on scaling, i.e., the establishment of agile approaches in medium-sized and large companies.

When choosing coaches, pay more attention to concrete project experience and ask for references. Whether the changeover will be a success depends significantly on the choice of the "engine".

4.2.2.2 Increase in Efficiency and Effectiveness

Experienced, committed testers might feel like they are in "Paradise" in agile projects. In traditional development projects, they have often tried unsuccessfully to be involved as early as possible in the project cycle, for example to review the requirement documents so that defects can be identified in the initial phase and potential errors can be eliminated. In the agile world, this is guaranteed from the beginning, since here the entire team, including the tester, must take all the steps together to be able to make a joint commitment.

The Paradise Is Not for Free

However, there is still room for improvement in agile teams, which is bigger the more the developers are anchored in old patterns.

For example, testers often complain that there is resistance, especially in development-heavy teams, to accepting testers as equal partners in the team, even to letting them have a say when it comes to implementation strategies. This is an unusual and new situation for some developers, but also for testers, and both must get used to it. An important catalyst is mutual acceptance and the recognition that the better we work together, the faster we will reach our goal. The sooner both roles realize that one cannot do without the other, the sooner they will be on the road to success.

One measure that can help here is an XP-based practice: "pairing." Testers can generate benefits for everyone in the team and thus increase their acceptance in the team.

Pair Testing
Pairing Tester: Product Owner
Testers usually look at the requirements from the same perspective as the end user or, in our case, the product owner. However, the "Tester's view" also ensures that the acceptance criteria are clearly formulated and can be clearly demonstrated. By critical questioning, stories can be brought into an actionable state more quickly.

Pairing Tester: Developer
An essential practice in Agile is TDD, Test-Driven Development (Beck, 2003) . Experience has shown that many developers find this difficult at the beginning. Technically inclined testers can actively support the developers here. We can advise them on the compilation of our test sets or do this directly.

One of the most important advantages is derived from the implementation of the functionality: The developers primarily focus on quickly implementing the basic required functionality. If testers and developers now work together on the same function, the tester can, for example, create the appropriate test cases and test data in parallel with the development, and thus carry out the test from a functional point of view immediately after completion by the developer. If deviations occur, the developer comes in and, based on the existing error situation, can quickly correct the error.

Working hand-in-hand, which has to be done in an appreciative manner, creates functionality with high quality from the start.

Pairing Tester: Tester
If we have several testers in a team, it is the same as with children: Alone they might be well behaved, but when there are several together, they can come up with the most creative ideas. These ideas enrich the test, and by passing on know-how, be it technical or methodical, the test procedure is constantly improved.

4.2.2.3 Team Composition
The following practical example describes how important it is to find the right team composition:

Practice
As part of a large project in the banking sector, it was decided to implement the project according to Scrum after an unsuccessful start using a traditional model.

Using this particular project example, we were able to observe four different phases of the team composition live (Fig. 4.1):

We distinguish the four phases as follows:

(continued)

Fig. 4.1 Complete overview "tester in a team" evolution

- "Quality is free" phase, freely based on the quote from PB Crosby (Crosby, 1980)
- "Highlander" phase: There can be only one!
- "The more the merrier" phase
- "Selectively appropriate" phase

The IT team was trained in agile methods and divided into agile teams. The special thing about this project or rather the team setting was that there were no dedicated testers in the IT team. The departments acted as saviors by promising to assign employees to test the new system in addition to day-to-day business. The interface between departments, the IT department, and the scrum teams was organized by a dedicated test coordinator.

For the implementation of the first stories, they followed what they learned in their Scrum training: A product backlog was created, the Task Board and Definition of Done were defined, etc.—but there were no dedicated testers in the team. This was ignored during team training, as is the case with many Scrum trainings since testing is not explicitly mentioned in the basic practices of the inventors of Scrum.

(continued)

Fig. 4.2 "Quality is free" phase

Phase 1: "Quality is free" (Fig. 4.2)

The teams started with the first sprints and quickly implemented the first stories. In parallel, but regardless of the order of the product backlog, the business department, accompanied by a test advisor, began to design test cases for the features.

The scrum teams developed one story after the next, which worked quite well at the beginning. Gradually, however, problems and errors arose, and nothing seemed to really fit together. Remedy: Each scrum team was assigned one person from the business department to take care of the tests.

(continued)

Fig. 4.3 "Highlander" phase: There can be only one!

Phase 2: "Highlander" (Fig. 4.3)

This business specialist, who was technically experienced and was also very committed, had very little or no test experience. The result: Things were going a little better, but the "almost done" stories continued to grow faster than the "Done stories."

During this phase, a test expert was called in to serve as overall test coordinator. Their task was to coach the testers in the scrum teams and, above all, to coordinate the creation of test cases in the business departments and the test activities downstream of the sprints. It quickly became clear that a more efficient structure was needed to get both the stories within the current sprint "Done" and "approved by product owner," and at the same time to quickly work through the debt of "Almost finished" stories. Despite some concerns, the decision was made to assign all available employees (from the business departments) to scrum teams.

(continued)

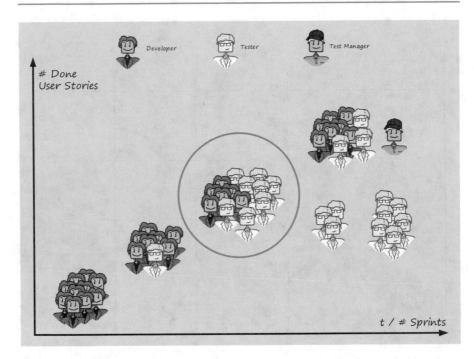

Fig. 4.4 "The more the merrier" phase

Phase 3: "The more the merrier" (Fig. 4.4)

The requirement was to bring the new stories to "Done and accepted" within the sprints and at the same time to process the collection of half-finished stories from the previous sprints—also lovingly called the "Almost-finished backlog."

However, the test coordinator supported the teams the more it became apparent that this approach did not have the desired effect.

In addition to the fact that the Stand-Up meetings lost efficiency and often exceeded time limits, the testers soon lost track of what was to be tested and how. As a result, a team spirit could also not really develop. The employees from the business departments were also not reporting to the IT department and had to follow the hourly schedules of their departments. In addition, the business specialists also had to cope with their day-to-day business. This always brought challenges to performing the test, especially if, for example, a few sick days in the departments and problems with a deployment coincided before a sprint end. Finally, it was decided to move to yet another project reorganization.

(continued)

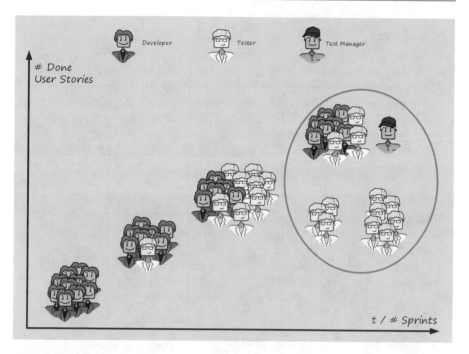

Fig. 4.5 Winning team phase

Phase 4: "Selectively appropriate" (Fig. 4.5)
After analyzing the situation and its advantages and disadvantages, the scrum teams were divided:

- **In sprint teams:** These core teams consisted of approximately five developers and two to three directly assigned testers.
  The goal of these (up to three parallel) teams was to complete the outstanding stories and to include at least one "Troubleshooting story" per sprint.
- **Out-of-sprint teams:** A separate team was set up for each department.
  Goal: Each team analyzes and tests the "Almost finished" stories that relate to the functionality of their business area in a structured manner and reports errors collectively.
  Subsequently, these teams also created cross-departmental test cases to ensure the bank's entire processes in the form of system integration and acceptance tests. These teams impressed everyone with their strong commitment and goal orientation, especially since they had hardly any IT know-how.
- **Other independent teams** took care of special topics that could not be accommodated in the sprints, e.g., security, recovery, load and performance tests, and special test series that were necessary to meet regulatory requirements (certifications, etc.).

(continued)

- With this setting, the tasks could ultimately be brought under control to such an extent that the final announced go-live appointment could be held, and the most important thing: to be able to exchange the heart of the bank unnoticed by customers.
- In this context, it should also be emphasized that all those involved, and above all the management, had very high-quality standards and placed these as the top criterion for the go-live.

Here is another case study to illustrate the point:

Project EMIL: Role of the Tester and Quality Management

Coming from traditional software development and under the organization of Quality Management, the integration of the testers into the agile teams was a challenge for all team members in this project. Where previously software modules were sequentially handed over to the test team every few weeks, agile development required much greater integration. The following activities were carried out to promote this integration:

- Define a common goal: While in the past the developers had the goal of having their software modules implemented as quickly as possible, and the testers worked toward evaluating the quality, a common goal has now been created and expressed: to develop a product that has high value for the customer. This common goal connects the team and motivates it.
- Joint requirements discussion: If requirement questions arise in development or testing, these are always discussed and clarified together, preferably also with the product owner.
- Reciprocal participation in trainings: In order to speak a common language, all developers in the team attended the ISTQB Certified Tester training together with the testers (ISTQB—International Software Testing Qualifications Board, 2018). In addition to understanding the tester's concerns, they were also given a methodological basis for designing their unit tests and code reviews. Conversely, the testers also took part in development workshops to gain an insight into their world.

At the beginning of the project, phrases such as "handing it over to the test team" and "reporting the development error" were often heard, but these have almost completely disappeared. This is also evident from the stronger cooperation:

- Testers support the code and design review with an outside view.
- Testers support the design of unit tests, especially in risky system areas.
- Developers support the automation and implementation of acceptance tests.

(continued)

This is how testers and developers grew together as a team.

The role of quality management was also defined: Quality management defines the framework for the development process:

- Which documents have to be created?
- Which artifacts are tested and how (test, review)?
- At what points are documents/artifacts handed over for the ongoing risk analysis?

The necessary agreements can be found in the Definition of Done. This ensured that regulatory requirements were met without excessive bureaucracy. This also required a sensible selection of tools. The Quality Management works best when team members do not notice it in their daily work.

As the example in the EMIL project shows, the change from the traditional to the agile world can be very successful if a common goal is defined and consistently pursued by all sides. And, as described here, it can and may be done in stages. A step-by-step changeover, which also allows those involved to get used to the new situation and approach, is often more successful than the "Big Bang" changeover according to the motto "Yesterday we were traditional—from today on we are agile."

4.3 Challenges for Testers in the Team

4.3.1 Testers in the Agile Team

The focus of testers in an agile team is to ensure the correct function and quality of the created features. With this focus, testers sometimes have a hard time asserting themselves in the project. Ensuring quality is often defined as showing quality deficits. And who likes to be told every day that this or that does not work or is faulty? This is especially true when a team has been newly formed and most of the team members only have experience with traditional development methods.

When a team is created, there is no real team structure in the initial phase—Bruce W. Tuckman calls this the "Forming" phase (Tuckman, 1965). In this phase, developers often still work according to their usual, traditional experience and mostly have only one goal: to fulfill the implementation of functionality and tasks as quickly as possible. If testers now come along and report errors that may even have to be rectified immediately, they can be perceived as slowing down progress. Not only do their efforts stop the ongoing development of new functionality, but they also show that developers have delivered incorrect code. According to Tuckman, the maturing team goes through the phases of "storming" and "norming," and this can be viewed more and more positively. The tester can grow into the role of a helpful partner who supports the team to "score the goal," i.e., to have the promised functionality accepted at the end of a development cycle. It depends on the type of communication, and above all on the maturity of the team, whether and how strong this cooperation is lived in a team. In the authors' projects, the testers often also took on a new role: that of a **Quality Coach**, also seen as **Quality Owner**.

4.3.1.1 The Quality Coach

The Quality Coach focuses primarily on the successful completion of a story: We could also call them "Story troubleshooters."

Quality Coaches focus on the acceptance criteria and their correct fulfillment— that is, depending on the general conditions (Definition of Done), they create test cases and carry them out as soon as possible.

When errors occur, the Quality Coach does not act as a "bad guy" but as a consultant and team coordinator. Which bugs must be fixed and which measures have to be taken so that the team can nominate the story as "Ready" and ultimately as "Done" for the final Sprint Review? Usually, it is also the testers or Quality Coaches who present the respective functionality to the product owner or end customer during the Sprint Review. Of course, we clearly reject the idea that testers or Quality Coaches present features strategically because "they know where to click and where not to click."

4.3.1.2 Tasks of Agile Testers

An important task of agile testers is to ensure that the right team atmosphere prevails. As Crispin and Gregory (Crispin & Gregory, 2009) emphasize again and again, testers have to advertise themselves in the team. The other team members (e.g., developers) must recognize the benefits that the testers bring for themselves and thus for the entire team. It is helpful if testers can demonstrate both business and technical competence. Very experienced and technically well versed testers may even know potential dangers, for example in JavaScript code from previous projects, or be aware of leaks in the respective development technology. The more they are able to speak the language of developers, the faster they will be accepted in the team. In an agile team, it is no longer just about testers who are only concerned with the operation of the user interface, but more about knowing what is behind it and being able to evaluate it in its entirety. This means that testers must have technical skills.

In addition to technical skills, agile testers must be familiar with the domain of the application. Every domain has its very special points of interest. In the case of travel booking systems, for example, it is the booking processes and the compliance with certain laws. When implementing production control systems, obviously the pro- duction processes are essential. Testers must be at least familiar enough with the respective domain so that they can identify blatant violations of business rules.

The testers therefore need much more technical and business knowledge than in previous traditional projects. The previous system test was more of a mechanical process, with the aim of performing as many test cases as possible in the shortest possible time. It is therefore not surprising that many of these tests have been outsourced, to areas with cost advantages. Most of these system tests have also been automated. This is less the case for the integration test level prior to the system test. The integration tester must at least be familiar with the technical environment. After all, they have to know how the components communicate with each other. For the unit test, on the other hand, the tester must be familiar with the development technology.

The role of agile testers can also be compared to the role of the integration tester in traditional projects. They should understand enough about the technology to be able to integrate the components that the developers provide and to run them under simulated conditions. For this they need suitable tools, and they must also be able to operate them.

Finally, there is the acceptance test, in which the testers test the entire system from the user's point of view on behalf of the end user. Here they change into another role: that of the business experts. They must judge whether the system is technically correct. Have all technical requirements been met and are they complete and consistent? In addition, they are also often required to assess the nonfunctional requirements of the software.

Given these many requirements, it is questionable whether one person can do all these tasks alone. In the traditional projects, there was usually a separate test team consisting of testers with different skills. There were business experts, others familiar with the used technology, and others who covered special topics such as security. The experts supported each other in such a specialized test team.

In an agile project, the few testers in the team are now expected to cover all these aspects, from the integration of the components to the performance of the overall system. It is therefore advisable to have several testers with a corresponding mix of skills in each agile project, where one tester is more business-oriented and the other technically experienced. In terms of numbers, the testers should also be in a balanced relationship with the developers. In practice, a ratio of five developers to three (+/− 1) testers has proven efficient because the fact that testing is as complex as development has not changed, not even through agile development. On the contrary: Due to the fast, incremental creation of the software, the test is more complex than ever since the frequent deployments and the "potential shippable products" naturally increase the regression test effort immensely after each sprint. This can only be managed with a good automation strategy.

4.3.2   Timely Problem Detection

Quick feedback from testers to developers is one of the essential advantages of agile testing. How the testers are best integrated into the team is a question of work organization. Ideally, testers and developers form a well-established pair. This means that when developers practice test-driven development they first create unit tests. The actual functionality gradually emerges, which is checked in by the developers after completion and a successful unit test in the central repository. In agile teams, "Continuous Integration" is now crucial: This means that the checked-in version is compiled, a new build is created, and the entire set of available unit tests is executed out. This gives the developers immediate feedback as to whether their checked-in code could be integrated into the overall system without errors. The result is a new build with extended or corrected functionality.

The aim of testers is now to examine this functionality from a functional point of view. Although this means that testers in an agile team still start testing with a time delay, they are still as close as possible to development, so that when errors occur, the developers are immediately involved to ensure that the available environment information (system settings, test data, log files) is available to enable rapid correction. Of course, test automation is also crucial, making it possible to repeat the regression test daily and to run functional tests of the latest components. This also ensures that not only defects of the currently worked-upon function are found, but also those regression defects that occur in the related environment. This is the decisive advantage over traditional, often bureaucratic quality assurance, in which it often took weeks for the error messages and defect reports to be returned to the developers.

This should no longer be the case in agile development.

If the team is still new and the "Hand in Hand" collaboration is not yet working properly, it can quickly lead to the testers having to struggle to keep up with the team. To avoid this as much as possible, testers should

(a) Familiarize themselves with the development environment
(b) Have powerful tools
(c) Have a good relationship with the developers

If these conditions are not met, testers cannot deliver the expected benefits, no matter how well they master testing methods. Agile testing demands more from the testers than was previously the case.

The main benefit of agile testing is the timely detection of problems and quick feedback to the developers. Therefore, testers and developers should work together as closely as possible (co-located). The authors of the agile manifesto placed great emphasis on "face-to-face" communication. If we look at large companies such as Google or similar companies that successfully operate in an agile way across many locations, we can see that "co-located" can also mean using the appropriate infrastructure, so the "co-located" team is available directly whenever needed.

At testing conferences and also in projects from our consulting environment, we see projects where work is agile, but the teams only work together virtually and are distributed around the world: The product owner might be located in Germany, part of the development team in Slovakia, another part in India, others in Austria, and the test could be covered again in India. If we take agile values such as "face-to-face" communication, the focus on individuals and interactions, the reaction to change, pairing, etc., the question arises as to what extent the agile idea can still generate benefits in distributed environments. Even though the collaboration tools have improved massively, we still perceive in our customer environment/project environment that "having a coffee together" is often more efficient than many forms of digital communication.

When setting up team structures, the most important thing is which work culture the teams are used to. As far as testing is concerned, one goal is paramount: the timely detection of errors and undesirable developments. In our experience, this is most efficient if the testers work as closely as possible with the developers. And this is often much more efficient if testers and developers sit around the same table.

If a team has too few testers, the developers have to be included in the integration and system test in addition to the unit test, which they should be conducting anyway. However, this will pull them away from their development tasks and might slow the implementation pace of the project. Otherwise, concessions may have to be made on an ongoing basis. Fewer tests would be carried out, which could ultimately lead to lower quality and stability of the entire system. Hence, one would need to accept that the system is of lower quality. This acceptance of risk accumulation has of course always existed in software development, but for some time now it has also had its own name: It is now called "technical debt." We take a closer look at this topic in Sect. 4.4.

Can this be reduced or even prevented by more testers in the team? Testers test, ... but not only that; they also see their role in testing and consulting. They should check the code and advise on the architecture of the system. In addition to the business requirements, they also focus on the nonfunctional quality properties of the software—the properties that the developers often seem to neglect. The testers need to make sure that these quality properties are not neglected when talking about architecture and solutions.

4.3.3 The Emergence of Technical Debts

To deliver what the users want, namely a working software product in the shortest possible time, the developers are often forced to make simplifications. They leave out one or the other feature in order to move ahead faster. A typical example is error handling. If a function is called that is located on another node, one would have to reckon with the fact that the feedback does not always take place. It may be that this node is overloaded or has failed completely. The developers must expect that there will be no response at some point and take this into account. For this reason, error conditions should be provided for all external function calls. The same applies to all access to databases and files as well as printers and other external devices. This leads to a lot of additional code. Experts estimate that over 50% of the code is intended for such exceptional situations if the developers consider all potential exceptions. This means that if they do not take them into account, they save half the coding and testing effort. Because if developers incorporate such exception handling into the code, they must also test it. The exception handling is often omitted at project start, especially in view of the additional testing effort. The user might not notice it at first. There first might need to be a very large load before some exceptional cases occur. Others appear after only a small load, but the user might not notice that immediately. Thus, if delivery as fast as possible is the top priority, one could simply omit many error messages. The developers often think they can add them later when they have more time. Unfortunately, this "Later" is almost always forgotten later and at the end.

It is the same with security. Secure code means more code to intercept all possible intrusions. We could check all calls from outside before we accept them. Every transferred parameter value can be checked. The developers can also check whether the number of values passed matches the expected number, so that no additional values are appended. They can also request an identification key as a parameter, which is confirmed every time. The SQL statements embedded in its code must also be handled very carefully, since these can be easily manipulated and are a popular "back door" through which hackers gain access to systems. There are several potential threats for which the developers must take countermeasures, but all these countermeasures decrease implementation speed. If such functions or tests are missing, the user might again not immediately notice, at most only once the customer data is stolen, as is often reported in the press. Only then is the damage that is caused (not including the damage to the image at all) usually many times higher than the minimum time "saved" in implementation.

We cannot really blame the developers for this. They are often under enormous time pressure. Do they really have to implement everything immediately? Frequently they are initially just working on a prototype that might end up as production code. Users might not even notice whether they are dealing with a prototype or a product. If it seems to work for them, they might not even notice what is still missing. The users cannot answer the question of what is finished because they have no idea what "finished" really means. They cannot recognize the many potential dangers in the software. Therefore, they need experts who decide this on their behalf, and those experts are, of course, the testers.

Testers are responsible for ensuring that the software is ready for production, that all exceptional conditions are dealt with, that all security threats are intercepted, and that all functions are accepted. The testers often also check the programming conventions (which are also part of agile projects). Especially when software is written for a safety- or security-relevant environment, the testers sometimes ensure that the code remains in an updated state through ongoing static analysis. To be able to work effectively, the testers must be familiar with the programming language and the development environment.

4.4   Agile Teams and Testers Working Against "Technical Debt"

4.4.1   What Is "Technical Debt"?

"Technical debt" is a term for defective software. It aims to express the problem of inadequate software quality in economic terms. Managers need to learn that shortcuts in software development might have negative consequences, which will later cost money. The term "debt" should remind us that we have to pay it off at some point, like the national debt. The level of national debt is measurable, both in absolute monetary values and relative to the gross national product. The same applies to the technical debt or the software debt of a project. It can be expressed in absolute costs or relative to the development costs of the project.

The term was coined by Ward Cunningham in 1992 at the OOPSLA conference. In the original description by Cunningham, technical debt is "all the not quite right code which we postpone making it right." By this he meant the inner quality of the code. The term was later expanded to include everything that belongs to a decent software system but is postponed due to time constraints. This includes error handling, exception handling, security handling, and emergency handling. The developers can initially leave out all of this and comfort the users with the promise of implementing it later—if they even ask for it. In his book *Managing Software Debt: Building for Inevitable Change*, C. Sterling addresses these omissions (Sterling, 2010). There are quite a few that occur several times during development. The longer one postpones their correction, the less likely it is that it will ever be corrected. It would be the task of the testers in the agile team to insist that the corrections are made as quickly as possible, at the latest in the next release. To do this, however, they must be able to recognize what is missing in the code. It is not shown by test coverage measurement, because functions that are not there cannot be measured either. The testers would have to search for them in the code, otherwise they would have to trigger every single fault, every exception, every possible security threat, and every emergency through testing. This would be far too expensive and is why agile testers also need good programming skills. It is about uncovering everything that belongs to the code and is not there. This accounts for most of the technical debt.

The other part of the technical debt is the quality of the code. That is what Ward Cunningham originally meant. The developers might make concessions on the architecture of the system and the implementation of the code to make faster progress. Instead of expanding the class hierarchy, they might deepen it because it is easier to add new subclasses. Instead of calling new methods, they might prefer to nest the decision logic because it is faster. Instead of using polymorphic calls, they might prefer to write nested case instructions and copy the same code into every case branch, except for a few variable names, etc. There are endless possibilities for the code to deteriorate, and stressed developers might make use of them if they are pressed for time. The result is a piece of code that is executable but can hardly be updated.

Recognizing that such coding practices can be a direct consequence of extreme programming, Fowler coined the term "Refactoring," and wrote a book about it (Fowler, Beck, Brant, Opdyke, & Roberts, 2012). Refactoring is what developers do to bend their "quick and dirty" written code back to what it should be. The classes are reorganized, the flow logic flattened, and the variables renamed. Case instructions are replaced by polymorphic calls, redundant code is removed, and individual parameters are summarized in container objects. There are endless possibilities to improve the code—which could have been avoided if the developers had had the time to implement them beforehand.

One can accept the hypothesis that developers cannot satisfy functionality and quality at the same time, and that they first address functionality and only then quality. But someone has to make sure that the second step actually follows. The former head of the QA Department at the US Department of the Navy, John Shore, claimed there were no developers one could really trust. They have good intentions, but under pressure they make too many concessions to code quality to move faster. Shore compares them to sinners who do not want to sin, but ultimately cannot help it. The only effective way to prevent them from doing so is to test and request corrections.

This software quality manager claim was made in 1975. The tendency to make concessions and to accumulate technical debt is often the same, especially in crisis situations. There are approaches to calculating the amount of technical debt and to implementing it in the workload.

In the past, this pressure came from outside, from an independent quality assurance group or from a separate test team. In agile development, this pressure now ideally comes from within, from the testers in the team. According to the collective ownership and team spirit, they are not entitled or encouraged to force developers to do anything, but if the common rules of the "Definition of Done" contain the stipulation that "technical debts" are to be avoided, testers can be very active and keep insisting on compliance with the rules. This might lead to conflicting goals such as functionality versus quality and quality versus time. The role of the tester in an agile development team is to represent the aspect of "quality" and to prevent quality from being neglected in the project or to build up "debts" for the future.

4.4.2 Dealing with Technical Debt

An important aspect of agile development is shifting of long-term quality problems in favor of short-term productivity gains. It is more important to involve the customer in the development with a semi-finished product than to wait until the product is finalized, only to discover that it is not the right product or that the customer has had different expectations. This approach is quite legitimate, because it is better to deliver the right product not yet correctly than to deliver the wrong product correctly. The emphasis here should be on "not yet correct." The difference between the current state of a product and the ideal target state is called technical debt. Debt must be processed, i.e., a product is only really "done" when it is also debt-free.

But who should define what the target state of a software product should look like? Most product owners would be overwhelmed because they lack the necessary technical knowledge in terms of software quality. We need someone to help us define an appropriate level of quality. In an agile project, this person is the tester. The testers help the product owners to define the desired quality level. All quality properties of a software must be considered, both external such as correctness, reliability, performance, and security, and internal such as maintainability, reusability, portability, and interoperability. To define quality goals, we need expert knowledge that a product owner rarely possesses. As already mentioned, this role can be assigned to the testers.

At the conference "Belgium Testing Days" in 2012, Johanna Rothman and Lisa Crispin dealt with this problem. The question was: What is "done"?

Johanna Rothman repeated our view that this is a team task, and specifically of the entire team. The team coordinates and determines collectively when a task/story is set to "Done." An important task of the testers in defining these "Done criteria" (also called "Definition of Done") is to enrich the discussion with arguments for more quality. Rothman claims: "You have to get the team thinking about what is done. Does it mean partially done, as in it is ready for testing, or fully done, as in it is ready for release?" Here you have to be aware that there can be a big difference between the quality that is sufficient to create a story to be completed in the Sprint Review as "Done," and the one that is needed to get the overall system extended with new functions and ready for production.

There is often a long way between these two states.

Testers can function as a "Lawyer" of quality, whose "Law book" is on the one hand the "Definition of Done" and on the other their claim that a function can only really be considered complete when it is also embedded in the overall system, in "End to end" scenarios, and was proven correctly.

It is important to diplomatically convince the whole team that this view is the more effective in the long term. One must not take one's eye off the "technical debt," pushing to keep it as low as possible. Sometimes it is also necessary to convince even the product owner that certain work or effort is required. In this case, "Sometimes good is not good enough". . . especially not when one thinks about the future.

If, for whatever reason, we are too careless here, we only postpone the problems to maintenance, as was the case with traditional development projects in the past.

In all their activities, the testers primarily have the done criteria in mind, meaning that the achievement of done criteria per story is the minimum that must be achieved for each story.

The functional state of a software product is easier to assess than the qualitative state. It is visible whether there is a functionality or not. However, the quality is not always easily visible. We can only know how many errors are still in the software once we have tested all of its functions. We can only assess how effective the code is after we have analyzed it in detail. And the quality of the overall system can only be assessed if it has been in use for a certain time.

Lisa Crispin points out that software quality is the "final" measure of agile development. Functional progress must not be achieved at the expense of software quality. Occasionally, but especially when creating security-critical software, it may even make sense to set up a separate quality assurance team, which works alongside the development team to monitor the quality of the software created and report to the development team.

Johanna Rothman believes that the testers must have a say in what "done" means—from the start of the project: "To be done also means that the quality criteria set by the team are met." As a result, these criteria are accepted by everyone involved. Everyone in the team must be aware of their responsibility for quality and do their part. "Everybody in the team needs to take responsibility for quality and for keeping technical debt at a manageable level. The whole team has to make a meaningful commitment to quality." In other words, the quality of the software is a matter for the entire team.

4.5   Experience Report: Quality Specialist at Otto.de

This story was provided by Diana Kruse of otto.de and she reports on her experiences in the transition from tester and test manager to quality specialist or Quality Coach, visualized through graphics by her colleague Torsten Mangner:

At otto.de there is at least one tester/test manager/QA member in every cross-functional team... whatever we might want to call the role of the person who is creating awareness for quality (Kruse, Lorbeer, Mangner, & Volk, 2016).

So far, the term "test manager" has been the dominant one—a very wooden, bureaucratic-sounding title. This should make it clear that the role does more than just carry out tests: They manage tests! In reality, the management of tests is only a small part of the added value that test managers generate in the team.

During a large workshop, this contradiction was picked up and worked on by two of our "test managers," Finn and Natalie. We quickly agreed that it was no longer enough to write the word "agile" in front of the role of "test manager." This created a new understanding of the testing roles in agile projects, which are defined in detail.

4.5.1   We Act as the Team's Quality Coach

We support the teams in understanding quality as a shared responsibility. We do not do this through lectures on general concepts, but through daily, intensive collaboration with all other roles in the team. In doing so, we establish knowledge and appropriate procedures for quality issues (Fig. 4.6).

Fig. 4.6 Team Quality
Coach

Fig. 4.7 Quality Coach
throughout the entire life cycle

4.5.2   We Accompany the Entire Life Cycle of Each Story

Together with the whole team, we ensure that our high-quality standards are considered long before our products are developed (Fig. 4.7).

During the conception of a story, we show alternative ways and point out possible risks. We avoid later edge case problems by considering them when creating the story. During the implementation, we pair with developers to test the right things in the right place. This means that we have more time during the acceptance phase to exchange ideas with our stakeholders and users. In production, we monitor and evaluate our software through suitable monitoring and alerting .

4.5.3   We Operate Continuous Delivery/Continuous Deployment

We bring our deployments to the production environment with as little risk as possible. We keep our changes as small as possible and roll out each commit automatically. In this case, we use Feature-Toggles to switch new functions on and off regardless of code changes (Fig. 4.8).

This has two large additional advantages: We can deliver our software to our customers at lightning speed and receive quick feedback about newly developed components.

Fig. 4.8 Continuous
Delivery/Continuous
Deployment

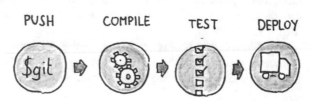

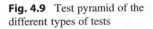

Fig. 4.9 Test pyramid of the different types of tests

4.5.4   We Balance the Different Types of Tests in the Test Pyramid

We know what is tested at what level of the test pyramid. We can use it as a guide to create many quick unit tests, a reasonable number of integration tests, and as few end-to-end tests as possible. As a result, not only can we accelerate our pipelines, but we can also carry out our tests as effectively and with as little maintenance as possible (Fig. 4.9).

We also find various types of tests (such as acceptance tests or feature tests, and explorative tests), methodologies (e.g., Test-First, BDD), and frameworks (e.g., Selenium, RSpec) in our toolbox. We use the respective type, method, and framework at all levels of the test pyramid.

4.5.5   We Help the Team to Use the Right Methods for High Quality

As test experts, we know the advantages and disadvantages of different methods and can successfully establish them in a team. We learned that pairing in a team leads to greater knowledge diversification, more communication, faster software development, and higher quality. In addition to pairing, test-driven development is one of the key methodologies to create our product with high quality right from the start (Fig. 4.10).

Flexible software is only created in flexible structures. This is why we convey to our teams undogmatically suitable process methodologies. We can then decide together which processes we actually need.

Fig. 4.10 Different methods
in agile teams

4.5.6   We Are Active in Pairing

We not only promote pairing between developers, but we also enjoy active pairing ourselves. In this way we can point out problems as the code is being created. In order not to encounter edge cases during development, we are happy to pair with business designers, analysts, and UX designers. In production, we monitor our software in collaboration with DevOps (Fig. 4.11).

Pairing with these different roles allows us to combine both our technical and professional skills.

4.5.7   We Represent Different Perspectives

By taking different points of view, we enrich one-sided discussions. We try to break through typical thought patterns by questioning assumptions about processes,

Fig. 4.11 Quality Coaches in
pairing

Fig. 4.12 Different perspectives

methods, features, and architectures. We can often point out possible alternatives when working out problem solutions. This helps us to reduce systematic errors, avoid cost traps, and weigh risks as objectively as possible (Fig. 4.12).

4.5.8   We Are Communication Talents

We are a point of contact for questions and information of all kinds, both within the team and externally. We also actively take advantage of the effect of informal communication, which is almost always present in large organizations (Fig. 4.13).

We see ourselves as an amplifier for communication. This can take place between a pair, between many or all team members, and across team boundaries. Through this coordination, we can significantly reduce ambiguities about features or integrations and thus develop our products faster until they are ready for production.

Fig. 4.13 Quality Coach as a talent for communication

Fig. 4.14 Hello! I am a Quality Specialist

4.5.9 We Are Quality Specialists

In the next step, this new understanding of roles was presented more and more to our "agile test managers," who were so enthusiastic right away that they wanted to apply again immediately. What was missing was an appropriate name. There are various specialists in each of our cross-functional teams. One of these specialists is the driving force for more quality: the Quality Specialist (Fig. 4.14).

"Quality Specialist" is a very fitting term for this grown role. Even though they are almost always distinctive generalists, their real strength lies in creating awareness of quality.

These were the first steps on an exciting journey that was now beginning. Next, with the other roles in the teams, we will work out what the changes mean for our everyday life and our cooperation in detail. We also know that we have not yet fully fulfilled this role. Hence, we will now grow into this role, reflect on the changes in our role and, moreover, continuously learn different amounts in different fields.

4.6 The Challenge of Change

When it comes to staffing agile teams, we repeatedly experience reservations about employees with predominantly traditional backgrounds. Agile is often equated with new, innovative, flexible, and dynamic, which are seemingly not seen in connection with traditionally structured approaches.

4.6.1 Starting Position

In an agile environment, traditional management structures are "out." The roles of scrum master and product owner are understood as coaches or supporters and not as managers. Instead of project decisions by the project manager, these are now made "from the bottom up," which means that they are made by the team that acts independently. The teams are self-organized and therefore do not need their own management or command hierarchy.

Experiences from Many Projects
We experience the following problems again and again in organizations after the introduction or transition to agile approaches.

Adherence to Leadership Role   The organization, or rather the management, clings to the leadership role it has had up until now and cannot accept the new leadership mechanisms. The background in many cases is insecurity that they no longer see the possibility of being able to perform a leadership role within an agile environment.

Some organizations see it as a certain risk to hand over the freedom of design and implementation to a team instead of a responsible manager.

Lost Career Model   Positions, responsibilities, and prestige that have been built up over many years are at stake. Job descriptions such as project manager, test manager, and group leader no longer exist in agile project organizations. Those affected must reinvent themselves so that they can work efficiently.

Additional Starting Difficulties and Possible Solutions   Especially in the initial phase, the agile team is challenged to quickly confirm and strengthen the trust placed in it. We recommend providing the team with an experienced agile coach.

4.6.2   Supporting and Challenging Factors on the Way to Agile Development

If we take a closer look at agile approaches, the following important aspects for working and collaborating in agile projects emerge.

4.6.2.1 Creativity and Flexibility
Agile means that a lot of creativity and flexibility is required to achieve the goals set. In addition to solution creativity, this also requires communication within the team, and with the customer (product owner).

It also takes a lot of imagination to understand how the individual pieces of a prioritized backlog will fit together as a whole.

Employees from traditional projects sometimes have to fight the prejudice that speed and creativity are not that important there. But be aware: Not only is this an inadmissible generalization, the signatories of the Agile Manifesto also came from such projects. And the average age of the signatories at that time was well over 40 (!)—just in case anyone has the bias that agile is only something for very young people.

4.6.2.2 Stuck in Old Thought Patterns

In the many years of experience with traditional approaches, some see the danger of employees getting stuck in encrusted thought patterns. Long-term planning and stability were also a companion that provided security for years. All that is being "thrown overboard" by faster pacing (iterative planning, backlog grooming, retrospectives, etc.), which also raises fears of massive uncertainty.

Processes that have already become very familiar often no longer exist or are heavily modified.

Due to the lack of a formal test concept in agile projects, test managers from traditional projects might initially be unsettled when asked about tools and processes for defect management. This is because nowadays bugs are often discussed directly with the developers in the team and, if possible, fixed immediately. Bugs that cannot be fixed immediately are entered directly into the backlog. These are all processes that take time to get used to.

Communication has also changed massively. Whereas communication used to be very document-driven, it is now a direct exchange between all team members and stakeholders. In addition, the use of various collaboration tools is constantly growing.

4.6.2.3 Sluggishness and Lack of Flexibility

A key sign of agility is constant learning in short feedback cycles. In daily Stand-Up meetings, there are continuous updates and presentations of what has been achieved and what has not. This means that riding the wave of others' achievements is not possible—not even for testers, as they are an integral part of the team.

Agile teams are always good for surprises, and for unconventional and new approaches. "We've always done it that way" is not a good argument in discussions to present ideas. If one has been infected by the inertia of development and decision-making processes in the past, it is important to get rid of it quickly. This is especially true for testers, as they have to show extraordinary flexibility in agile projects. This applies to active involvement and "having a voice" in the planning meetings, continues with the daily status updates in the Stand-Up meetings, and extends to intensive communication with the developers. Since testers often do not have the technical background in the beginning, i.e., rarely speak in the "language of the developer," they also have to prepare to ask the right questions.

4.6.2.4 Work Environment

The work environment is completely different in agile projects: If we had "worked our way up" to become a test manager with our own office, we now might find ourselves in a large office with all the other team members. There is a constant coming and going; everything is public and transparent.

New values are established in a collaborative culture. The self-organized team also changes roles.

Teams commit to and are then collectively accountable for the results to be delivered. This requires a willingness to work with a high level of openness and mutual support, to learn and share each other's knowledge.

Those who see the knowledge they have built up over the years as "their" capital must now be willing to give up potential egoism and free themselves from competitive thinking between colleagues and agile teams and consider it a privilege to make their experience available to the team without reservation.

4.6.2.5 Changing Roles of Senior Testers/Senior Managers

Are experienced testers and test managers now "discontinued models"? In our opinion, not at all! After all, the faster, more optimized, and more creative the approach to solutions, the more important experience and knowledge are—from a technical and business perspective, but also in terms of organizations.

Over the years, senior testers may have developed the ability to look at things from a holistic perspective and to master critical situations with routine, calm, and composure.

Experienced testers and test managers have come across many new "cure-all remedies" that then turned out to be "castles in the sky"—they are therefore more resistant to blindly following every trend. This does not mean that new approaches are blocked, but rather that they are questioned on the basis of experience, and as a result even better solutions can often be found.

Qualities that the senior testers must bring with them in this case are willingness to learn, flexibility, creativity, and, above all, the much-cited common sense to adapt their specialist knowledge and sound experience to current situations.

4.7   Helpful Tips from Project and Community Experience

We regularly encounter a fascinating phenomenon, especially at conferences:

Someone appears who presents a "new, innovative method" in colorful slides, which will fundamentally change the agile community. Agile newcomers might be intrigued, but experienced testers and test managers will often quickly recognize that it is just about long-established practices with new names.

Even though the focus of tester professionalization schemes like ISTQB has been primarily on the traditional approach, this has resulted in testers mastering many tried and tested (test) techniques. If such experienced testers now understand how to use this extensive knowledge flexibly in agile projects, they can generate enormous benefits in a team.

"Modern testers" (Tester 2.0) are, at least in most companies where professional IT project development takes place, actively involved in the project life cycle: from early phases of the project when reviewing the requirement specifications, through the involvement in planning and estimation, and the methodological, structured test preparation and implementation up to the error correction and delivery processes.

Summarizing the essential strategies for project involvement:

- Testers must get involved in the process as early as possible—i.e., ensure the quality of the backlog items with the product owners (uniqueness, testability, etc.).
- Testers are equal team members.

- Testers should actively communicate in the team, approach the other team members, speak to them, and clarify ambiguities immediately.
- Testers bring enormous added value for a team—if the team does not (yet) recognize this, the tester should make this benefit visible/conscious, i.e., in retrospective meetings.

In addition to these success factors that have been known for many years from a wide variety of process models, these essential strategies also contain helpful tips:

- One of the agile mantras is "If something generates a benefit for the end result or if it is imperative due to regulations, it must be considered part of the deliverables."[1] This can be anything—for example, a test concept or a test design guideline, but also detail specifications or architectural design.
- "Keep the test artifacts lean." Consider whether the project requires detailed test manuals, concepts, or plans to be created in advance.
- Testers approach the test based on experience and exploration, ideally drawing from their entire test know-how.
- Testers focus on useful tests—that is, every test case that is performed must be useful for the project. Test scenarios that deliver errors but are far from any reality are often a waste of time and should be avoided.

A major change of mindset for testers in an agile environment is the general objective of the test. We have all heard it before: "We break the system!" or "The tester is only there to find errors!"

In reality, this has to be: "We help the team to deliver the optimally possible and desired quality together." The tester's task is still to find errors, but with a different objective. Testers focus on the quality of the currently available feature, the delivered story. It is important to ensure that the acceptance criteria specified by the customer representative (product owner) is met. Experienced testers use all established test case design techniques (boundary values, decision tables, etc.). In addition, testers also cover the robustness (fault tolerance) of the features or the system with targeted exploratory tests. Therefore, one thing is clear: There is still plenty of work for experienced testers and test managers in agile projects.

---

[1]Especially if the end product (such as in a safety-critical environment) has to go through a certification audit and has to provide certain evidence here.

Agile Test Management, Methods, and Techniques

5

Management includes the tasks of planning, organizing, directing, and controlling activities. A project manager is someone who plans, organizes, monitors, and controls a project. To be able to do this, they need knowledge, experience, information, and competence. To understand the management of agile testing, we first have to take a careful look at how agile projects work: In most agile process models such as Scrum, Kanban, Extreme Programming, and Lean Management (details on these can be found in Chap. 2, "Agile Process Models and Their View on Quality Assurance"), testing is not is explicitly addressed as we know it from traditional models—it is implicitly assumed that this is of course covered by the agile teams.

The test is therefore inextricably linked to the development. There may be testers, i.e., specialists with a focus on quality assurance and acceptance testing, but a separate test track does not appear in most process models (Kanban deliberately leaves this open). Team members with a test focus thus cover several roles: on the one hand that of the tester; on the other that of the test manager and finally that of the quality manager. We have already described which tasks they perform in Chap. 4, "Role of the Tester in Agile Projects." As this is essential, it should be mentioned again that testers in the agile world practically manage themselves. If there are several testers in a team, they usually divide the coordinating tasks among themselves (Beck, 2000).

Regardless of the development model, whether traditional or agile, there are a variety of activities that testers perform in projects.

5.1 Test Management

The term test management serves as a collective term, which we roughly break down into the following individual topics to describe it more precisely (Fig. 5.1):

© The Author(s), under exclusive license to Springer Nature Switzerland AG 2021
M. Baumgartner et al., *Agile Testing*, https://doi.org/10.1007/978-3-030-73209-7_5

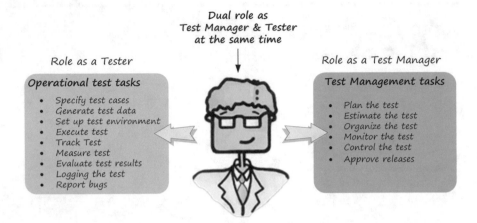

Fig. 5.1 Tester as manager

- Test planning
- Test estimation
- Test organization
- Test creation, implementation, and approval
- Test monitoring
- Test control

5.1.1 Test Planning in a Traditional Environment

Before we look at test planning in an agile environment, it is helpful to roughly review the test planning methods in the traditional project environment. In traditional software development projects, the test is usually planned as an independent activity. The test plan and test specification are often considered part of the mandatory delivery. But how did the test planning work in practice in these projects?

According to a survey on software testing in practice among public organizations and companies in German-speaking countries (Haberl, Spillner, Vosseberg, & Winter, 2011), in traditional projects a test manager will be nominated who will then begin with test planning.

Test planning is hardly possible without the often very time-consuming, tedious task of document inspection, and therefore the nominated test manager is well advised to first start looking for:

- Architecture diagrams
- Requirements documents and specifications
- Specifications on functionality, services, and masks
- GUI prototypes
- Style guides

- Use case descriptions (verbal, graphic)
- Big picture
- Project planning
- Project and quality management manual
- Test data strategy
- Risk management plan

In short, every documentation that can be found for the present project.

With these documents as a basis, the test plan, mostly based on the IEEE 29119 template (formerly IEEE 829) recommended by ISTQB, can be defined.

At the same time, the test manager is often required to estimate the test effort that is to be incorporated into the overall project planning. This can be challenging since the requirements are often incomplete or described only vaguely so that no reliable estimate can be derived from them. Another aspect that makes initial estimates error-prone is the fact that at this early stage in the project it is not yet entirely clear which seemingly trivial requirements might suddenly become tedious and effort-consuming.

Experienced test managers often use their experience with similar projects from their past as an estimate. Another approach that is also often used is the 20 to 30% thumb estimate, meaning that about a quarter of the estimated total project budget should be calculated for the test activities.

The authors' experience shows that such approaches may provide time and budget for the test, but the reality might look very different: Planned testing often serves only as a buffer for delays in the preliminary implementing phase. This practice continues to this day in traditional projects.

> **Note**
> A modified quote from Socrates seems fit to describe test planning in traditional projects: "I don't know what I don't know."

5.1.2 Test Planning in an Agile Environment

As we have already described in detail in Chaps. 1 and 2, the aforementioned dilemma is one of the initial sparks of the agile movement. A radical change in the way projects are carried out also has a serious impact on all phases of the test, from planning, design, draft, and implementation to the control of testing itself.

Even if the role of the tester and especially the test manager is controversial, it is obvious that in a professional project environment—no matter whether traditional or agile—many tasks have to be performed to ensure quality and also have to be carried out according to the principle: "Trust, but verify."

For agile approaches, we would adapt this statement as follows: *Trust is good; verification with continuous and constructive feedback for improvement is the best.*

The activities to ensure quality extend over the entire agile project period and are to be carried out by the entire team. Nevertheless, many of the projects surveyed by the authors show that quality aspects are only dealt with sufficiently when someone actively takes care of testing.

Ultimately, it does not matter what the role that carries out all these tasks is called. For the sake of simplicity, we will call them test managers and/or testers and the activity "Testing."

> **Note**
> Here the same principle applies that we already know from the traditional projects: "The earlier you are involved in a project as a tester or test manager, the better."

In an agile environment, this means that long before a project is started, product ideas can be collecting and entered in the product backlog.

To quickly come up with suitable user stories, one can consciously choose to put the cart before the horse: first collect specific examples of a requirement and only then summarize it in one or two explanatory sentences (Adzic, 2011). This is how an initial user story is created—more is often not needed, besides making sure that it is testable even in its initial state.

Only stories that can be tested are deliverable and, above all, only those that are of real benefit to the end customer should be included in delivery.

Often the next logical question arises: "When we talk about planning, what about the technical requirements such as response time, stability, and the like? Where do I define these quality features?" These features are of course also an important part of a product and sometimes more complex to implement—just think of any data migration that might be required or the switch to a new framework.

If one follows the statements from the agile community, these aspects—formulated in the form of acceptance criteria—should be assigned to the user stories, since only the stories can be assigned a real benefit. Short "technical stories" do not belong in a backlog. More on this later.

A specification of how quality is to be ensured in the project depends on the team structure (note: examples according to Scrum notation):

a) **One team on one project**
   The primary task in this case is to ensure to what extent the team should guarantee quality. It depends on the deliverables agreed with the customer/product owner regarding the proof of quality, whether extra reports or documents have to be prepared, or whether, for example, the proof of correctness in the context of the sprint reviews and the team-defined, serious Definition of Done (DoD) is sufficient.

b) **Multiple teams on one project (Scrum of Scrum)**
Basically, the same applies as in point a), but companies that have been using such Scrum of Scrum teams for a long time attach importance to the way in which the quality verification is carried out. Also, it should be uniform across teams. The only exception is that the customer representative/product owner orders other quality certificates. Once the project has been completed, the teams collate the results, documentation, quality certificates, etc. and archive them. If there is a further development in the future, the previous history, i.e., how the product was initially created, is irrelevant—it must be "as if from a single source."

c) **One or more teams in an organization**
In many, especially larger, companies, there are uniform quality specifications, be they based on ISO specifications (900x) or a set of rules such as CMMi, which requires specific results. Therefore, when introducing, setting up, and establishing agile procedures, it is essential to ensure that these framework conditions are observed and fulfilled. Here the quality assurance officer or test manager is required to provide the framework for the teams.

d) **Teams that are bound to special framework conditions**
Companies/teams that produce software that are subject to statutory regulators, such as in a medical, pharmaceutical, or safety-critical environment, are used to having to produce more detailed test and quality certificates. These will not become obsolete just because we are now agile. Thus, the creation of this evidence is integrated into the workflow by the team right from the start. How teams handle this varies individually. Some see this evidence as a deliverable of every sprint; others integrate the creation of quality evidence into their Definition of Done.

In most of the companies known to the authors, it is important that work is carried out consistently, regardless of the variants just described.
This brings the following advantages for the companies and teams:

- **Cross-team resource balancing**
  If the team, for whatever reason, identifies a resource bottleneck and addresses it as an impediment in the Daily Stand-Up Meeting, the ball is in the Scrum Master's court. If all teams in the project or organization are working according to similar (test) specifications, members of other teams can integrate into the impeded team with manageable familiarization effort.
- **Using synergies in technologies and methods**
  Shared technologies and methods also lead to reduced overall efforts, be it for tool procurance, configuration, or training.

Overall: The more teams work in a uniform manner, the more flexibility there can be across teams. For example, resources in other teams can help if there is a need. Here it should be clearly stated: Standardization should of course not go so far that teams can no longer work individually.

5.1.3   Test Plan

How could a general test plan look in a team working according to agile principles?

It has proven useful to design the general test plan like an organization-wide test directive/test policy, i.e., at a high level of abstraction. Within the test plan, the test manager defines the principles, procedures, and key goals of an organization related to testing that must be followed for each project.

This could look like the following example:

Practice

Test guideline from QualityIsOurSuccess Ltd.[1]

1. **Definition of testing in the organization**
   Our products stand for quality. We coordinate every customer requirement with our customers, identify together those that are most important to our customers or bring the greatest benefit, and deliver them quickly and with proven quality. This quality is demonstrably lived in the entire development process.

   In a nutshell: *"Ensuring the software fulfills its requirements."*[2]

2. **Definition of the test process**
   From the collection of the requirements to the approach of Test-Driven Development, there should be accompanying quality assurance by testers in the teams that ensure the quality of each individual requirement from the end-user perspective, automation of the acceptance criteria, and regression tests of the existing functionality.

   This must be ensured in detail as follows:

   - **Backlog Item Quality**
     Every entry that is included in the product backlog must be checked to ensure that it has the correct story format and corresponds to the agreed depth of description.
   - **Testable acceptance criteria**
     Ensure that every backlog item or user story has testable acceptance criteria—static test techniques such as reviews are to be used here and clarified with product owners, developers, and business analysts until all criteria are clear.

   (continued)

---

[1]Fictional example based on specific test guidelines.

[2]TestingExcellence.com is the source for this and all other brief descriptions.

- **Consider test effort**
  Introduce the test view at all planning meetings, i.e., the estimates ensure that the test activities are also considered.
- **Test design and implementation**
  During the development cycles (sprints), test cases must be designed, documented, and carried out for each acceptance criterion depending on the criticality.
- **Acceptance test**
  Ensure that at least one test case is created for each acceptance criterion.
- **Traceability**
  Each test case is clearly assigned to a story.
- **Sprint review**
  At the end of each sprint, the functionality of each story that has been reported as "Done" must be demonstrated to the product owner or end customer as part of a sprint review. The proof is considered successful if the acceptance criteria could be presented without errors.

In a nutshell: *"All test plans are written in accordance with organization policy."*

3. **Ensuring quality (Test evaluation)**

- **Guidelines for teams for development:**
  Each function is to be developed using TDD (Test-Driven Development/ Test First approach). The unit and integration tests created in this way must be carried out continuously as part of the Daily/Nightly Builds. If errors occur ("Broken Build"), these must be rectified immediately.
- **Completion criterion:**
  A story is only finished when all the criteria of the Definition of Done have been met (e.g., the team has successfully carried out all tests (unit tests and functional tests) ("Green Bar").
- **Proof of quality:**
  Evidence must be provided in a test protocol.
- **Team composition:**
  The team consists of members with cross-functional skills. To take the end-user view into account in the teams, at least one tester must be permanently integrated in each team.

In a nutshell: *"Effect on business of finding a fault after its release."*

(continued)

4. **Quality criteria to be achieved**
A "Done" status for Stories ensures that there are no errors classified as "Blocker" or "Serious Error." This ensures that this functionality is ready to use.

In a nutshell: *"No open high-severity faults prior to products release."*

5. **Improvement process**

Our goal:

- Learning from experience, we aim for continuous improvement in all areas of the development cycle.
- Each development cycle (sprint) must be concluded with a retrospective, in which potential improvements are defined.

In a nutshell: *"Project review meetings are to be held after project completion."*

Explanation of Terms
Broken Build Unit tests, which are carried out automatically after a build has been created, produce errors. The reason is that the last checked-in component is not yet compatible with the other components.

Green Bar In the Continuous Integration system (e.g., via tools like Jenkins or Hudson) the results of the automatically running unit and integration tests are shown in a report. The aim is that the result bar for the test of each build is error-free, i.e., green.

The test guideline forms the general framework for all projects processed in the organization, is binding for everyone, and is usually created long before a project is initiated, or a project team is set up. Companies that have been working according to this procedural model for a long time see this guideline as the essence of previous experience, which is also continuously updated. That is, none of the points listed is set in stone; on the contrary, the principle "inspect and adapt" is used very strongly here.

Now we finally start with a project. The team is assembled, takes shape, and goes into the project start phase.

5.1.4   Test Activities in Iteration Zero: Initialization Sprint

Just like in surgery all devices are prepared so that they are within reach during the operation. We prepare the entire environment so that the team can concentrate on the goal in the sprints: to deliver deliverables.

"Every Path Starts with the First Step"
This first step is often called Iteration Zero and should already include test preparation activities.

These test activities must be considered for all phases and explicitly planned. For this purpose, we have supplemented the following "Checklist Iteration Zero" with test activities (the list does not claim to be complete, but is a good starting point to create a project-specific list):

General team task	Test activities and considerations
• Development/expansion of the product backlog—prioritization of the backlog items	• Review of items for testability • Consideration of the end user perspective • Check that there are acceptance criteria that are formulated clearly, unambiguously, and without contradictions Important: Can these also be tested? • If the entries in the product backlog are already given rough estimations or story points, it must be ensured that test aspects are also included
• Setting up the environment(s) – Development – Continuous Integration (CI) – Test – Pre-production	• Has the CI process been set up? • Has it been ensured that the unit tests (for TDD) are integrated, and the results are transparent (reports, dashboard, etc.)? • Is the CI process clearly defined for the test environment(s)? • Is the test to pre-production process defined?
• Selection/definition of the development process	• Create a suitable test concept
• Recruiting/forming a team or finalizing team building (including all roles)	• Are testers on board? • Do they have sufficient know-how?If not, then outline the rough training concept
• Defining the working environment (premises, equipment, etc.)	The same applies to test environments
• Tool selection: Ideally, this is done via the proof-of-concept checklist of suitable tools (software) for development including GUI, unit tests, code analysis, CI, collaboration, test automation	• Define test management tooling • Is there a concept for test automation and test automation tooling at system and acceptance test level?
• Automation: Are unit test frameworks available and usable?	• Is a test automation framework available and usable?
• If the team is already available: Develop how collaboration is ensured: Where is the task board located? What does it look like? etc.	• Clarify how ticket handling will be done: – Are there separate implementation and test tickets, or are tickets transferred directly from development to the test, like a relay run? – Is it transparent when the implementation is done and when testers can take over? – How do testers organize their test activities? Do they use the same task board as the team or a separate one? – Determine how defects are communicated and which task board/tool is being used
• Working together to define the Definition of Done	• Focus on quality, testability, and measurability • Are the given constraints (such as statutory regulations) covered in the DoD?

5.1.5   External Support for Test Planning

In agile teams, planning activities are usually completed by the team and carried out in the individual sprints.

In some cases, it is necessary to set up or implement certain specifications that are difficult or impossible to implement within the team. These include, for example:

- Partner systems (third-party systems that are required for the comprehensive process test; time window for using such systems, etc.)
- Test data (such as specific data to be supplied by third-party systems)
- Definition of detailed components that are subject to special framework conditions (safety and security criteria, compliance guidelines, interfaces where, for example, accessibility is required)
- Special architectural specifications (regarding performance, failure safety, etc.)

Whenever long-term planning or preparation is required, it has proven worthwhile to take the support of a person outside the agile team who can pursue and carry out these activities for the team.

5.1.6   Test Estimation

In traditional projects, testing and quality assurance were only present in organizations with a high level of maturity already integrated in the requirement phase, whereas for agile projects this should be true in any case.

In agile projects, one of the first tasks in the project initialization phase is to fill the product backlog with requirement stories. In addition to the story description, these early stories already contain rudimentary acceptance criteria, the business value,[3] and a rough initial assessment of the complexity of the story. This complexity is usually specified in story points[4]. It is often the case that, in addition to a review of the user stories (in terms of testability), the testers also request a rough estimate of the complexity, i.e., how many story points are required for the implementation and testing in comparison to the other stories.

Regardless of whether we look at it from a development or test perspective, the following approach has proven to be efficient and effective:

From the existing stories, choose a story that is as simple as possible—and can be easily estimated from a test perspective—as a reference story.

---

[3]Business value is a guideline with which the product owner can weigh the stories. The higher this value, the more benefit the functionality brings to the user.

[4]Story points are a popular method of estimating the size of a story. In our experience, this depends on the scope, risk, clarity of the story, and experience of the team, but also overall complexity. The Fibonacci series, which was adapted by Mike Cohn using the following values, has established itself as a scale for Story points: 1, 2, 3, 5, 8, 13, 20, 40, 100. The higher the value, the more complex, ex-tensive, risky, etc. is the story.

This story might have, for example, the following key characteristics or acceptance criteria:

- Five to ten test data records (simple type) must be created.
- Result values can only be verified against a set of reference values.
- No data from external systems is required.

This story could now be given the complexity rating of 1 or 2 story points. If automation is required at the acceptance test/system test level, the next higher value should be used.

1. For all other stories, compare them to the reference story to get an initial complexity assessment—from a test perspective.
2. The values obtained in this way are to be understood as a rough estimation of complexity but can already be a measure of whether the story is appropriately "cut," i.e., whether it can be realistically implemented within a sprint.
3. However, the actual estimate can only be made during the sprint planning meetings, when all team members contribute their views on each individual story. Here, the testers need to play an active role, as the goal is to have every story available as part of a "potential shippable" sprint, which means the testing activities are an inseparable part of every story.

    Sometimes a story seems to require minimal development effort, but could still entail extensive (regression) testing activities. Here the testers may have to convince the entire team if the awareness on test activities in the team is not yet established.
4. The testers should also contribute their expertise while continuously re-evaluating the stories still in the product backlog ("backlog grooming").

5.1.7   Test Organization

In Chap. 4 we got to know different team compositions—including those that have proven successful in some of our projects.

Each agile team should have at least one or two trained testers. If necessary, the team can also have several additional support teams or individual experts who can be consulted for special topics.

A security, recovery, or load and performance expert or team can join the agile team whenever stories require testing of these (mostly nonfunctional) quality features. This means that the team is temporarily expanded, and the temporary team members should have the same rights and obligations as all other team members—and commit to the sprint result.

An alternative approach is to have these stories or test activities carried out by other organizations or teams outside the agile team.

The situation can be similar with other supporting roles such as DB modelers, system architects, etc. If such special skills are required in an agile team, these

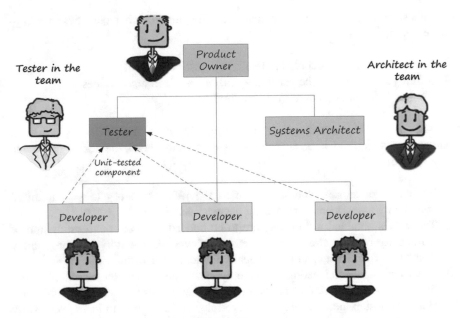

Fig. 5.2 Team composition and position of the testers

specialists are temporarily engaged in the team and then carry out these tasks either as an external supplier or even as a temporary team member during the current sprint.

The agile team composition can follow a simple structure as depicted in Fig. 5.2:

5.1.8 Test Creation, Implementation, and Release

If agile teams are set up co-located, they can generate a significant advantage: direct communication. This added value is often massively underestimated, but it becomes very clear when the additional effort that distributed teams have to put up with every day being spread across several locations is made visible. This starts with the review and the estimation of stories during the initial filling of the backlog, and continues with the release and sprint planning, through the preparation for the sprint review to the acceptance of the story and ultimately the release. The more direct communication is possible, the more efficiently a team will work. Of course, there are plenty of tools supporting distributed teams, but while these can help to virtually bring a distributed team together, nothing beats an exchange of experience face to face.

If we now look at the test, we can see that in all of the above phases the entire team is required to work on the common goal. The more the team understands how to work hand in hand, the more efficiently and quickly it will reach the goal of fulfilling the acceptance criteria of each story. Testers lead their team to success by specifically identifying weaknesses and problems and directing the team to eliminate these weaknesses.

As for the test execution itself, not much has changed. It is important to find as many errors or deviations from the expected behavior as possible in the shortest possible time. This needs the explorative test approach described in more detail below, but also methodically defining good test cases, mastering test executions (with preparation and follow-up), and finding and managing test data. The only difference to traditional projects is that teams primarily create more detailed test case descriptions if it is useful for them or if the project environment requires it—for example, if legal regulations are to be observed.

For **load and performance tests** different approaches can be chosen:

In-team handling: We often find this in early phases, when it is primarily a question of verifying the chosen approach of the system or database architecture, for example whether a request really has the desired performance due to the selected layer structure. These tests can be carried out with a few parallel users and can also often be carried out on the development environment. The focus of these early tests lies in the performance of individual transactions.

Support team handling: If the test goal is to verify the predicted productive performance of the system, the test setup can look very different. The aim is to provide evidence that the system created can cope with the "real world," i.e., whether users can still operate the system within the acceptable response times even under full load. There are many popular open-source tools that are well suited to generating load and evaluating minimal measured values. But if serious, in-depth analysis is needed, considering the effects on the entire system environment, the use of professional load and performance test tools is essential. Manufacturers of such commercial tools have now taken the market's criticism of the past years into account and already offer powerful tools with attractive purchase and rental models.

The execution of load and performance tests including evaluation and analysis of the system behavior follows its own rules. If these tests are to be conducted seriously and professionally, they are often difficult to force into the fixed timing of iterations/sprints, which is why these tests are often also outsourced to support teams in a test organization. The necessary experts, the systems, and the networks required to simulate a production-related environment are usually available in those support teams, and not in agile implementation teams. Based on nonfunctional requirements, these teams can handle the tests and ultimately return the results and detailed analysis to the agile implementation team. The agile implementation teams then evaluate the results and, if necessary, derive measures from them, which they either implement directly or add to the backlog as a "Ticket."

We can see in this chapter so far that test planning had to change for agile projects, but what about the test methods? Has there also been a change?

5.2   Test Methods in an Agile Environment

Ten years after the publication of Lisa Crispin's first article on agile testing in America, Markus Gaertner describes another way of practicing agile testing in the "Object Spectrum" journal. He was looking for an answer to the legitimate question of how testers can keep up with rapid development cycles—two to six weeks—given the often-proven declaration that testing software takes longer than writing software

Fig. 5.3 Testing methods for agile teams

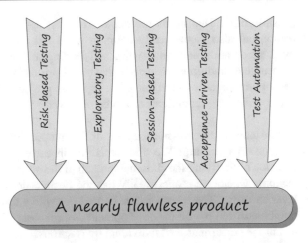

(Budd & Majoros, 1978). When looking for an answer to this question, he came across multiple promising approaches, including:

- Risk and value-based testing
- Exploratory Testing (ET)
- Session-based (exploratory) testing (SBT)
- Acceptance Test-Driven Development (ATDD)
- Test automation

It is up to the testers to select the appropriate approach or combination of approaches for their respective project situation (see Fig. 5.3).

5.2.1 Risk-Based and Value-Based Testing

Gaertner already found that agile development with its short release intervals presented the previous test methods with a problem that was difficult to solve, if not impossible. There is hardly any time to find, document, and execute test cases for all functions. It is therefore important for testers to compromise on test efforts and test coverage: less testing due to the shorter test time—but to still test just enough to find the most serious errors (Menzies & Cukic, 2000).

Risk-based testing provides a way to do this, by letting the tester select the high-risk points in a system and address them in a targeted manner.

So much for the idea, but how does the team know which components, functions, stories, or processes mean which risk for the end customer?

An extension of the above-mentioned approach is to base test coverage not only on risk but also on the value of the respective functionality. This means that the more business-critical the failure of a functionality, the more intensively it must be verified with test activities.

It is usually the product owner's responsibility to share all important information when filling the backlog or to disclose it to the teams at the planning meeting at the latest. Based on this information, the testers carry out a risk analysis of the components classified as critical together with the rest of the team. Every new function of this component is checked for its risks. The potential impact of an error in the function is classified and the probability of an error must be calculated. The impact times the probability gives the priority of the test (Bach J., 1999).

> **Note**
>
> A creative "joker" had an even more efficient idea:
>
> "Just prepare and run tests on the parts that contain errors. We can safely economize the test of the other, flawless parts."
>
> Whoever manages to implement this idea successfully and consistently will surely be the new star in the testing community—we are still working on it. . .

Another type of risk can result from implementation: If, for example, central modules are developed that represent the heart of the entire system, these are of course much more critical and therefore need to be tested more intensely than other "normal" functions.

Working closely in an agile team makes it easier to identify the high-risk parts of a system than in traditional projects when testers only received the finished product.

The measurement scale for the factors' impact and probability is the same:

4 = Very high
3 = High
2 = Medium
1 = Low

If a function has a high impact factor = 3 and a high probability of becoming faulty = 3, a priority of 9 can be calculated. If it has a medium impact factor = 2 and a low probability of becoming faulty = 1, priority would be 2. It is important that the entire agile team is involved in determining the impact and probability.

Given this approach, the exit criteria for a test run might also be "test period ended." This means that only as many test cases from the prioritized test execution list are processed until the time frame is exhausted. The longer the test time, the less risk remains in the then smaller "untested" part of the system. For example, it can happen that only half of the functions are tested in a new release. The chosen risk- or value-based test approach then at least ensures that the functions are tested that are most business-critical or pose the greatest dangers for performing the core business in case they are faulty.

If there are errors in the remaining functions, in the worst case they will appear in production at some time. However, since—if the risk assessment has been made correctly—they are hardly or not at all critical to the business, they will be entered into the backlog and the team corrects these errors as part of the maintenance.

More important than the absence of errors in every functionality is that the users can use high business–value functionality in time.

Does agile development functionality take priority over quality?

Professor Mario Winter described the topic of risks and testing in one of his presentations (Winter, 2009) as follows:

What Are Risks?
Risks are problems that can arise both during development and during use of the product and could have undesirable consequences.
• Project risks relate to the management and control of a (test) project, e.g., lack of human resources, tight time frames, changing requirements, etc.
• Product risks are directly related to the software product and often result from quality defects.

Project and product risks are often considered according to the software quality as per DIN/ISO/IEC 9126 (note by the authors: this standard has been replaced by ISO/IEC 25000).
The influencing factors are very broad and can hardly be influenced in some cases (Fig. 5.4):

Fig. 5.4 Risk influencing factors

Value-based or risk-based testing means:

- **Targeted testing** by considering system functions depending on the benefit that these functions represent for the organization. In addition, the risk level must also be considered, i.e., the probability that this risk will occur. Both the choice of test method and the depth of the test are decisive.
- **Prioritized testing**, whereby areas with higher risk are given a higher priority in test planning and are tested accordingly early and intensively.
- **Quantify the residual risks** in test reports, risks that remain when the software is delivered despite shortening the test or waiving the execution of planned tests.

5.2.2   Exploratory Testing

Exploratory testing has long been hailed as an alternative or supplement to structured testing using a specific method. Experienced test experts such as Cem Kaner and James Bach advocate a creative test approach according to which the testers are controlled by their intuition and not by a method or tool (Kaner, Bach, & Pettichord, 2002). An effective, creative tester will be able to guess where the mistakes are. This approach can be considered "exploring" the software. The testers push into the system and follow paths that can possibly lead to errors. If they do not find an error, they return and follow a different path. Due to their many years of experience, the experienced testers will know where to look. Similar to the term "code smell" in development, where developers "smell" suboptimal code, one could say that testers perceive a "bug smell."

This experience-based approach is already becoming more structured: Testers are focusing on concepts such as "features," "complexity," "configuration," and "interoperability"; these offer clues from which testers can start their tours through the system.

James Whittaker compares exploratory testing to being a tourist in a foreign country who has the opportunity to discover the area on different tours (Whittaker, 2009), for example:

Landmark tour: In this case, we look at the sights, i.e., the most important features, and test them in many ways and sequences—just as tourists visit the sights according to their interests and preferences.

Money Tour: This tour primarily focuses on the functions that bring the greatest benefit to the customer, perhaps like an art lover who is primarily interested in museums in every city but not all their sights.

Intellectual tour: This is the tour of the inventors who want to find out the limits of the system, essentially the "traditional tester approach," where the primary aim is to find as many errors as possible, even with particularly tricky input combinations.

Saboteur Tour: Destructive testers who use every situation to bring the system down specifically feel at home here.

FedEx Tour: Like parcel tracking, testers follow the data through the system and pay particular attention that it arrives at the right places.

Guidebook tour: This tour is particularly appropriate if there is documentation about the system. Testers follow the paths given in the documentation and find out whether the description and system fit together and work correctly.

James Whittaker discovered several other tours in his book that a tester may be interested to learn about as a software tourist.

However, exploratory testing remains essentially what it is: a manual search process for experience and instinct. Either the testers have the right experience and instinct or they do not. If the testers have it, they can significantly shorten the test time relative to the test result. If the testers do not bring this with them, this test approach is not justified (Wallmüller, 2004).

Exploratory testing, especially when it is practiced as session-based testing, is a highly efficient method that also enables a separation of roles for testers and business experts.

5.2.3   Session-Based Testing

To make exploratory testing more sustainable and, above all, measurable, Jonathan and James Bach developed their own extended test method in 2000: session-based testing (SBT).

Note

J. & J. Bach describe their motives as follows:"From a distance, exploratory testing can look like one big amorphous task. But it is an aggregate of sub-tasks that appear and disappear like bubbles in a Jacuzzi. We would like to know what tasks happen during a test session, but we do not want the reporting to be too much of a burden. Collecting data about testing takes energy away from doing testing." (Bach J., 2000)

To be able to follow the "bubbles" in a more comprehensible manner, the explorative testing approach is followed in principle, but the testing and processing of results follows a predefined structure, so-called session sheets. This has several advantages:

- The creativity in the exploratory test execution is not restricted.
- The test runs are understandable because they follow a rudimentary structure.
- Test results can therefore also be measured.
- Repeatability, a kind of regression test, is possible.

Another big advantage is that session-based testing can be easily adapted. If the team recognizes potential for optimization, they can simply adapt the basic session sheet.

This test approach is often also found in companies whose test process is not yet fully developed, but whose test teams still need a measurable and controllable process.

How Does SBT Work?

The session-based test approach (SBT) requires the testers to plan short work periods in which they test intensively.

At the start of the session, the testers receive a briefing from the experts or team, in which the key data of the test session to be carried out is defined—a session sheet (according to Bach), which includes the following categories, has proven helpful:

- **Session Charter:** This includes a mission statement, a short definition of which goal should be pursued with the test in the test session. This can include, for example, the strategy/tour (discovery, bug detection, bug retest, "Simply on it") and the session duration (short: 60 minutes; normal: 90 minutes; long: 120 minutes).
- **Tester name(s):** Assignment of who carries out the tests.
- **Date and time:** When the test session starts.
- **Task Breakdown:** These are the key figures of the test:
  - T(ime—duration, i.e., duration of the test session)
  - B(ugs—number found during the session)
  - S(ession setup—which environment conditions are effective for this session)
- **Data files:** that are required or have been created.
- **Test notes:** Everything that appears important is documented. (Step by step or in brief, which behavior did the system show? Which one would have been expected?)
  Experienced testers can, for example, supplement individual test ideas and approaches with traditional test techniques: Especially if acceptance criteria are tested, it could look like this:
  AC01: Key-value input must meet dependencies on the input field xyz (according to Appendix XY)
  - Verification of the input field using a decision table (according to the supplementary sheet)
  - Verification of the different areas (according to the limit value analysis)
- **Issues:** Questions, deviations from expected behavior.
- **Bugs:** Defects that were noticed during the test execution/session This can be the defect ID if defects were recorded in a defect management tool, or testers can attach all the necessary log files or screenshots to the session sheet that are required for analysis and correction.

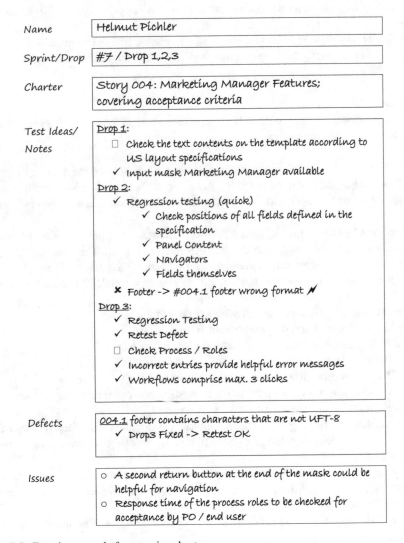

Fig. 5.5 Exercise example for a session sheet

Figure 5.5 presents an example session sheet from one of our sample projects:

At the end of the session, the testers report their experiences to the experts or the team, which is efficiently possible due to the orderly, although mostly keyword-like, documentation of the results.

The knowledge gained from this then flows back to the implementation team. If it turns out that testers, for example, have made incorrect assumptions or "got lost" during their exploratory testing, it can be quickly resolved, and the charter adjusted accordingly.

Based on the test results, experts or teams decide on further test areas and define further test sessions.

This method combines risk-based testing, structured testing, documentation, and sensible separation of roles (experts have to invest comparatively little time)—in other words, everything that can help achieve higher quality.

SBT is widespread in the agile testing community, which uses SBT as a basis for advanced techniques or builds on them and sets their own key figures on them. For example, James Lindsay developed a very interesting approach (Lindsay, 2003), based on SBT, in which he derives improvement models by determining and using test points and can thus control the test with simple means. SBT is therefore a relatively simple and very effective method that makes exploratory testing of agile projects more professional.

Summary
Session-based testing (SBT) includes:

- Managed and controlled, exploratory testing
- Limited time (time boxed)
- Explorative orientation
- Logging the test activities and findings

5.2.4 Acceptance Test-Driven Development

In Acceptance Test-Driven Development, the entire agile team analyzes each story in the sprint planning meeting or in the Grooming Session and discusses the acceptance criteria predefined by the product owner.

Specific examples for interpretation of the Stories are discussed—such as "If the customer Harry orders a book with the title 'It was a long time ago,' he receives the message that this book is no longer in stock." If different interpretations of a story appear within the agile time, these examples serve the team as a basis for discussion when coordinating with the product owner.

As soon as the team has a uniform view and understanding of how the given acceptance criteria are to be understood, the testers formulate relevant test cases from the complete set of examples, which are now considered "concrete acceptance criteria." In future, these will serve as the only valid acceptance criteria for acceptance, e.g., in the sprint review.

The entire team therefore has these acceptance criteria right from the start, which help sharpen the common understanding of the stories.

Elisabeth Hendrickson, one of the masterminds for agile testing, sees it as one of the most important practices in an agile environment (Hendrickson, 2008).

With his book *Specification by Example* (Adzic, 2011), Gojko Adzic has given a new impetus to this topic. Adzic clearly shows which approach leads to success and provides very understandable examples.

5.2.5 Test Automation

Test automation is an indispensable component of agile testing. It must therefore be introduced and trained before the project begins. When the first iteration takes place, the testers must be able to handle implementing and executing automated tests. Of course, not all test activities can be automated, but a large part of them, especially including repeatable tasks such as test data generation, test result checking, test procedure logging, and test run repetition, should be. The testers should be freed from time-consuming activities so that they can concentrate on creating test ideas.

For Gaertner, test automation is the culmination of the agile test. It may be different in every project, but every project team must find a suitable solution. The testers will only be able to keep up with development with automation, and this is the conditio sine qua non for testing in agile projects. The maximum test coverage must be achieved in the short time of an iteration.

> "To automate or not to automate that's the question." Freely based on Shakespeare

If we want to successfully handle projects in an agile environment, the quote would be:

> "But if we want to be successful with agile projects there's no option: Automation is a MUST have!"

Since this topic is essential in agile projects, we have devoted an entire chapter to it (see Chap. 7).

5.3   Significant Factors Influencing Agile Testing

For agile teams to be able to work efficiently and effectively, some practices and processes must be ensured. Continuous Integration and deployment, short delivery cycles, and a common code base, to name just a few, must be set up and run like clockwork. Only when these processes "run smoothly and stably" can an agile team focus on successful implementation of stories.

One might interject here that "This is primarily relevant for the developers, so these are development topics!"

True, there might be limited direct connection to testing, but still, it is the basis for the overall project process. Whether the team and thus also the testers regularly receive the latest versions depends on the functioning of these tools and processes.

Let us therefore take a closer look at these processes and their history:

5.3.1 Continuous Integration (CI)

Continuous Integration is a term from software development and is considered a "must-have" in the agile world. CI is a practice based on XP (Extreme Programming) and the basis for delivering high-quality software.

While in traditional projects and development models the code base is usually made available to the test at a later point in time relative to implementation, agile methods pursue the approach of continuously testing the software to identify errors very quickly and thus fixing them right away.

Experience from various software projects shows that the late handover of the software to test teams poses many problems. It is fairly common that the software does not get sufficiently tested on lower test levels during development. The software handed over to a test team very often still contains teething troubles, which are the cause of frequent, unnecessary delays until the software has reached a state to enable efficient testing on higher test levels. The consequences of this are higher costs in the test phase, increased personnel costs, delays in the delivery of the software to the customer, and quality deficits in the operation of the software.

Continuous Integration is one way to remedy this, with a simple-looking process (Fig. 5.6):

Continuous Integration is an essential part of an agile test strategy: If the development works with a test-driven approach, the developers adapt their code parts until the locally created unit tests run without errors. They then check their new or modified executable source modules into a configuration management tool (Version management)).

The Automatic Build
After every change in the source library, a new build run is usually started immediately after checking in, which automatically versions the new software builds according to a predefined scheme and stores them in the software repository. Then the tool automatically starts all unit and integration tests contained in the central repository that have been created and checked in so far.

This is where it gets exciting: Are all test cases still running successfully—is the result bar green ? Or does a code change cause errors in other components? This is also referred to as Broken Build.

If errors occur in the build, the team has the highest alarm level! The primary goal now is to correct the errors as quickly as possible.

Build Process A separate build manager is often responsible for the administration of the entire build process. This build manager adjusts the build routines, controls when and how many sanity tests are started automatically, and defines when more complex functional and nonfunctional tests are started automatically as part of the build process. In many teams, this is usually done only once a day, and preferably overnight (Nightly build). This means that a completely new build is created, and all unit and integration tests are executed—and if they have produced a green bar, the

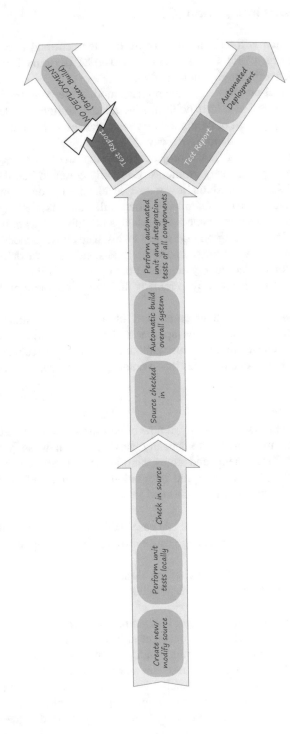

Fig. 5.6 Continuous Integration—build process (simplified representation)

more complex functional tests then run automatically. In the end, the team will have both a result report and a completely new version in the early morning.

There is also excellent, in-depth literature about Continuous Integration and build process such as Pichler, Roock, & Havenstein (2011) where Andreas Havenstein breaks down the topic of Continuous Integration in detail and with a high degree of practical relevance. After an introduction to the topic, he goes into the general conditions that are necessary to operate this technology. Furthermore, he dedicates an extensive chapter to the topic of feedback since quick feedback is the basic principle behind CI. He also describes in detail which framework conditions should be observed when introducing and "living" CI and what can cause issues for agile teams.

5.3.2   Automated Configuration Management

Any development team, be it agile or traditional, needs automated configuration management with versioning capability. The check-in and check-out procedure should ensure that the current version is always available and that previous versions are archived. The workflow from sources to executable components must be clearly defined. Both the customer and the agile suppliers benefit from defined processes and infrastructure standards. They make it possible to deliver new releases in easy-to-integrate installation packages.

Agile teams need to be able to convert their software into installable packages and should strictly structure and standardize the data needed for it—only then can the applications be effortlessly imported into various environments for system test, integration test, and production. The necessary configurations should be made via environment and software parameters without changing the code itself. The information on this should be documented on delivery and, if possible, provided automatically.

Most build tools provide workflow and integration standards that should be common to all releases. Usually, a single state-of-the art tool can cover the essential requirements. Even if a team communicates daily, as is the case with Scrum or Kanban teams, the build scripts should always be versioned. This procedure also provides revision security and versioning makes it possible to automatically pass on fixes for production to new releases.

A similar procedure to that for versioning a build can be used for the deployment. A single comprehensive installation routine should contain all the steps that are necessary for the deployment. This routine should be the same for all projects and is already integrated in every software package during the build process. This approach is not only less complex and error-prone than manual adaptation for each individual application, but also much faster. Changes carried out on the central overlay are automatically transferred to each individual package. If developers change the code during an agile development process, the deployment tool can react immediately.

The deployment tool usually allows an immediate check of the availability of an application—server, databases, target scheme, and the required queues—saving time and effort. If errors still occur during delivery despite successful tests, their probable source is related to the environment.

5.4   The Special Challenges of Testing of IoT

The Internet of Things (IoT for short) does not necessarily have anything to do with an agile approach. Nevertheless, many IoT developments are carried out in an agile manner, and IoT presents testing with very special challenges, which we want to deal with here.

5.4.1   What Is the Internet of Things?

With the Internet of Things (IoT) many very different areas of application of software are summarized, in which many individual devices (e.g., sensors, control devices, household items, medical devices) communicate with one another and with a central server via a common network and thus allow central data collection or control. The most well-known area of application is the control of lighting or other electrical devices, from a mobile phone or tablet PC. The range also extends to sensors that pass on the wear and tear and defects of rented construction equipment to the distributor or manufacturer, so that maintenance can be carried out in a targeted manner or billed according to use. The networking of implants in humans (so-called cyborgs) is still in its comparative infancy, but is already a reality.

According to Beecham Research (Beecham Research, 2021), there are nine different industry areas where very different IoT solutions are offered: building management, energy supply, consumer goods and home, health care and life science, industry, transportation, trade, personal and public security, and IT and networks. This list alone makes it clear how wide the application area of IoT is. The potential that lies in networked individual devices for the economy and ultimately for our society cannot be overestimated. Accordingly, IoT is becoming one of the megatrends in IT—especially since it is often used in conjunction with other megatrends such as big data and cloud services (Fig. 5.7).

IoT solutions usually not only consist of the software in the networked devices or components, but also the management of the required network, central server applications for processing the data, applications for evaluating the information, control applications, and finally the cloud services for flexible connection. Thus, IoT applications are often complex IT systems in which the latest technologies including mobile apps and micro-services are used.

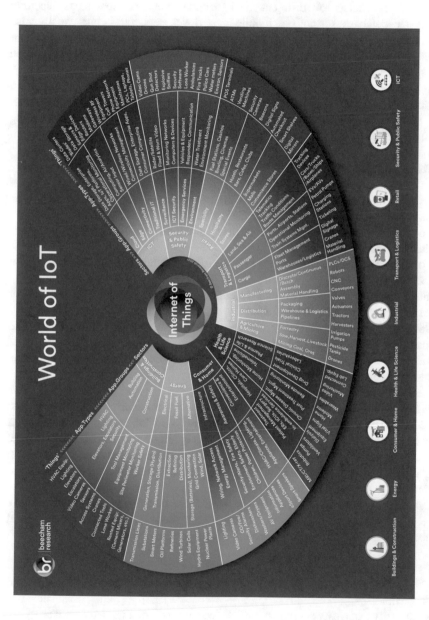

Fig. 5.7 The most diverse areas of application of IoT (Beecham Research, 2021)

5.4.2   The Challenge of Testing IoT in Agile Teams

IoT requires extremely interdisciplinary teams, in which interdisciplinary not only means IT specialists of different backgrounds (network specialists, security specialists, database specialists, mobile app developers, etc.), but usually also specialists from electrical and mechanical engineering—and possibly even sector specialists like medical professionals. This must obviously be considered when organizing an agile team for IoT.

It would now seem logical to leave the testing largely to the specialist team members and not add additional test specialists to keep the team size manageable. Still, the opposite is advisable: Especially for IoT someone needs to take on testing and its challenges holistically.

The challenges for the testing and quality in IoT projects are typically:

- Security and appropriate design of the data connection (correct and secure encryption, reliable coupling, sufficient bandwidth)
- Correct use of big data solutions for many small devices (load and performance characteristics)
- Correct assessment of the user experience for users and alignment of the solution accordingly
- Interoperability of devices and interchangeability/expansion of devices or subsystems—in short, compatibility
- Ensuring of reliability, stability, and robustness of the solution, thus dealing with (partial) failures, dead spots, etc.
- Increased regulatory requirements, such as to protect personal data, resilience, and emergency plans

Many providers of current IoT solutions have a particularly painful experience related to quality risks, because a comprehensive view of quality and testing has often been neglected. Test specialists who advise quality across teams and contribute to testing are an important part of IoT teams. A community of practice for testing, in which an exchange of QA methods can happen across teams, can be useful and important.

Surprisingly, so far, we do not see the need for new testing methodologies in IoT projects. Existing methodologies can cover all needs, if they are selected and combined in accordance with the project's requirements.

- Use of nonfunctional tests:
  - Targeted load and performance tests that detect cross-system or end-to-end weaknesses
  - Security tests, especially penetration tests by well-qualified specialists
  - Usability tests, e.g., in order to run through certain scenarios with typical user profiles
  - Reliability tests, which primarily target bandwidth fluctuations and misconfiguration by the end users

- Robustness tests, where resilience is checked, for example stable behavior even in the event of partial failure of the overall system or individual sensors
- Shift-left when testing:
  - Take the review of requirements and design specifications seriously and/or design the sprint planning very effectively (preferably in several steps).
  - Schedule tests of subsystems as early as possible and work heavily with mockups or simulation environments.
- Plan creative exploratory test sessions which bring together many (unfavorable) influencing factors at once (e.g., failure, reduced connectivity, incorrect operation, misconfiguration, or even deliberate external attacks).

Finally, we would like to mention one very important aspect for IoT projects: ethics. This is obviously not an additional quality feature and cannot really be tested, but testers should nevertheless pay special attention to ethics in IoT projects that bring information technology to new areas or sectors. There is still no general "Code of Ethics" in IT, such as in medicine; however, testers should adhere to the ethical code of ACM and IEEE which is also part of the ISTQB training (ISTQB— International Software Testing Qualifications Board, 2018).

Agile Testing Documentation

6

One of the Agile Manifesto's core principles is: "Working software has priority over comprehensive documentation." Unfortunately, this declaration of principles is understood by many as a waiver of documentation. What is meant, however, is that the documentation is reduced to a minimum or postponed if time is tight. Living code is more important than dead documents. Later, the creators of the Agile Manifesto tried to put this statement into perspective, but their intention is clear: Documentation is secondary.

The authors of the Agile Manifesto may not be entirely wrong with this point. Documentation has always been a controversial topic in software development. Decades ago one key notion was that the only valid documentation for a program is the program code itself, and to describe everything that a program does, additional documentation would need to be as extensive as the program itself, i.e., including all conditions and branches and loops. Accordingly, the documentation would be the same as the program code, only in another language.

On the other hand, additional documentation is often indispensable. Without a second description of the automated process, it is often impossible for users to understand the system, let alone operate it, and they need a definition of functionality in a language that they can easily understand. There is often little point in confronting users with UML diagrams, which are useful for communication between the developers. Users need a structured, natural language user manual that takes their view of the software into account. Testers need documentation as well, an oracle to which they can refer: Since a test is always a comparison of actual behavior with a desired behavior, it presupposes that the desired behavior is described somewhere.

6.1 The Role of Documentation in Software Development

Documentation is always an abstraction of a real system. Abstraction means leaving out details—but what details should these be? For some users, the algorithm for calculating a price might be more important than the general architecture of the program in which this algorithm is embedded. But this algorithm can often only be understood at the instruction level. Documentation is supposed to convey information, but what that information is can only be defined in connection with an information need.

It follows that documents must meet a specific need for information to be useful. This means that as many types of documents are necessary as there are different information needs. If we take note of how quickly software changes, then we must also recognize how much of a hopeless endeavor it is to keep all the necessary documents up to date with the code. The authors of the Agile Manifesto were right when it comes to the ongoing documentation of a constantly evolving IT system: It is hardly worth creating it, at least not manually.

However, with reverse engineering tools—tools that automatically derive useful documents from the source code—we can create documentation while minimizing manual efforts. Structure trees, structure diagrams, flow charts, and data flow diagrams are extracted from procedural code. Class diagrams, , sequence diagrams, state diagrams, and component diagrams can be generated from object-oriented code.

Architectural trees and call hierarchies can even be derived from the source directories. These documents do little to help a manager or filing clerk understand the application, but they can help maintenance programmers find the places they should correct or change. These tools can document entire systems in just a few minutes.

What the authors of the Agile Manifesto also had in mind was to create the documentation prior to the implementation of code. This means detailed requirement specification and the technical design documents that should serve as guidelines for the developers.

For a long time in software development, far too much time was invested in describing technical and functional solutions without knowing whether these solutions were even practicable. All too often, it was not until the implementation phase that it was discovered that these solutions were useless. As long as users only see design documents and specifications, they can nod their heads and think: "Just keep going," but when they finally see a working system, they may realize that they didn't mean it. After all that had been invested in documentation with SSD or UML, this was a bitter experience. And going back and revising the documentation was not an option either. Hence, they threw away the documentation and just worked with the code until the user was finally satisfied.

6.2   The Benefits of Documentation

"As much as necessary, as little as possible"—this principle applies particularly to documentation in software projects. As banal as it sounds, its concrete implementation is difficult. Unfortunately, many agile projects like to use the statement "Working software over comprehensive documentation" (Beck, et al., 2001) as a killer argument for not dealing with this question at all. However, this can be disadvantageous—it is therefore the task of every (agile) project to deal very consciously with the topic of documentation. The basic value of agile approaches, the continuous creation of corresponding benefits and values, must also be applied to documentation. Especially since the corresponding documentation can be viewed as part of the software according to the definition of software (IEEE Std 610.12–1990, 1990). For the purposes of this standard, a software document is therefore a document whose object is the production, maintenance, or use of software or its results (DIN 66270:1998–01, 1998).

In addition, documentation must not be created just to create documentation. It must be read and understood by someone and be useful to the target audience. Therefore, it must also be created in accordance with the audience and be current and valid at the time of use. There are in fact different audiences for software documentation:

- The users who will use the system in the future
- IT or data center operations that will install and operate the application and databases
- The users in the project, who create and read project documents in their role
- The developer in the project who translates stories and requirements into code
- The developer in maintenance who was not already on board in the project
- The tester in the project, who in turn must derive test cases from requirements
- The architect who keeps an eye on the software architecture
- The business analysts supporting the user representatives
- External bodies such as an audit or the United States Food and Drug Administration (FDA), which require detailed software documentation

The consideration and analysis of these requirements should result in a "storyboard of the documentation," whose implementation, but also ongoing adjustment and prioritization, can be carried out within the product backlog and the planning of the sprints (Fig. 6.1).

The figure given below shows some result types of a project as exemplary, which, apart from code, arise in connection with the development and use of software. Every project would do well to get an overview of the documents to be created and agree on their concrete, beneficial characteristics.

		Construction – Project	Evolution – Maintenance	Use – Operation	Results of use or processing
User	requires			• User manual • Online help • Help text	• User manual • Online help
	creates			• Error messages	
Operations	requires			• Installation instruction • Operating Manual	• Operating Manual
	creates				
User in the team (Product Owner)	requires	• Requirements of the specialist departments • Specifications		• User Feedback	
	creates	• Stories • Requirements • Product Backlog • Decisions & Reasons		• Product Backlog	
Architect	requires	• Requirements	• Existing architectural design	• Technical data from operations	
	creates	• Architecture • Standards • Conventions • Decisions & Reasons	• Refactoring guidelines		
Developer	requires	• Stories • Requirements • Product Backlog • Error descriptions • Development guidelines • Architecture	• Stories • Requirements • Product Backlog • Error descriptions • Development guidelines • Architecture		
	creates	• Inline documentation • Unit Tests	• Inline documentation • Unit Tests		
Tester	requires	• Stories • Requirements • Product Backlog • Error descriptions • Information about bug fixes	• Product Backlog • Stories • Changes • Information about bug fixes • Regression test set • Test data description		
	creates	• Test cases • Concretization of requirements • Error descriptions • Retest results	• Test cases (new) • Specification of requirements (new) • Error descriptions (new) • Retest results		
Analyst	requires	• Requirements of the specialist departments • Specifications			
	creates	• Stories • Requirements			
External authority	requires			• Standardized evidence for product testing and the manufacturing process	• Standardized evidence for product testing and the manufacturing process
	creates				
Management	requires	• Project status • Data on development efforts and costs	• Data on maintenance efforts and costs	• Data on operating efforts and costs	• Data on (market) benefits of the application
	creates				

Fig. 6.1 Storyboard of documentation

Project EMIL: (Test) Documentation

In a regulatory environment such as the health care industry particular importance is placed on documentation, as it is the only way to obtain product approvals and audits. Thus, it seems rather strange at first to use agile development in such an environment, when the Agile Manifesto estimates the value of *working software* higher than that of *comprehensive documentation* (Beck, et al., 2001). However, the examination of the documentation during the project quickly led to two insights:

1. All the documentation that is required by regulation is fairly simple and should be created in every project. Even more so: Looking back on older projects, it became apparent that some of the written documents were of no benefit to the project or product, nor were they required by regulations.
2. Documentation that is consistent with the development and test results is much easier to achieve with agile practices, since the documentation should always have the same status as the implementation.

Which documents are really needed was determined outside the project—in quality management? The project then had to implement these requirements. The central storage of the documentation in the EMIL project is the "Polarion ALM" tool for Application Life Cycle Management (Siemens Product Lifecycle Management Software Inc., 2017). In addition to the documentation of user stories, defects, and the design, the following test artifacts are also documented:

- Manual and automated acceptance tests
  - Test cases for checking user stories and design
  - Test results per sprint
- Results of unit tests per build
- Results of user story reviews, design, and code reviews

Traceability is an important requirement for all documentation. The tool that was used provided a simple way of navigating through dependencies and relations by linking the artifacts, for example:

- User story ↔ Test case ↔ Defect
- Epic ↔ User story ↔ Design ↔ Software Unit ↔ Source Code

Since Polarion also logs all changes historically, it was also possible to state what the release X documentation was and who made which changes. This enabled quality management to aggregate information for documentation without disrupting the workflow of testers and developers. These in turn had a simple and partially automated tool that helped them to achieve their Definition of Done.

6.3   Documentation Types

Documentation is part of a software product like the dashboard is part of a car. A software system without documentation is like a complex electrical device without operating instructions. It may be that too much has been documented in the past, especially at a time when users were not sure what they wanted. The alternative, however, cannot be to work without documentation entirely. It is still used, according to Fig. 6.1, in several ways:

- From a manufacturing, development, and maintenance perspective
- From the point of view of use and operation

In relation to the key stakeholders, the manufacturers, and users of the software, the following types of documentation are of importance:

- The description and documentation of the requirements as a specification for the development and as a test oracle for the testers
- Documentation of the code and its architecture as well as associated standards as a basis and support for the developers of the project, or for developers who are new to the project or who take over the product for maintenance
- The test documentation including the test case descriptions for the execution of the tests, but also the regression test at later, recurring times and the error documentation as the basis for an orderly troubleshooting and execution of the retests
- The user documentation for the end users as well as an operating manual for the operation of the software, if applicable

Each type of documentation shows a different view of the software.

6.3.1   Requirements Documentation

In traditional projects, the requirement specification, i.e., the specification of use cases, functional specification, or technical concept, was the document that defined what the software had to fulfill. It was often created by the users themselves or by their representatives, the business analysts.

We want to use Scrum to briefly explain how requirements are defined and documented in an agile environment. A key success factor in the collection and documentation of the requirements in Scrum is the "sprint planning meeting." It consists of two parts:

- **Sprint Planning 1 (briefing, analysis):** Sprint Planning 1 is the basis for high quality requirements. This meeting is about defining the goals and the range of functions to be delivered for the upcoming sprint. The product owner presents his or her goals and must be well informed about the project status and the backlog items. The entire team and one or more "users of the application" are present at this meeting to conduct a requirements analysis. This meeting can be compared to a requirements workshop. Based on the product backlog, the team members carry out a requirements analysis together with the user and the product owner. The requirements are recorded and documented in an appropriate form, for example on story cards. At this point the acceptance criteria are also defined and the first test cases are already described.

- **Sprint Planning 2 (design):** In Sprint Planning 2, design, specification, and architecture are developed based on the goals and functionalities defined in Sprint Planning 1. It is common for the team to be divided into several groups to discuss specifics and work out specific topics such as architecture and data elements.

At the end of the sprint planning meeting, tasks are defined and presented transparently using the task board to get an overview of the upcoming work in the Sprint.

User stories, i.e., the requirements in the language of software users, can be described as the cornerstone of the requirements specification in Scrum. In keeping with the agile approach, they are deliberately kept very short. Use cases can be derived from the user stories. User stories are a heading for a specific scenario and use cases contain several of these scenarios. The description of use cases is just as important, as these are essential for the implementation of the software to be developed.

The stories, use cases, and scenarios should be sufficiently detailed so that they can be understood and implemented by the developers in the agile team. In the past, developers were often creating software based on less concrete and possibly still unclear specifications with the help of implementation creativity. Developers will often be satisfied with simple story cards, while these—including the acceptance criteria—are usually far from being formulated in a detailed enough manner to serve as a test oracle for the tester.

Testers in the agile project are now faced with a choice: They can take the stories or use cases only as items in a processing list and test the supplied software against their own interpretation of the stories, or they can be responsible for getting a test oracle themselves.

"We get to the heart of the requirements!" This has often been the statement of testers in the authors' projects. Whether in traditional or agile projects, many requirements become clear and precise only when specific (or abstract) test cases are formulated. This means that the tester specifies comprehensible test cases in addition to the stories.

It is therefore logical to see the technical test cases as part of the requirements documentation since test cases are usually kept more up to date than extensive specifications in a Word document. This is especially true if these test cases are automated. It is important to note, however, that the tester should never specify the requirements: This is done only by the users or their representatives. Through the documented tests the requirements are merely detailed and concretized. This activity can also be understood as an atrium for test-driven development.

Fig. 6.2 From the user story to the test case

In principle, we can speak of a classic language transformation here. It starts with an inaccurate vision of an IT service. At the end there are one or more executable code blocks and the corresponding test cases. One path leads from the user story to the individual code blocks. A second way leads from the user request to the use case to the action step to the processing rule to the test case (Fig. 6.2).

6.3.2 Code Documentation

Code documentation is written by developers for developers. It is intended to describe how the code is composed and where one can find which code blocks. It can explain what the code blocks are implementing—but that would be better kept in the code itself. Good code with module headers, comment blocks, and comment lines should be self-explanatory. In keeping with the "Clean code" philosophy, every developer should take the time to annotate their code properly. If they do this, developers only need to keep an overview of architectural models to find out where individual modules are. It would be best if there were no paper documents or static diagrams. The system documentation should exist in the form of a repository that is fully searchable. This repository should emerge from the static analysis of the source code. Whenever the source code changes, the repository is updated. The repository thus always contains a current map of the code landscape, which developers can use to determine the status of the code.

There can be no difference between repository and code. The repository is built and maintained by the developers. In a larger project, there could be a separate role for this—the technical documenter. This role should not be confused with a system architect. The system architect is more responsible for the overall design and less for the documentation of the details. In any case, the effort for this documentation should be kept to a minimum. If the developers require UML diagrams, they can at least partially generate them from the code. It is not worth investing too much manual effort because experience shows that they are quickly outdated and would need constant maintenance—an effort that the fathers of agile development wanted to avoid.

6.3.3 Test Documentation

6.3.3.1 Test Case Description
In addition to the functional and nonfunctional requirements, the traditional requirements documentation defines the business objects, the business rule, the system interfaces, the system actors, and the use cases. This information serves as

the basis for the development of a test plan, the draft of a test design, and the derivation of abstract and subsequently concrete test cases. In addition to the test case steps, the description of a test case includes the test data and the corresponding pre- and post-conditions. The effort for this test preparation can easily amount to 50% of the total test effort, i.e., as much as for the actual test execution (Sneed, Baumgartner, & Seidl, 2012).

In an agile project, the effort for the test preparation—the test case design—is divided into many small units, the stories and features of the individual sprints, but the question remains as to how much of the time available should be invested in the "theory" and how much in the "practice" of the test implementation. In terms of the agile principle, it would be better to find ten errors than to document five test cases—a misleading principle:

The recording of a test case design and the formulation of a test case should primarily serve to clarify and quality the tests. The form and detail of the description should be such that the testers feel that it helps them to optimally support the test execution. Future retests and regression tests should also be considered. It will therefore make sense to record elaborately analyzed facts, specifications, framework conditions, or creative ideas to have them ready when they are needed again later. A routine description, however, can usually be spared.

Sometimes, however, it is also necessary to meet test documentation requirements that are brought to the project from the outside. In this case, the team should make sure to meet the minimum requirements—but not more.

Exploratory tests aim at finding errors as quickly as possible with as little preparatory work as possible. But here, too, it is advisable to provide orientation along documented scenarios to keep a rough overview of the technical test coverage.

In most agile projects, we observe a mix of systematic and exploratory tests. The systematic test often provides more and deeply hidden errors, while the exploratory test often finds errors faster.

As far as the documentation of test case creation and the logging of the execution is concerned, it is quite common in agile projects to use integrated tools. This is particularly necessary in larger projects or in the complex interplay of several projects, especially in connection with error management. If the (planned) test cases are documented accordingly, they can also be prioritized. On a documented basis, the knowledge of which tests may not be carried out, the risk can be better assessed than just from a gut feeling.

The more test automation is implemented in agile projects, the fewer questions about the documentation of technical tests arise. Automated tests are a detailed and sustainable description of the test cases, the test data, the processes, the expected results, and subsequently the test execution.

6.3.3.2 Test Execution Documentation

The test execution documentation is the description of what was tested and its results. Stringent logging of tests carried out is sometimes prescribed from the outside, for example in order to be able to obtain appropriate certificates for the tested product. But apart from this, logging the test execution provides valuable information for development and testing.

A simple but important test metric results from the test execution documentation: the ratio of the test cases executed to the required test cases. Since the requirement-based test cases fully describe the functionality, the functional test coverage can be derived. It is particularly important for a risk-based test approach to be able to assess risk. This can be derived, for example, from the lack of functional test coverage. However, it is not enough to count only the test cases; their results must also be considered. The correctness of an application results from the number of correct results relative to all results. This number is extremely valuable for controlling and prioritizing the test activities and for evaluating the quality status of the application (Sneed, Baumgartner, & Seidl, 2012). If almost every test case leads to an error, the test cases can be formulated in an unspecific manner, or the application will be in a miserable state. If only every hundredth test case leads to an error, the test cases may be too granular or unnecessary, or the application may already be running without errors.

6.3.3.3 Test Coverage

In current systems with a lot of foreign code and external libraries, code coverage no longer plays the role it used to play. Test coverage should now be measured at a different level: at model level or at requirement level. This registers how many of the potential connections in the model or how many of the requirements are tested. A practical solution is to derive rules and paths for all requirements and then measure which part of these test cases is executed without errors. The same applies to model-based tests for test cases that are derived from the design model. This requirement coverage or model coverage report gives an indication of achieved coverage. Of course, the goal of an agile test cannot be to test all possible cases and reach 100% coverage for every requirement. The tester may only reach 60% coverage, but using a coverage report also gives the knowledge what was tested and what was not. This plays an important role in the decision to release a version and in updating the backlog.

Project EMIL: Metrics

Metrics usually provide a higher-level control and steering function. However, the developers and testers used them as an aid in the project as well:

- When developing unit tests, test coverage is used to determine where unit tests should be changed or added.
- In refactoring, various measures of complexity and quality metrics are used to better assess certain code parts.

(continued)

However, these measures are not documented in the project. Design patterns and rules of clean code are used, which implicitly include metrics, e.g., regarding method size or modularity. These are checked during code reviews (Westphal & Lieser, 2013).

The calculation of velocity based on the story points was done for a few sprints, but then stopped by the team.

6.3.3.4 Defect Documentation

The logging of found defects is also part of the test documentation. This documents what needs to be corrected and these are added to the project's to-do list. If the fixes cannot be done in the current release cycle, they will go to the project backlog to be fixed in a later release. Dealing with defects must also be regulated in an agile development project. It turns out that the use of a defect management tool also makes a lot of sense in agile teams: The communication of defects and their correction on mere calls may work only in individual cases, in small teams, or in small quantities. Most of the time, the developers are not waiting to fix a defect that has been newly reported, and are in the middle of the implementation of another feature when a tester reports a defect. The reverse applies to the tester if the defect has been rectified and a retest has to be carried out. Defect finding and troubleshooting are mostly asynchronous and are often also distributed locally. The agile team can decide in which form and with which details a defect is to be documented. If the team cannot agree, it can still rely on the IEEE standard—or use it as a baseline for further simplification (IEEE Std 829–2008, 2008).

Project EMIL: Defect Management

Defect management represents a central communication medium between developer and tester. It is not just the factional content that is relevant (Is it really a mistake? Is it correctly and adequately described?), but also the way in which it is communicated. No matter how much attention one pays to objective formulations, it can always happen that (missing) information or the choice of words triggers misunderstandings. While more time can be invested in traditional development processes due to the long phases for defect management, it is essential in the short sprints of agile development to eliminate errors quickly, which amounts to more direct communication between tester and developer. However, the regulatory requirements in the presented project still required the documentation of discovered defects. Therefore, two ways were established in the team to deal with errors: In both cases, the defect is first communicated and discussed directly, either immediately when it is found or at the latest in the next daily meeting. If it is of low severity or a triviality that

(continued)

can be fixed immediately, this will be done. However, if the defect is due to an incorrectly implemented requirement, it is documented and, if possible, rectified in the same sprint. It is important for everyone to first address the defect and only then to log into the defect management system. This was not only handled by the testers, but also by the developers in the team.

The lofty goal of having no mistakes left at the end of the sprint was also part of the Definition of Done at the beginning. However, it soon became apparent that there are defects that cannot be resolved ad hoc or that contradict the expected behavior, which was previously not thought through in depth. These defects are recorded in the backlog and clarified and resolved in one of the subsequent sprints. Nevertheless, the scrum master continuously provided assurance that these are just a few defects, that they do not increase, and that they do not remain open for a long time.

6.3.4 User Documentation

User documentation is still expected today, even if many user interfaces are self-explanatory. Gone are the days when the user documentation was printed out as a thick manual. In modern IT systems, the documentation is online or in the system, mostly distributed to the interaction points where the user needs them. However, it still consists of individual texts in the language of the end user, and someone has to write these texts. It is very unlikely that this is the developer, and this would be undesirable because developers often have a different view of the software than the user. The analysts used to write the user documentation in traditional projects but might no longer be available in an agile development team.

The user representative in the team could write their own documentation, but often they lack detailed knowledge. The tester, who works with the system up close from the very early stages, usually has the best overviewed and detailed knowledge of the system. Therefore, the tester is often the best candidate for creating this type of documentation. From this perspective, the user documentation is a side product of the test.

As already mentioned, user documentation consists of many small text explanations on the individual steps in dealing with the software system. Where extensive reports are required, the documentation must explain the content. Where system interfaces occur, the documentation must describe them exactly, and if the user wants to take their own actions, the documentation must explain how to proceed. In addition, the user must know what to do in the event of an error. Nobody is better able to explain this to users than a tester, who already gets to know the error situations during the test. Some of the user documentation can be found in the test documentation. These parts might just have to be worded differently.

User documentation is not just an instruction manual. It must also explain what the system is good for, how it works, and what it does. The "What for" part must be learned by the tester from the user representatives in the team. The testers get to learn the "How" part from the developers. The "What" part results from the testing of the system. The tester can collect this information and summarize it in a suitable, understandable form. This analytical work also benefits the test because the tester gains deeper insight into the system and can better assess its behavior. This shows even more how test and documentation complement each other.

In larger projects, which have several agile teams involved, there might be a technical editor who is documenting the product in parallel with the development. This documentation often includes the installation instructions, the user manual, and the operating manual. The technical editorial team has to work very closely with the testers in the individual projects. They provide the operating instructions in a rough format and the technical editor refines them. In this regard, the tester serves as a supplier for the technical documentation.

In traditional projects, the documentation is very often postponed to the end of the project, i.e., shortly before delivery, which is challenging for the responsible roles. They might not get the information they need in time. The users only know how the system should behave, but not how the system really behaves. Anyone who creates the documentation has to improvise.

In agile projects, documentation is carried out in parallel to development, by the tester and the technical editor. They get to the basics they need for their documentation work very early on and can get involved in early stages of the project where they can influence the development, in the direction of testability and documentability. As soon as new components take shape, they are tested and documented. This means that the documentation is always up to date. If for any reason the project is canceled or put on hold, the documentation is complete and up to date with the code. However, everything comes with a price and the price for this is increased testing and documentation capacity needs.

6.4   The Tester as a Documenter

The worldwide test community has ensured that testing is included as an independent activity within agile development. The defects found by the testers are recognized earlier and reported back. With the documentation, the developers have less insight. Documentation stops and is often seen as tedious or unnecessary. However, at some point someone has to describe what the programs do and how they are used. Otherwise nobody would be able to use them, let alone understand them. Testing and documentation are both important, accompanying activities that contribute to the quality of the product.

For this reason, it is recommended to have testers on the team who are also able to create documentation. Several resources may be needed. In this case, the increased effort serves the quality of the product that is better tested and documented. Both activities help to reduce the follow-up costs of the project and increase the sustainability of the product. The client, represented in the project by the product owner, has to decide which is more important, to save costs now or later, considering that better documentation can save costs in product maintenance. For this reason, a balance between developers on the one hand and testers/documenters on the other should also be striven for in agile development.

This approach may be unusual, and the fact that the tester also acts as a documenter is usually not found in any job description for software testers. Nevertheless, nobody is better able to create the user manual than the testers. They have to deal intensively with the system and see the system mostly from the outside as a black box. They therefore have an end-user perspective and can pass their experience on to a real end-user. To add a technical writer to the project when the tester could perform this role would be inefficient. The tester's language skills must then of course be sufficient to formulate the requirements and the user manual clearly and precisely in the language of the end user.

6.5   Importance of Documentation in Agile Testing

Even if the documentation is behind the executable code in the priority list of an agile project, it still has meaning for the project. Nobody can work entirely without documentation. This also applies to test documentation. A minimum of test documentation is required to investigate the causes of defects and to determine the status of test coverage. Few people want to go back to the time of traditional projects when projects produced more documents than code or test cases. It is to be welcomed that agile development is going in the opposite direction—still, we cannot completely do without documentation. End users still need their instruction manual and testers needs their test documentation. It is all well and good if the user representatives are able tell their stories easily, but someone in the project needs to record and formalize them and create a test basis.

The ideal candidate for this documentation work is the tester. In her first field report and later in her book on agile testing (Crispin & Gregory, 2009), Lisa Crispin points out this additional burden on the tester. However, she speaks out against the tester being pushed into the role of the project tracker. The documentation is more of a side product—in a positive sense—of the test work. The tester must make sure the requirements are specified in detail to derive test cases from them. They must document the test data status and test procedures to prove the correctness of the system. After all, nobody is better suited to writing the user documentation than the tester, who has to go through the software in all its variants anyway. For the testers, the writing of the operating instructions coincides with the recording of their scenarios. The agile team therefore does not need additional documentation capacity and can remain lean.

Agile Test Automation

The consistent use of test automation is the only chance to ensure the quality of each potentially deliverable product at the end of each sprint. However, many aspects must be clarified and defined for maintainable and efficient test automation. These include the organizational and technical integration into DevOps environments and processes, the selection of suitable automation tools, the design of an automation framework, and the organization and planning of automation activities and automated test executions within or synchronized with the development sprints. If required, test automation know-how also needs to be established within the team. This is a challenge to most teams, but this investment needs to be considered as there is no successful agile testing without test automation.

7.1   The Trouble with Tools in Agile Projects

Tools related to software development are a dime a dozen, and they all claim to make our project work easier. However, we came to see that most of the tools have similar characteristics, as a bucket excavator in open pit mining (Fig. 7.1).

Why do we use this comparison? Large bucket excavators used in open pit coal mining usually take up to a week to adjust correctly to a new mining direction. Only once they have been adjusted, they work with the amazing effectiveness we know them for. This means that any kind of reorientation pauses or slows down the production process at first and should therefore be carried out only if absolutely necessary. Anyone who takes a closer look at this giant piece of equipment on chain wheels is sure to notice that a complete production line with finely tuned machines and conveyor belts has been set to work. It is not something that can be changed quickly.

The use of tools in software development follows similar characteristics: It optimizes a very specific function but can take some time to be ready for use (training, configuration, integration with other tools, etc.). Unfortunately, countless tasks exist that would not be possible without tools or could be done only with

© The Author(s), under exclusive license to Springer Nature Switzerland AG 2021
M. Baumgartner et al., *Agile Testing*, https://doi.org/10.1007/978-3-030-73209-7_7

Fig. 7.1 Tools used for software development are like bucket excavators in open pit mining

ridiculously high effort and expense. Here, too, the use of tools is like in open pit coal mining.

Of course, such a characteristic is anything but favorable for agile teams. Agile procedures require an increased degree of flexibility, and must, therefore, consider carefully which tools should be used and which ones are more of an obstacle. The following principles always apply to agile test tools, regardless of the project:

- The test object is a moving target.
- Process flows must never be rigid (or solidified).
- Tests should run with every build if possible.
- Tools must therefore be lightweight and flexible (which is a clear challenge for the "bucket excavators" among the tools) (Fig. 7.2).

The consequence is that many mature tool solutions from traditional project environments are extremely unpopular in agile teams and sometimes even frowned upon. This is certainly also the reason for the disrespectful attitude of the Large-Scale-Scrum Framework (LeSS, 2017) toward traditional test automation tools. Other types of tools have been developed for this purpose, which make a more flexible working method possible. These tools particularly include xUnit frameworks and continuous integration servers as well as Wikis for project documentation and test documentation.

All in all, we should bear in mind that agile approaches always have to deal with short iterations that change something over and over again: be it the code, the

Fig. 7.2 A tool approach for agile projects must always be lightweight and flexible (like a hunting cheetah)

architecture, or even the used approach. Paradoxically, this iterative approach, the courage to get along with change and a certain degree of fast pace in working, requires reliable tooling solutions, since we would not be able to do it manually. This becomes particularly clear in the testing phase: Iterations require an extensive regression test of functions that have already been created in previous iterations, otherwise we would have to deal with massive quality problems. It is therefore true to say that only the current range of tools has enabled us to work consistently in an agile manner.

Anyone who wants to reasonably master testing in agile projects cannot avoid using tools. It can of course be the case that some tools are only used temporarily and are later put out of use again due to self-optimization measures in the team. Under these conditions, comprehensive rollouts of uniform tool solutions within an organization are doomed to fail. The smarter way is to pilot tools and approaches with test tool experts in the organization, to refine them later when needed and finally to keep them ready for any kind of new requirements that may arise. Test tool experts should be familiar with testing in agile projects and should know the portfolio of potentially suitable tools well—just as a craftsman knows their toolbox and has it always at the ready.

7.2   Test Automation: How to Approach It?

Project EMIL: Test Automation

Test automation was hardly a topic in the organization in the past, so experience was thinly spread. While at the level of unit tests and unit integration tests automation was inherently provided by the development environment in which a unit test framework was integrated and used extensively, the lack of automation of the acceptance tests hit the testers with full force after a few sprints, as the necessary regression tests could no longer be conducted manually. This "blame" was dealt with jointly by testers and developers:

- The developers actively addressed the issue of "testability" and promoted the automated testability of the software through better object identification and a test API.
- The testers evaluated various automation tools directly on the software by automating the first test cases.

As commercial tools were ruled out due to the training period and sometimes due to the huge effort and costs involved in test settings, AutoIt (AutoIt Consulting Ltd, 2017) was the first choice, as know-how was already available in the organization and good results could be seen even for complex test cases after only a short time. AutoIt may not be a highly specialized solution for acceptance tests, but it was a viable solution for the team to automate acceptance tests.

However, automation problems arose also at the unit integration test level. Due to the chosen integration strategy, it took almost an hour for all integration test cases to run through, which caused the development flow to slow down. Therefore, the existing integration strategy was discarded and a more modular architecture was implemented as part of the refactoring of the unit integration tests. Thus, the time required for a complete run-through could be reduced to a few minutes.

In general, the image of test automation changed considerably among the team during the project: from the simple automation of test execution to support for all activities in the sprint. An entire range of test activities are automatically supported with a few suitable tools:

- Preparation and housekeeping of the test environment
- Creation and processing of test data
- Installation and configuration of the test object
- Test execution at various test levels
- Evaluation, filtering, and preparation of test results

(continued)

> • Export of relevant information from a regulatory point of view regarding the various tests from the systems
>
> The tools used in this case range from individual scripts to smaller open-source applications to larger frameworks (see also Chap. 8). Here too, changes were possible at any time if the need arose and the expected benefit justified the costs for a tool change. Great care was taken by the team to ensure that the use of a specific tool did not become self-perpetuating, but rather promoted the development of the product or solved an existing problem.

As is evident from the example of EMIL test automation, test automation in agile projects not only has the task of making regression testing cheaper and, thus, feasible with frequent test cycles, it is also an integral part of the working method and influences the software development process itself. Also, it is rarely solved uniformly (e.g., by a certain tool), usually consisting of different techniques optimized for the respective tasks. It is not uncommon for in-house developments to be mixed with open-source solutions and commercial tools.

An agile project without any form of test automation is always incomplete! Test automation must, therefore, be planned in the iterations right from the start and must be consistently expanded. It is always a common task for all team members and not limited to the testers.

7.3   Test Automation with Increasing Software Integration

Even if agile teams dissociate themselves from the mode of thinking of a V-model, they must acknowledge that software has to be integrated and this is best done in a step-by-step manner. Because the steps are executed again and again within and with each iteration, the terminology for these tests becomes blurred for most teams.

Many teams like to talk about unit tests, but they don't merely mean component tests, for which according to ISTQB the term unit test is only a synonym (ISTQB-International Software Testing Qualifications Board, 2020); they can use it to describe tests that use an xUnit framework, such as JUnit. Framework and Fixtures, both being terms related to working with xUnit frameworks, are often used for working with tools that specifically automate user interfaces and are another successful test automation technique.

Before different techniques for test automation are introduced in more detail later in this chapter, our focus will first be on their use in the respective integration stages of the software. Another note about the four test quadrants of Crispin/Gregory (see Chap. 3): Unit test and component integration test are more likely to be technically oriented team support tests (first quadrant), while system test and system integration test are more likely to be in the other three quadrants.

7.3.1   Unit Test/Component Test

The unit test or component test focuses only on one class/method; everything else is done by the so-called placeholders like stubs, mocks, etc. (see Sect. 7.5). Typically, correct calculations or plausibility checks are the goal of these tests.

The xUnit frameworks, such as JUnit, have proven themselves in unit tests and component tests, whereby some placeholders can also be custom applications or scripts. Test automation makes absolute sense in this case and is most often created in this way. However, we must be careful with classes that are purely integration classes, such as wrappers, web service connection classes, or database access layers. These can usually only be tested automatically in the next integration stage.

7.3.2   Component Integration Test

In the component integration test, several classes/methods are tested together. Classes/methods whose integration is not the subject of focus are simulated by placeholders. These tests can often be automated with xUnit frameworks and independent placeholder routines. For example, in this case, we could test whether a class reacts correctly when an event occurs in another class, or whether a certain functionality is correctly exposed via a web service.

At this level, good integration servers play an important role as they ensure secure builds and qualifying automated tests, thus enabling a CI (Continuous Integration) strategy.

7.3.3   System Test

In the system test, an entire system or the entire application is tested. Here, we could test, for example, whether a new customer can be created in the system. These tests already achieve the level of acceptance tests, wherein stakeholders, like the customer as well as the product owner, are to be convinced of the quality of the implemented function.

This can also be automated with xUnit frameworks and placeholders, whereby at this integration level we prefer to use the adjacent systems themselves for testing, thus not needing the placeholders. The tests at this integration level are already largely controlled via user interfaces or a service interface, which is why specialized test automation tools are also used.

Intensive load tests and performance tests with load drivers and monitors make sense at this level; however, it is important to be cautious in this process, as many performance problems only become apparent when several systems interact.

7.3.4   System Integration Test

The system integration test is a test across several systems that, for example, work together via web services or exchange data intensively using batch processes. Here, too, we can simulate adjacent systems with placeholders, if the interaction with these systems is not the focus of the tests. A typical test case in the system integration test would be whether customers receive an invoice from the accounting department if they had previously placed an order in the ordering system.

xUnit frameworks only play a very minor role in this case, while test automation tools for service interfaces or user interfaces are used more often. In some cases, test automation is no longer very useful at this level or might need a very mature system- and technology-spanning solution. Even though test automation is certainly possible and often useful at this integration level, tests are more often handled with manual test techniques, such as explorative testing.

The last stage of the system integration test is usually an end-to-end test in which no components are simulated anymore. In this case, even printing lines would be integrated that print the invoice on a trial basis and send it to the testers for checking. If test automation is used here, it is used usually only for the preparation of tests, for example, by creating test data using automated routines. Surely, the question is also whether such tests are really necessary to a significant extent or whether they are to be limited to only a few test runs before Go-Live, which can then be carried out manually or semiautomatically.

7.4 xUnit Frameworks

XUnit frameworks such as JUnit (for Java) and NUnit (for .NET) are the most commonly used test automation technologies in agile projects. They can be used in almost all test levels from component integration testing to system integration testing but have their greatest strengths and broadest use in component and component integration testing. This situation leads to this technology also being used in an inflationary manner in system tests or system integration tests, whereby the limits of efficient use are quickly exceeded.

The core task of xUnit frameworks is the control of developed classes or methods through tests, which are written in the same programming language and managed in the development environment. All the modern programming languages (such as Java, .NET, C++, PHP, Ruby, etc.) now have reliable xUnit frameworks, which is why it is incomprehensible for development teams to work without them altogether. They enable adequate test coverage in the first place, particularly in component testing.

Although we have also seen teams conducting manual unit tests, most teams use these test frameworks, which are now readily available and combine both automated test runs and drivers/placeholders. Tests are created with dedicated test classes,[1] which

---

[1] Test classes means that the programming language must support object-oriented development. As can be seen very well in case of the PHP-Unit, the actual test object itself does not have to be programmed in an object-oriented basis. However, a consistent object-oriented programming method is recommended so that the tests are not perceived as foreign bodies.

- Bring the test object, i.e., a component or even an entire system, into a controlled initial state (usually also referred to as setup, initialize or before)
- Execute the test (a separate method for each test), by calling the unit/component or system interface to be tested and providing it with suitable parameter values
- Evaluate the test (mostly with standard methods "assert" or "verify") and present the results in the form of an overview (failed/passed)
- Reset the tested unit/component or restore data (usually also referred to as teardown or after)

For most programming languages now, there are reliable test frameworks that are relatively easy to integrate into the development environment (e.g., as an add-in in Eclipse) or are integrated from the start (e.g., in the case of Visual Studio). What most of them have in common is that they are usually based on an object-oriented programming technique. Test objects written in procedural languages can also be tested, which is often the case with legacy applications or embedded systems, but tests itself are programmed on object-oriented basis. Figure 7.3 shows a Java example of a JUnit test in the Eclipse development environment, wherein the code coverage is measured simultaneously.

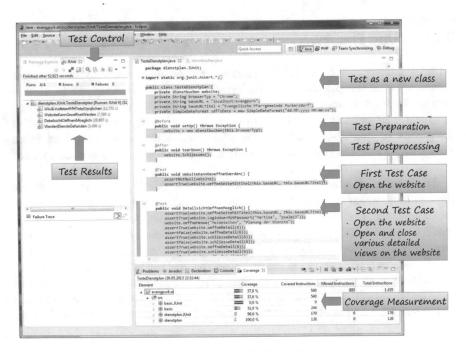

Fig. 7.3 JUnit test case for an automation script in Eclipse with coverage measurement

Since white-box techniques such as statement, branch, and path coverage or condition and decision coverage are typically used as testing techniques for unit and component testing, the corresponding counters and monitors for coverage metrics are available as add-ins to the testing frameworks. These tools can now also be obtained and integrated relatively easily for the most common development environments.

Unit and component tests as such do not require any specific test management support. They can be handled via a simple execution list with result display and a few test control switches, since the tests are mostly carried out by the developers or automatically in the build pipelines and the troubleshooting usually takes place immediately. The test cases are usually managed together along with the code and therefore do not need an additional management level.

Nevertheless, agile teams should think early about a suitable test infrastructure in the development environment. This is because xUnit frameworks will soon also be used for higher test levels such as system testing or system integration testing. In addition to the test frameworks shown above for automated test execution, several tools, most of which can be custom-scripted, are also required for higher test levels:

- Test data provision
- Resetting the local test environment
- Starting services and background programs that are required for test execution
- Management of more complex test results (e.g., files, data extracts)

An agile team should also agree upon a uniform procedure for the execution of tests with xUnit frameworks. It is to be determined how the test cases are to be named and filed. In agile teams, but especially in XP-based practices, other team members should easily be able to find and understand the tests to adapt the code themselves (so-called "collective ownership"). It is often neglected that a uniform standard for the usage of coverage metrics is also required. Time and again, we come across teams for which one test case per method in the component test seems completely sufficient as test coverage target. Why so, if instruction coverage and branch coverage can be checked relatively easily in the development environment?

Practice: Measuring Test Case Coverage

A method is written to calculate the value-added tax rate to a net price (which should then be invoked at different points in the application). The first three digits of the product number provided (representing the product category) are decisive for the assessment of the default or reduced value-added tax. Only five product categories are allowed, of which two are reduced and three are

(continued)

subject to normal taxation. According to architectural requirements, the method must be robust enough to handle inadmissible product categories with an exception routine.

The developers construct the method in a way that they first filter out the permissible product categories in two stages:

- Do the first three digits form a number?
- Is this number one of the five product categories?

The tax rate is then applied at the default rate, and only then it is checked whether it needs to be reduced due to the product category. Finally, the tax portion is calculated based on the determined tax rate (see also Fig. 7.4).

If we want to achieve instruction coverage in this relatively simple example (each instruction is run through once in the test), we need the following three test cases:

- Exception 1: Product category cannot be determined from the transferred product number.
- Exception 2: Product category unknown.
- Reduced value-added tax (also run through the default assignment with a normal tax rate, just as the developer programmed the method).

If we want to achieve branch coverage, we will also need the additional test case

- Normal value-added tax (because the branch which skips the assignment with lower rate would otherwise not be covered).

Depending on the structure of conditions in the if-queries, a condition and decision coverage (even optimized as modified condition and decision coverage) would require significantly more test cases.

If we would only stay with the team requirement to write at least one test case per method, we would move all the other test cases, and thus any necessary error correction, to the integration test or acceptance test. In addition, the team would miss the opportunity to discuss the required level of failsafe code and possibly leave the decision about normal or low tax rates to the invoking procedure (possibly making the object relationships simpler and less error prone).

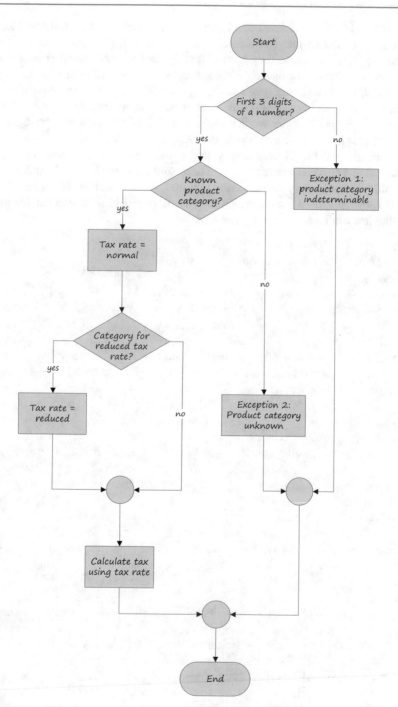

Fig. 7.4 Structure chart for the code example "value added tax"

In some systems, an isolated development environment (local) causes problems if we want to test in an integrative manner from within it. Automated tests are very sensitive in this respect, as they cannot flexibly deal with changing environmental parameters or varying availability of peripheral systems or adjacent systems. On the other hand, it is usually not worth setting up extensive placeholders (stubs, mocks, fakes, etc.) for each interface to other units or components already for the unit tests. In this case, it may be more worthwhile to use skillful hierarchies of configuration files and processing scripts to make the peripheral systems from the integration environment available in such a way that a unit test or component test can be conducted in a stable and detailed way. These solutions are also application specific and can, therefore, rarely be purchased and integrated as standard solutions. There are also several applications in which the extensive mocking or implementation of placeholders can be economically justified.

Practice: Local Test Environment Using the Integration Test Environment

A development team must provide various services for various applications in the organization, which provide electronic forms from a central database to the invoking application based on certain parameters that are pre-filled.

In the local development environment, work has been going well with mocks that simulate the invoking applications for a while. Stubs have also been written for the database, which always return the correct templates for the test case (without a database working behind them). This allowed the developers to thoroughly test their components in the local environment before delivering them to the integration test environment (Staging).

Unfortunately, expectations for the services increased in the course of time, without the team being able to assert itself. The query data had become so complex that it was difficult to comply with mocking, and the template variants in the database were so comprehensive that the stub would soon have needed a database itself.

The primary response was to reduce the tests with the existing placeholders to a minimal, economically feasible, set which in turn reduced coverage. A separate test database for unit tests was not available for the team and access to the other applications in the integration environment was taboo (mainly because of the uncontrollable status changes and data changes in the invoking applications).

The team took the initiative—initially hesitantly, but after the first success very intensively—to use the applications and database from the integration environment for local tests by means of reconfiguration. The risk of returning critical data and states to the applications from the test was prevented by smart measures and reserving certain data ranges for the unit test. The icing on the cake for the team was that the reconfiguration was automatically removed during the build, and thus could not accidentally get into the integration environment.

A challenge are legacy systems, which may work very successfully with procedural languages and for which there are few convenient test frameworks. In many cases, these systems have never been designed with testability in mind, and functionality was often added layer by layer without consistent architectural considerations.

In dealing with legacy systems, a team should carefully consider how much time it takes to create individual solutions for each individual component. Test automation without a general test framework for the entire application quickly becomes highly time consuming and expensive. Agile teams, however, will not get very far with manual unit tests or component tests alone, since frequent regression tests are part of the agile principle. Simply shifting the tests into the integration test level can lead to overstraining of the tests in later integration stages. The increasing number of unit test frameworks, even for relatively rare development languages and technologies, shows that it is almost always worthwhile to set up and use a general and flexible test framework.

7.5   Use of Placeholders

Placeholders are technical devices (mostly software, but in embedded systems also special hardware devices) which simulate the existence of other systems, for the (sub-)application to be tested. For example, an insurance policy can only be created by an application if another application for insurance mathematics is invoked via a service that calculates risk-based premiums. Without the availability of the invoked application (e.g., if it is not finished yet), the testers must simulate the interface appropriately.

Very few agile teams manage testing without placeholders, as they develop partial applications rather than entire applications (otherwise the optimal team size would quickly be exceeded) and because they must test their code early on with integration. After all, every Sprint, if we take Scrum as example, is supposed to generate potentially executable software.

According to Linz (2013), placeholders can be separated into the following five types:

- **Stubs**—These return a predefined result in response to a (predictable) request from the application to be tested, which perfectly mimics the behavior of the non-existent adjacent component or application.
- **Spies**—Stubs which can additionally record and analyze the requests of the application to be tested in order to use them later for evaluation of the test result.
- **Mocks**—Stubs containing logic routines, which can also perform calculations and are usually created for more dynamic dialogs between components/applications to be tested and simulated.
- **Fakes**—Replacement for a missing component/application returning a very simplified result, as the returned result has no relevance for the test.

- **Dummy objects**—Replacement objects, replacement pointers, replacement data objects which, like fakes, have no further influence on the outcome of the test but must be there for the test to run smoothly.

The first three types play an integral role in test cases and their results, while the latter two types are only auxiliary constructs that are necessary for the executability. In general, however, it is the principle of placeholders to display a simplified image of the missing component or application with as little effort as possible. Agile teams should pay attention to the principle of simplicity: It must just be possible for the planned test cases to function correctly. Exaggerated flexibility quickly makes placeholders complex and is a potential source of test errors (e.g., false-positives).

Particularly in more complex system architectures, such as IoT solutions, microservices, and big data usage, it is hard to imagine executing tests without simulation of entire processes with placeholders. These solutions, now known as service virtualization, make it possible to test sections of a route for robustness at an early stage. This shifts error detection to an early stage in the product life cycle (so-called Shift-left), where defect elimination is more cost-effective. In addition, the complexity of end-to-end tests is reduced, which can quickly grow exponentially in the situations mentioned above (Binder, 2016).

All of the most commonly used test automation tools are suitable for implementation of the above principles. The choice ranges from open-source tools, like SOAP UI (SmartBear, 2017), Selenium (2021), or Cucumber (Cucumber Ltd., 2017) to commercial tools, like UFT One (Microfocus, 2020), Tricentis Tosca (TRICENTIS Technology and Consulting GmbH 2017a), or Microsoft Visual Studio (Microsoft, 2017)—to list only a few, far from being exhaustive.

Nevertheless, in the case of all the tools used, a lot of effort must be invested in the development of the virtual interface. This is rarely implemented with a few clicks, requiring systematic development. We should also pay special attention to the reuse of more complex logics, so that the effort for each new virtual service remains manageable.

7.6   Integration Server

Integration servers are particularly important in agile teams since builds are created very frequently and are often delivered in system integration environments or production environments. The main function of this server is the integrated compilation of the application, without forgetting parts or integrating obsolete components. Continuous integration technology has resulted in very mature integration servers that understand automated tests as an integral part of their automated integration processes.

One example is the standard integration cycle of an Apache-Maven-Integration server (The Apache Software Foundation, 2017):

- **Validate**—Checking if the project structure is correct and all necessary information is available.
- **Compile**—Compiling the source code of the project. Further static analysis can also be carried out optionally.
- **Unit test**—Executing the assigned unit tests with the corresponding test framework.
- **Package**—Packaging the compiled code for distribution/forwarding to appropriate formats (such as JARs).
- **Integration test**—The finished software package is provided in a suitable integration environment and (if defined) the automated integration tests run there accordingly. Manual integration tests can also be conducted afterward.
- **Check**—Checking the whole software package for valid structure and performing additional defined static analysis for the quality of the software.
- **Install**—Installing the software package in the local repository so that it can be used by other locally installed projects.
- **Ship**—Installing the software package in an overall integration or pre-production environment to be ready for acceptance or system integration testing.
  Although this is possible, it is rarely used in more complex systems because the risks for the target environment are often too big due to automated assembly. Sometimes tool and database upgrades are due, and special arrangements need to be made that are difficult to implement in an automated way.

Although this relatively generic minimal process flow clearly relies on semiautomated integration, in which unit and integration tests are firmly scheduled, only the unit tests are fully automated. For continuous integration, however, servers have been designed that

(a) Can use different modular compilers, configuration management systems, and test frameworks (depending on what is suitable for working in the respective team)
(b) Collect the results of all process steps (e.g., test success) for monitoring and controlling progress, and display them in a dashboard

For testing, this makes it possible to run more complex integration tests automatically and to monitor their results in an orderly manner. In this case, the most commonly used tools include Hudson/Jenkins (Kawaguchi, Bayer, & Croy, 2017), Cruise Control (2017), or Team Services (formerly Team Foundation Server) from Microsoft (2017).

A challenge for inexperienced teams is often the appropriate configuration and adaptation of integration servers to their own needs. Also, the installation and operation of most integration servers is relatively complex because the setup of (virtual) test environments, the integration of code management systems, the control of test automation, and ultimately the entire build process depend on them.

However, even for experienced teams, a new project can be a completely new challenge, as the requirements for the process, the hardware, and the tools to be integrated can always be completely different.

Therefore, agile teams should use their first iterations to set up the build process with automated unit tests and integration tests as accurate and reliable as possible. It is possible to make corrections later, but ill-considered or half-hearted solutions at the beginning can discourage the team to run test automation later on, which ultimately harms the effectiveness of testing in the entire project.

7.7   Test Automation in Business-Oriented Testing

After extensive testing at the unit or component level, and after the successful integration test has shown that the units/components also run correctly and can be tested together, the application (or the functionalities that have been implemented up to that point) must be tested from a business point of view.

Test automation is also more suitable in this case for team-supporting tests, i.e., those tests that are simply intended to prove functionality that has already been planned. These particularly must be tested very repetitively and frequently in constant quality, so that the team has the freedom to make changes without compromising in terms of functionality and quality.

Although test automation can also be used in critique-product business tests such as explorative test sessions, it is usually not flexible enough for test execution and is, therefore, mostly limited to test preparation and test post-processing work (such as loading or resetting test data).

> **Hint: Test Automation Only for User Interfaces?**
> Test automation has to be closely evaluated for user interfaces, since in these cases
>
> - it is particularly difficult to implement in a maintainable way but
> - it promises to save a lot of efforts in test execution.
>
> However, it should be noted that all other test automation options (e.g., API control, communication via a service interface, batch jobs, etc.) are equally important and should often be preferred. Mike Cohn, one of the agile pioneers of Scrum techniques, once explained how a test should be distributed among the different possibilities (Cohn, 2009) (Fig. 7.5):

(continued)

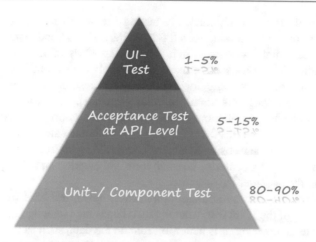

Fig. 7.5 Test Automation Pyramid according to Mike Cohn

This distribution may not be easy to implement in some projects, but agile teams should be careful not to invert the proportions (which unfortunately happens often).

When we mainly talk about test automation for user interfaces (UI) during functional tests, this is simply due to the special challenge for agile teams. However, this should not obscure the fact that most test automation should already take place without UI integration.

The trick with test automation in business testing is to translate the automation script to a business test case perspective. The following illustration shows an example with FitNesse (Fig. 7.6):

Fig. 7.6 From the business test perspective to automation using FitNesse

This example is about automatically testing the search for certain terms on a website. Thus, the testers want to search for "Galleries" and hope to find several hits. Sometimes they might want to search for "Metaphysics of morals" and end up finding nothing. These tests have many variants, but only one sequence with a somewhat more complex logic for evaluating the results (how many hits and, more importantly, which hits are hit in what sequence). Therefore, these tests are an ideal object for test automation, especially for business-oriented tests.

In this case, Selenium is used as a test automation tool to automatically control the interface elements of the website. Selenium is invoked again from a Java class and is "remote-controlled," e.g., entering a search term and clicking on the "Search" button or evaluating the hits after the search.

Now we could simply program additional test cases, test case by test case, as often is the case of the JUnit test, whereby test data is then included in the code. For the business tests, however, it is better to separate the data, such as the search terms and their results, from the detailed script sequences. Therefore, the technical automation perspective (the so-called fixture) is separated from the functional test case perspective, that usually only consists of a table with the relevant test parameters.

Thus, the tester can now concentrate on the many variants of the search and the facets of use from the point of view of the user. Ideally, this perspective is then still linked to the requirements or acceptance criteria of the user stories. The advantages for the technical test are obvious:

- The role or perspective of a business-oriented tester can be separated from the role or perspective of a developer (also helps developers who have to implement code but also test with a business-oriented view).
- The test cases concentrate on technical aspects (such as the process flow or data variants).
- The tests can usually be easily managed together with requirements, e.g., by storage in a Wiki such as FitNesse.
- It sharpens the view for testability of an application during the development itself.

However, this additional level of abstraction in test automation is not for free: The team must create their own fixtures and maintain/update them whenever changes are made. This results in additional error potential, which one must get under control as soon as possible. Kaner, Bach & Pettichord therefore recommend creating these fixtures as well as the rest of the code by test-driven development (Kaner, Bach, & Pettichord, 2002). The simple architectural structure of automation scripts (fixtures) makes test-driven development relatively easy.

It becomes clear that test automation which is used in business testing needs additional infrastructure and must also be integrated differently. In the following, we will take a closer look at technical support through tools, get to know typical agile techniques and point out special features of continuous integration.

7.7.1 Test Automation Frameworks

While in technical testing the test cases for test automation are largely created by code (possibly with underlying data tables for data variations for the specific sophisticated solutions), in business-oriented testing, as explained in this chapter, mapping of the technical view to the business-oriented view is required.

Three main approaches (Bucsics, Baumgartner, Seidl, & Gwihs, 2015) can be used to automate business-oriented test cases:

1. Programmatic test case representation and Capture & Replay
   Test cases are created in the form of code as in the unit test. In the case of user interfaces, the code can also be created by simple capture of a manual test. This method limits variables to central parameters, such as the base URL of a website, which can be configured centrally when changes are made to the test object.
2. Data-driven test case representation
   The script is initially the same code as the first method, only this time all test data is replaced by variables. Due to data tables (e.g., a CSV file), the variables are then assigned values and the script is repeated line by line. The so-called Decision Table given below in the example of FitNesse and Selenium (see Sect. 7.7.3) is a typical representative of this method.
3. Keyword-driven test case representation
   The script is broken down into individual sub-steps so that the tester can combine these into a more complex sequence as desired. As in the case of the data-driven test case representation, the test data in the script is replaced by variables, which are subsequently fed with values from test case tables at test runtime. However, each line of the table represents only one sub-step, identified by the keyword and followed by the test data to be passed. The so-called Script Table below in the example of FitNesse and Selenium (see Sect. 7.7.3) is a typical representative of this method.

Based on these principles, more sophisticated methods can then be developed, which enhance the controllability of test automation for a business tester without in-depth technical knowledge.

These techniques can also be optimized in such a way that access to the application, e.g., to a certain API or a certain mask in the user interface, is delegated to central classes, so that any changes to the application can be maintained at one point in the code and not in all individual test cases. Some test automation tools offer their own customization wizards for this, which make maintenance even more convenient and possibly even easier for less technically skilled testers.

The third characteristic that a test automation solution must have is the ability to handle large amounts of test data. Not only must the transaction data in the test be well managed in as many variants as possible, but the expected results for comparison during and after the test execution must also be readily available. A good idea when using "transient" transaction data in a test is to automatically "check" the transaction data used, so that the automation script automatically uses the next available set on the next run. For example, an account terminated in a test cannot be terminated several times in a row. Therefore, at the beginning, the test automation is given a list with many terminable accounts in the test database, which it processes one after the other and marks which accounts it has already "used up" in tests.

The more comprehensive a test case portfolio for automation is, the more likely it is necessary to create a test framework that fulfills the three functions mentioned above. Some commercial tools claim to have most of these features, but even in that case we need some effort to activate them and make them usable according to the project's specific needs.

Agile teams find themselves in a traditional dilemma in this case: The more flexible they want to be, the more frequently it happens that the test automation solution violates the principle of simplicity. In practice, we have set the threshold in the case of a test case portfolio of about 1000 test cases where we would strongly recommend a team to invest in a framework. Depending on how variable the test data is, the limit can significantly fluctuate upward or downward. But generally, one should not draw the line too late, otherwise simple test automation scripts can soon be dead code.

7.7.2   Agile Versus Traditional Automation of User Interactions

In agile projects, unit tests and integration tests have simply been extended in the established technology (test framework, placeholder) to be able to offer test automation for functional tests as well. As already mentioned at the beginning, this approach might soon meet its limits, particularly when the scripts make it difficult to take a close look at business aspects.

Traditional automation tools for black box testing usually offer these capabilities by nature but have not been particularly suitable for agile projects: They are complex in terms of installation/configuration, usually need more extensive training, and often cannot react fast enough to changed software.

As a result, a new generation of rather lightweight test automation solutions has emerged, which we call agile test automation. But how do they differ from the traditional solutions, given that they are supposed to serve the same purpose?

7.7.2.1 Agile Test Automation
The main difference is that in the case of agile test automation tools, the actual automation is mostly written by developers or by dedicated technical test automation

engineers. Instead of using a separate test script in a tool with its own objects and methods indirectly via a test recording, agile teams can directly access their code during test automation and write automation classes or automation methods for it. Very important: Knowledge of the inner workings of a test object makes test automation simpler and more direct. On top of that, if used consistently in the sense of acceptance test-driven development (ATDD), developers will account for the technical testability of their (sub-)application from the beginning.

Another difference is that the management of the tests (different test runs per release, per hotfix in production, etc.) is kept lean and the reporting is largely limited to a passed/failed list with concise debugging protocols. More complex reports, such as the coverage measurement of requirements, the coverage history through tests, etc., are therefore often not provided in agile solutions. The reason behind this lies, on the one hand, in the requirement of simplicity (only as much as necessary) and, on the other hand, in the immediate processing of test results in the team. An agile team often does not need more complex test management solutions or more sophisticated test reports.

The following illustration explains the function of an agile test automation tool. It is limited to providing a framework for

(a) The interface between requirements and the test automation code (Fixture) and for
(b) Test execution and logging of the same

The test code and the test execution routines (including the logging of details) must be created by the agile team (Fig. 7.7).

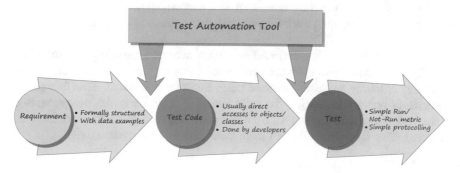

Fig. 7.7 Structure of agile test automation tools

The benefits of this agile test automation solution are as follows:

- Support of acceptance test-driven development (ATDD).
- Test cases are already written in the requirements draft and hardly need to be refined afterward.
- Test cases can be presented in a way that is easy to understand for end users or business experts, depending on the variant (e.g., in the case of Behavior-Driven Development, BDD, see Sect. 7.7.4 below).
- The tools are easy to install/configure.
- The solution is tailored for development and integrates the skills of developers extremely well (mostly integrated into the development environment and working directly with the developed objects in the code).

7.7.2.2 Traditional Test Automation

As already indicated, we cannot ignore the traditional test automation tools in agile projects. In many projects, mixed forms have also been emerging for a long time (as illustrated in the Sect. 7.7.3). The focus of traditional test automation tools is on the following aspects:

- The primary goal is the functional regression test before large releases.
- Large test portfolios with several thousand test cases can also be managed and maintained.
- Long test runs with meaningful logs are supported.
- The operation of several tools is also reasonable for experts of the business or representatives of the end users.
- Especially in the case of complex integration stages (up to multisystem) the tools can be well organized (who tests what and with which sub-applications).
- There is good reporting even for external stakeholders of the test.

The core of these tools is the excellent object detection regarding user interfaces (see Fig. 7.8). Many tools offer convincing solutions for the diverse platforms, such that there is hardly any user interface that cannot be automated. This feature can particularly be very interesting for agile teams, if they work with components or frameworks from third parties, whose inner workings they do not know or have not mastered. That is why we also call them black box test automation tools.

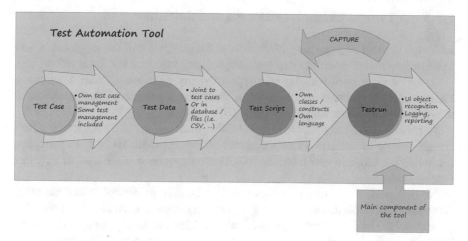

Fig. 7.8 Structure of traditional test automation tools

Another special feature is that these tools provide a working environment in which test cases can be created, test data for the tests can be defined and/or managed, and test scripts can be conveniently recorded, adapted, and modularized.

In addition, many tools can be integrated into a test management tool in which different test projects, releases, test suites, and test runs can be distinguished. This allows us to provide a very comfortable (semiautomatic) reporting about which test case has been successfully tested in which release or has not yet been tested.

Nevertheless, the focus still lies on test execution, where the tool has to recognize the UI objects to be tested reliably, address them quickly (minimize the runtime), and report comfortably regarding the test results (with detailed information including videos or screenshots). Test execution, in this case, also means only the tests via a user interface, possibly also via a web or database service.

Particularly in the optimization of UI tests, one weakness of the tools comes to light: They usually come along with a rather complex structure of tool-immanent functions and test scripts, which cannot always be easily adapted to changing software. According to the principle of simplicity, an agile team must clearly distinguish between a simple necessity in the project and unnecessary comfort. There are certain constraints in the project that impose to work with traditional test automation tools. Typically, they are needed in projects with the following characteristics:

- Regulatory constraints (e.g., specific reports/proofs for external stakeholders)
- Contractual constraints (e.g., use of joint tools with supplier or customer)
- Technical constraints (e.g., use of components, third-party frameworks)
- Non-flexible organization (e.g., separation of test automation from development team)
- Reporting exceeding the project level (e.g., regular reports to a multi-project office, the executive board, etc.)

7.7.3 A Typical Example: FitNesse and Selenium

Although we will be presenting other tools in Chap. 8, we will use an example here to show how "lean" solutions can look like for user interface test automation.

A tool widely used and the prototype of many agile automation solutions is FitNesse (2021), a cross-over between a Wiki and a framework for execution of self-written automation scripts.

According to the test pyramid by Mike Cohn, such self-created automation scripts should mainly be used to directly control the internal methods of the application (or the APIs). Graphic user interfaces (GUI) should only be automated in very few cases.

Nevertheless, the same technology can also be used to control traditional black box automation tools that integrate between the automation script and the application to be tested (or its user interface). In this context Selenium is very popular (Selenium, 2021), if only web interfaces in a web browser are to be automated. The advantage of Selenium is its easy handling for recording (Selenium IDE as a plug-in in the Firefox browser) and its easy integration as a stand-alone application in various programming languages (Selenium WebDriver).

The automation process flows usually as follows:

1. The developer of a test automation script (so called fixture) may possibly record a test flow using the Firefox Selenium IDE plug-in with the help of the business tester. It already ensures that suitable test points for the test result are entered (e.g., verifyText for checking whether a certain text appears in an element of the user interface).
2. The developer makes sure that the recorded test script is executable by automatically reproducing the test as many times as possible.
   Note: The developer should make sure that the elements of the website to be tested are identified as well as possible and maintainable. Fully qualified XPath expressions can quickly become outdated when the user interface is changed. On the contrary, CSS or id accesses can be more stable. The trend here is clearly going in the direction of CSS selectors.
3. The developer copies the steps from Selenium IDE to the clipboard and inserts them initially as a comment into a new class in the development environment. In Selenium IDE, the programming language in which the script is to be copied to the clipboard might have to be set first. For FitNesse, Java/JUnit4/WebDriver should be set.
4. The developer now writes a test-driven fixture for FitNesse from the transferred automation commands, which should have a certain structure (see examples below) and stores the functionality of the fixtures together with the unit test cases.
5. The finished fixture is copied (usually with simple copy/paste) into the FitNesse directory (or FitNesse accesses the development environment directly via path settings if it should remain simple).
6. The business tester starts FitNesse with a shell script. A local Tomcat server is started, via which the business tester can access the FitNesse Wiki via a browser.

In most teams, a central Tomcat server is installed relatively quickly and shared between the testers.

7. The technical testers create a suitable project hierarchy in the Wiki on pages in which requirements, user stories, and other notes can be written down. They describe the test feature on a few pages, with which their content can become an executable test. On these test pages they can now create an HTML table (with simplified Wiki syntax), which first names the fixture to be used in the first line, and then provides data for executing the fixture.

8. The business tester starts a test execution (via the page menu). The result of the test execution is highlighted in color (passed = green, failed = red) in the test table. Thus, the business tester knows what went well or what needs more investigation.

9. Using the history function, the testers can also specifically view previous test execution results of each individual test page.

FitNesse is thus a tool with which the business testers can concentrate fully on their work and way of thinking, and the Java IDE (such as Eclipse) is the working environment of the developer. If a test is missing, the business testers can order it from the developer. The developer creates test-driven test scripts and provides them to the business testers to complete the tests.

Note: Fixture Types

The test framework SLIM integrated in FitNesse (SLIM, 2017) recognizes multiple different table types. They certainly all have their functionality and can be very useful, but there are essentially two main types: Decision Tables for data-driven automation and Script Tables for keyword-driven automation.

Here, one example with two test cases (search on a website) is defined in both table types:

Decision Table (Data-Driven Automation)

Each line after the column headings (starting with line 3) corresponds to a specific test case, which should achieve a successful hit in the first case and should not achieve a successful hit in the second (negative) case.

com.teaching.tdddemo.TDDMainSite		
Search text	Result contains	Result?
Gallery	Photo gallery of the summer camp	True
Gallery	Welcome home	False

And this is the fitting fixture for Selenium:

(continued)

```
public class TDDMainSite {
  private WebDriver driver;
  private String baseUrl;
  private String Search term;
  private String ResultContains;
  private boolean Result = false;
  public TDDMainSite() {
    driver = new ChromeDriver();
    baseUrl = "http://localhost";
  }
  public void setSearchtext (String value) {
    this.Searchtext = Value;
  }
  public void setResultContains (String value) {
    this.ResultContains = Value;
  }
  public boolean getResult() {
    return this.Result;
  }
  public void execute () {
    driver.get(this.baseUrl + "/TDD-DEMO/");
    driver.findElement(By.name("query")).clear();
        driver.findElement(By.name("query")).sendKeys(this.
Searchtext);
      driver.findElement(By.xpath("(//input[@name='action'])
[2]")).click();
    try {
        this.Result  =  driver.findElement(By.xpath  ("(//div
[@id='content']/ul/li/a)[1]")).getText().matches("^[\crs\crS]
*"+this.ResultContains+"[\crs\crS]*$");
      } catch (Exception e) {}
      driver.quit();
  }
}
```

The column headings in the table have corresponding methods in the fixture with set as the prefix for inputs and get as the prefix for results (which are to be checked, marked with question marks in the column heading). They only pass data to internal variables or return the values of the internal variables to FitNesse. The actual script is then stored as an execute method and only needs to use the internal variables (for input as well as output).

(continued)

Script Table (keyword-driven automation)

script	com.teaching.tdddemo.TDDMainSite		
Search	Gallery	*With result*	Photo gallery of the summer camp
Close the browser			

script	com.teaching.tdddemo.TDDMainSite			
Reject	*Search*	Gallery	*With result*	Welcome home
Close the browser				

The same two test cases as above are now stored in separate tables. The tester would also have the option to vary the sequence (if the fixture has more keywords/methods). To mark the negative test case, the password *reject* must be inserted before the step that has to fail, so that FitNesse evaluates the failure as a successful test.

```
public class TDDMainSite {
  private WebDriver driver;
  private String baseUrl;
  public TDDMainSite() {
    driver = new ChromeDriver();
    baseUrl = "http://localhost";
  }
  public boolean SearchWithResult(String search term, String
ResultContains) {
    boolean result = false;
    driver.get(baseUrl + "/TDD-DEMO/");
    driver.findElement(By.name("query")).clear();
            driver.findElement(By.name("query")).sendKeys
(Searchtext);
        driver.findElement(By.xpath("(//input[@name='action'])
[2]")).click();
    try {
        result   =   driver.findElement(By.xpath   ("(//div
[@id='content']/ul/li/a)[1]")).getText().matches("^[\crs\crS]
*"+ResultContains+"[\crs\crS]*$");
    } catch (Exception e) {}
    return result;
  }
  public void ClosetheBrowser() {
    driver.quit();
  }
}
```

We can use the keyword even further: Each odd column (1, 3, 5, ...) in the table is recognized as a part of the keyword, while the even columns (2, 4, 6, ...) successively specify the input parameter values for the method. Thus, we can turn the method *SearchwithResult* into the keyword *Search ... With Result ....*

This popular solution based on well-maintained open-source software offers a good compromise between scalable test automation and a simple solution. However, it must be mentioned that Selenium is being used less and less in view of interesting new tool developments and this solution also has its limits:

- The test data management in fixture tables allows only little complexity (few versions for data, no images and documents without additional effort, etc.).
- Complex comparisons with expected results are difficult to generate from fixture tables. Especially when document contents such as invoices or reports must be evaluated, more sophisticated comparators must be used.
- Extensive and sophisticated business processes are rarely easy to simplify in fixtures.
- FitNesse is a good basic framework, but considerable additional effort is necessary to transform it into more mature solutions.
- The data types that can be used in the FitNesse tables are only limited to the general basic data types. There are projects where numbers and strings are no longer enough, and more complex structures or arrays would be desirable.

Many teams can live well with these limitations and it is a good starting point for test automation. Nevertheless, the use of automation tools should be planned with caution. Unfortunately, we have seen several agile teams that were quickly deterred by limitation and then lost the courage to undertake test automation of user interfaces.

7.7.4   Behavior-Driven Development with Cucumber and Gherkin

If the example from Sect. 7.7.3 with Selenium (for test automation) and FitNesse (for the technical tester) is consistently further developed toward the user story, then the question arises why it is not possible to derive the tests automatically from the acceptance criteria. The advantage would be clear: the requirements in the form of user stories and acceptance criteria would serve as test cases. A change in the requirements would automatically result in a change in the tests.

This automated generation of tests from acceptance criteria would have another advantage: The acceptance criteria should be defined in an as detailed and testable manner as possible. At first glance, this may sound rather cumbersome, but it does lead to important discussions about the requirements at an early stage and avoids misunderstanding between the business and the developers. Therefore, it is now regarded as best practice in agile development teams (Adzic, 2011).

This procedure is referred to as Acceptance Test-Driven Development (ATDD) (Gärtner, 2012): writing the acceptance tests first and then developing based on them! If the acceptance criteria can be evaluated automatically and executable automated tests can be created from them, we refer to it as Behavior-Driven Development (BDD).

A specific example of the technical implementation of BDD is the Gherkin language, which, in contrast to Ruby, Java, or C#, is not intended for applications or unit test cases, but for expressing functional acceptance test cases, which are then automatically reinterpreted into automated tests. The automation tool Cucumber then forms the framework for machine processing (Cucumber Ltd., 2017).

The business expert, tester, or product owner then writes their user story in the Gherkin language as a so-called feature:

```
Feature: Search for pages related to specific keywords
    As a viewer of the web portal
    I would like to find pages on certain topics
    To be able to inform me specifically about a certain topic

Scenario: I can search for photos from the summer camp in
the portal
    Given the user has accessed our portal in the browser
    And it is not on the registration form right now
    When the user enters the term summer camp in the search
    field
    Then at least the page photos from the summer camp is
    offered to him or her

Scenario: I cannot search for topics with special characters
etc.
```

The keywords at the beginning of each line are important. Table 7.1 provides an overview of the keywords and their meaning in Gherkin.

In this way, a user story with its acceptance criteria is provided in a more structured format without having to forego free formulation. Everything is kept together and only needs to be changed in one place. The business experts are required to be more specific about the acceptance criteria, but therefore can rely on the fact that these will then by and large be tested automatically. In addition, we see immediately what should be tested, compared to the complicated specification of steps in the FitNesse example above.

Now, however, the automation scripts must be created from the records of the business expert. For this purpose, test automation engineers simply prefix their routine with a recognition pattern (with regular expressions) for records which can then be assigned by Cucumber.

Table 7.1 Keywords for acceptance conditions (test cases or scenarios) in Gherkin

Keyword	Purpose
And	Linking of several preconditions, assumptions, or expected results
Background	Precondition for multiple scenarios (applies to each following scenario)
But	Synonymous with "And" (but sometimes better understandable when reading)
Example	Concrete example illustrating a business rule An example is not only a specification and documentation, but also a test case. Pattern for Examples: – Describe initial context (Given steps) – Describe event/conditions (When steps) – Describe expected results/outcomes (Then steps)
Examples	Section in "Scenario Outline" The "Scenario Outline" is run for each row in the examples table.
Feature	Title and high-level description for a software feature Grouping of related scenarios
Given	Defines the initial context of the system, the preconditions for a scenario
Rule	Representation of a business rule to be implemented
Scenario	Synonymous with "Example"
Scenarios	Synonymous with "Examples"
Scenario Outline	With this keyword the same scenario can be executed multiple times with different value combinations. The scenario is described with placeholders/variables, which are then filled/detailed by an examples table. (Scenario Outline is thus executed for each table row). Every Scenario Outline must include an Examples/Scenarios section.
Scenario Template	Synonymous with "Scenario Outline"
Then	Describes an expected result/outcome for the scenario
When	Describes a basic action or trigger/event for the scenario

```
@When("the user enters the term (.*) in the search field")
public void search_for_expression(String Searchtext) {
    ...
}
```

Gherkin also supports decision tables. In this case, the business expert has the real values in the scenario replaced by variables and adds a simple Wiki table below. The whole script is referred to as a "Scenario Outline," which is nothing more than a scenario with a decision table (examples). The following is our scenario from above as a scenario outline with examples:

```
      Scenario Outline: I can search for specific topics in the
   portal
      Given the user has accessed our portal in the browser
      And is not on the registration form right now
      When the user enters the term <Search text> in the search
   field
      Then at least the page <Page title> is provided

      Examples:
        | Search text | Page title          |
        | Summer camp | Summer camp photos  |
        | Contact     | About us            |
```

Ultimately, this type of test automation not only supports testing, but also promotes the analysis of user stories and team discussions about the content. At an early stage, all those involved must consider how the required functionality is to be tested at the end. This can help with the required quality early on and will save annoying troubleshooting cycles at the end.

However, it is important to mention that BDD does not make additional tests unnecessary. The BDD only provides an initial framework, which then needs to be refined or deepened in unit tests, further acceptance tests, non-functional tests, explorative test sessions, etc.

7.8   Test Automation in Load and Performance Testing

Load tests and performance tests usually require a completely different tool than functional tests. We want to point out an important feature, which leads to misunderstanding particularly in the case of agile teams:

Agile teams tend to limit the use of tools to the essentials and use proven and familiar solutions rather than piloting new paths in the tight timeline of iterations. Unfortunately, this often leads to an attempt to simulate and observe load situations with the limited means of the manual test or the unit test.

This may still be useful at the component level and to measure the performance of our components (e.g., when accessing the database). But at the latest when the system is already partially integrated, such a solution is no longer sufficient.

It is important to understand that load scenarios have two important characteristics:

- They always depict only a limited section of the "real" world, but this section is chosen so skillfully that it hits the suspected weak points in a targeted manner. Most importantly, the background load in a system must be skillfully approximated, as this can rarely be reproduced at 1:1 compared to production.

- They define suitable monitors that make the load behavior visible and measurable or loggable at the various points of the system. These monitors must be perfectly synchronized with the load generator so that it becomes possible to compare exactly what happened when and how.

The challenges of functional testing, such as the simulation of a surface or comparison with expected behavior, rarely must be covered by load and performance testing solutions. The tools usually interface a level below the client software (and thus below the user interface) and only validate the reaction of the application as far as it is necessary for the further test steps.

We therefore recommend that all agile teams take a close look at load test and performance test tools before prematurely reusing the existing automation solutions.

7.9   The Seven Worst Ideas for Test Automation

Instead of the usual well-intentioned recommendations, we want to take a new course this time. We shall simply list the worst ideas we have encountered in practice in connection with test automation. In the sense of a self-organizing team, we should be able to choose our suitable strategy with caution, whereby the traps and snares listed below show how much room for maneuvering we still have. Of course, we could not resist giving a few recommendations at the end of each section.

7.9.1   Expecting Success After Just a Few Sprints

It is best to go to the project sponsors (i.e., the customer, the business experts, or simply the product owner) and sell them the value of the introduction of test automation for UIs and APIs as backlog functionality. This may turn out to be successful, but it is a complete lie. Test automation has no direct value for the sponsor; it is a technology that assures lower maintenance costs and higher quality.

Accordingly, everyone will of course wait impatiently for the successful yield. Impatience is all the more reason not to invest in a suitable solution. Instead, we try from the beginning to achieve the much-sought Quick Wins. As usual, the first test case is still quite successful. Thereafter, the team becomes disillusioned as nobody really has the patience to work out the solution and to comply with all due diligence obligations. Usually, after four to eight weeks, everyone from the team to the sponsor loses patience and test automation is stopped like an unfinished building.

Perhaps it would have been better to always see the costs for test automation as ongoing development costs without calculating the return on investment. When the team runs out of breath, it is better to stretch the automation implementation a little and make it a possible task. When choosing the tests, too, we should perhaps focus on those functions that will most probably have to be maintained in the coming iterations. During maintenance, test automation does pays off the most.

7.9.2   Trusting Test Tools Blindly

Many tools prove to be tempting for the team by reflecting the best practices of the entire industry. The worldwide use, or quite a broad use of the tools, indirectly suggests this. Therefore, it is best to invite someone to demonstrate the use of tools as impressively as possible. This should then immediately inspire all project participants equally. Even if someone fails to do so, supporters will quickly come together. A general staff plan is drawn up and the use of the tool is rolled out, preferably organization wide. After all, the more people participate in the use of tools, the lower the costs per project for acquisition, implementation, and maintenance appear to be.

After the first weeks of enthusiastic work, the limits of the tool and especially the considerable remaining workload, which was probably not quite foreseeable at the beginning, soon start to show up: Not only do many colleagues need to be trained, but a suitable deployment must also be agreed upon. Should the test tool only automate certain UI or support the entire test management? In addition, the artifacts created in the tool (tests, data, etc.) must be maintained.

The enthusiasm soon drops, since the tool, even though a convincing solution, unfortunately fails to be one for the specific project problem. The other users in the organization have similar experiences and start complaining out loud. As a proponent of the solution, we cannot avoid defending the meaningfulness of the use against better knowledge.

Next time it would be ideal

- To carefully select the tool based on our own needs
- Pilot the operation as a precaution (in case of success we can then roll out gradually)
- Be aware that when checking the test result, elements such as formal display errors (like logo placement, invoice layout) are poorly detected by many tools and, therefore, such checks must still be done manually

7.9.3   Considering Writing the Test Scripts as a Secondary Job

Test automation is easy for developers, especially if the scripts are written in a familiar programming language. They are quickly created at the end as a replacement for manual tests, turning tedious manual testing into creative automated test scripting.

It quickly becomes apparent that writing good fixtures is not easy but needs a lot of experience and care. In addition, providing the appropriate data is not as easy as it should be. In order not to get slowed down by the test, only the most essential things are implemented. After about three to four sprints, it turns out that the fixtures of colleagues are hardly maintainable; after another three sprints, one can say the same for one's own fixtures. The vigor comes to a standstill. Automated testing is considered too expensive. It is looked at as a luxury. The fact that this also negates the opportunity to implement more extensive changes to the code without risk, because the quality-assuring test harness is missing, is dismissed.

Wouldn't it have made more sense to see fixtures for test automation from the outset as a necessary part of the code, which is, of course, secured by unit tests, or even better by test-driven development? Perhaps even the production of tests is then sometimes more expensive than the production and/or adjustment of the actual code. But this investment is certainly profitable.

7.9.4   Burying the Test Data in Test Cases

Test cases are the easiest to maintain if they are implemented directly, as the unit test, and the data is entered in the script in a legible and clear manner. Anything that requires additional abstraction of the tests is only a risky source of error and should therefore be avoided!

The success of the automated business tests proves the team right. After half a year, there is already a test portfolio of about 700 test cases that runs regularly and stably. That is when the unexpected happens: The customer number in the inventory database is converted. That is not a big deal. Only, the customer number can be found under very different object names in the test scripts and the search becomes very tedious. Unfortunately, such changes occur again and again. In particular, the sample department used in test cases now gets moved to a different unit—just for business reasons. Now even data relationships in the test cases must be traced.

Very soon, it comes to light that this is probably the easiest way to simply recreate all the tests. This time, however, the test scripts immediately access the central test data tables or decentralized CSV files, which can be adapted in a targeted and structured manner like a database.

7.9.5   Associating the Test Automation Only with UI Tests

We constantly come across projects that want to commit themselves to test automation for the first time and start with the biggest challenge at the same time, i.e., the automation of user interfaces. The principle behind it is clear: Manual tests on the user interface are usually the most obvious, especially from the end user's perspective, which is why we can quickly achieve decent success in this case. The rest can be done well with spontaneous scripts.

Unfortunately, it usually turns out that the user interface is a tough nut to crack for automation. Such surfaces are often also less then optimally developed and should urgently be subjected to refactoring or redesigning.

Although the first test runs go quite well, the stability and maintainability quickly become a challenge. In this case, the paradoxical situation arises wherein it is not possible to reset the data in the test environment, as the scripts are missing (which could have been implemented in two to three weeks). Instead, months of work are spent on getting automated UI test cases, which can handle variable test data, to run stably.

Once we have invested so much work, we will rarely have enough patience to continually invest when it comes to planning meetings in test automation.

7.9.6   Underestimating the Comparison with Expected Results

It is tempting to quickly build a series of automated test cases that leave the verification of the test result to the tester himself. The only stupid thing about this is that we can very quickly automate those test cases where it is not enough to evaluate the return code of the application or the title of the subsequent window. Checking the correctness of a printout of a life insurance policy document can certainly be mastered by an expert tester. However, there is little enthusiasm when regular regression test runs bring about 1000 different policies to the table, which must be found to be right or wrong again each time.

It gets even better when an intermediate result is read from a table in the middle of the test (e.g., sales forecast in online banking), before we can continue (e.g., with the output of the last account statement). This can get annoying if the tester finds out while evaluating the logs that many tests should have stopped at the sales forecast to preserve test data that would otherwise get "used up" for the regression test.

Usually, as a response to this, complex comparators are built, which can determine the correctness of extensive documents flexibly and unerringly depending on the input data for the respective test run. The constantly changing date of the day is recognized as accurately as new key data (such as the customer number). At the latest, during the maintenance of these comparators it becomes frustrating. Results change at least as often as the input options of an application.

It would be better to make the tests repeatable from the start, with the same data status/data inventory, and to only use result parsers where there is no other way. The correct formatting of a printout can also be quickly checked manually if the content has been automatically compared in advance.

7.9.7   Accepting the (Un)testability of the Application

We have seen automation experts proudly demonstrate how well and accurately their scripts are now able to find UI elements that have constantly changing properties like a chameleon (although technically they always remain the same). It is, in most cases, a technical masterpiece that costs a lot of time and effort to create and maintain. Such "moving targets" unfortunately arise again and again and are easily accepted in traditional projects or with third-party software.

But it is quite amusing when these UI elements are implemented and maintained by the colleague in the next room who belongs to the same team. We then often ask why such elements are used in development and get quite conclusive answers from the development team—albeit from a development perspective. The next question is obvious: What would it mean to work without these elements or to make them more recognizable? The effort and expense for this is usually many times less than the automation effort for the test. In most cases, the solution also meets best practice standards. For web interfaces, it is very common to request the use of unique IDs, which has also long been required by the W3C consortium.

So, remember: Design for testability is an imperative of simplicity from the overall project perspective. Simplicity does not only apply to development.

Use of Tools in Agile Projects

8

As with traditional process models, the choice of tools also plays an essential role in their later success or failure in agile projects. The approach for agile projects described in the previous chapters places special demands on the tools used to support the test process. These include:

- Low administration effort
- Short training period/low training effort
- Flexible tool adaptation options (processes and terminology)

In contrast, however, especially in larger organizations, there is a requirement to create or maintain a unified, cross-project, long-lasting, and standardized IT infrastructure. This influences the decision-making process when choosing a tool and may lead to not always making the optimal choice for a project.

As testing is no longer seen as a separate, independent activity, but rather as an integral part of the development process, not only tools that are directly aligned with the support of the test process are to be considered, but also tools that serve test activities (such as test execution or test specification) only indirectly. This holistic view is particularly advantageous in agile projects since individual team members are increasingly involved in a wide variety of activities (e.g., requirements collection and test execution) to achieve the project goal as efficiently as possible and to be able to perform optimally (Crispin & Gregory, 2009).

In the following sections, we will cover the general description of tool selection in agile projects and its special aspects. We also propose an exemplary selection for the implementation using a specific tool. This does not represent an assessment, but rather serves as an example implementation of the previously discussed aspects and considerations. It should also be noted that all the tools presented in the following chapters are not only designed for the (test-) activities described, but they also cover a wide variety of functionality that is not directly related to test activities. In this chapter, it is important to the authors that a tool is not only viewed and evaluated from all perspectives, but also to provide an overview of the currently available tool support options and their specific innovations and approaches to agile procedures.

8.1   Project Management

Just as in traditional projects, project management in agile projects is strongly influenced by the method used. As recent studies show, Scrum or variations of Scrum are the predominant procedural models in the agile environment and are used in over 85% of agile projects. In addition to Scrum, Kanban has also become increasingly important in recent years (SwissQ Consulting AG, 2017). Other methods that are frequently used in practice are XP, feature-driven development (FDD), or lean development.

The following criteria and aspects should be considered in the evaluation of tool use in agile projects:

- **Iterative-incremental planning**
  Many traditional procedural models require an exact specification in an early project phase, which must be implemented by the individual team members in the later course of the project. Necessary changes to this specification are by no means excluded, but they are always considered an exception. It follows that most of the specification is fixed at the start of the project and is no longer adapted during implementation.

  In contrast, a principle in agile process models is the acceptance of changes in every area (process, requirements, and framework conditions) (Beck et al., 2001). It is assumed that the detailed project goal is unclear in early project phases and therefore cannot be specified exactly. Many decisions cannot be made at this stage because the necessary information is not yet known. The specification is only created and adapted iteratively and incrementally (Highsmith, 2004; Oestereich & Weiss, 2007).

  In addition to the content or organizational changes described above, the prioritization of tasks, requirements, or activities in agile projects is subject to constant change. Requirements that are considered essential during the initial planning can, for example, become obsolete through the first customer feedback.

  When evaluating tools to support project management, it should therefore be ensured that these agile principles are considered. The management of requirements and specifications should be trivial without much effort, but at the same time the traceability must remain intact.
- **Agile project management**
  Since the team's self-responsibility and the resulting self-regulation are demanded and promoted in agile process models, the project manager is no longer a regulatory force. The scrum masters described in Scrum should not assume this role, as their task is to support the team in their work and to help clarify methodological questions.

The control of agile projects must therefore be done in a different way. To cover all or a part of these tasks, the following techniques are used in practice, which are also often used by tool manufacturers:

- Burndown or Burnup diagrams for progress control
- Product backlogs, sprint backlogs, or impediment backlogs to collect, prioritize, and estimate requirements or tasks
- Daily sprint meetings, Sprint Review Meetings, Retrospectives, and especially for Kanban even WIP (work in progress) limitation to facilitate continuous process improvement

When introducing these techniques (regardless of whether this is done using tools or not) it is important that the entire team is involved, and the results are made visible to all members. Otherwise, the self-regulation of the team will be inhibited or even prevented, and the team will fall back into old behavior patterns.

- **Customizable reporting**

When introducing tools in agile teams, the adaptability of reporting plays two roles: making project progress visible and promoting continuous improvement within the team.

It can be used to communicate project progress to the team or organization and the content of these reports differs greatly depending on the organization and project. A tool should therefore offer a wide range of options for adapting the existing reports to specific requirements. Possible configuration options for these adjustments are:

- Report format (PDF, Word, online dashboard, etc.)
- Content (costs, schedule, effort estimates, list of open points, etc.)
- The presentation of the reports (colors, layout, charts, etc.)

Even if these requirements apply equally to traditional as well as agile process models, we feel the need to explicitly mention them here, since these aspects are often not adequately considered in evaluations and can therefore lead to problems in the further course of a project. Especially in agile projects, where exact adjustment is essential for the efficiency of the project team, these aspects should be considered at an early stage.

Moreover, reports are increasingly used as a tool for change (Forrester Research, Inc., 2012) in agile projects, and the extensive data collected in today's tools can be used to represent a continuous improvement of a team or organization. Large ALM tools represent a valuable data source. But even with more complex infrastructures with different, specific tools, data can be collected and evaluated centrally. To facilitate this integration, when evaluating tools, it needs to be ensured that the data collected therein can easily be combined with other data sources (for example, through SOAP/JSON web services, and export interfaces).

- **Agile cost estimation**

Another challenge in an agile environment is the estimation of efforts required to implement a requirement to increase the accuracy of resource and time planning. To optimally support this, tools offer different estimation aids that can be used by one or more team members depending on the estimation method.

An important aspect is that the costs are not estimated in absolute units (e.g., in person days), but in relative, team-specific units (e.g., in story points or T-shirt sizes), and that the results of an estimate are always communicated together with the indication of an estimation accuracy (Confidence interval) (Hummel, 2011).

If formula- or metric-based methods for effort estimation are supported by the tool (e.g., COCOMO and function point method), it must also be ensured that their calculation logic is adaptable to be able to incorporate empirical values into new estimation tasks.

8.1.1   Broadcom Rally

CA Technologies acquired Rally Software in July 2015 and rebranded the Rally product of the same name as CA Agile Central; after the Broadcom acquisition, the product is branded as "Rally" again. Broadcom's complementary products offer a wide range of agile and DevOps tools.

The essential functions of Broadcom Rally include:

- Capacity planning
- Portfolio management (Kanban)
- Iteration and release planning (Timeboxes)
- Management of backlogs in hierarchical levels (Portfolio Items Hierarchy)
- Feature backlogs
- Real-time status tracking
- Risk management
- Team planning
- Performance metrics and report
- Collaboration platform

Agile principles are applied by Broadcom Rally in each of these areas, which is why it is also named in the Gartner Magic Quadrant for Enterprise Agile Planning Tools (Gartner Inc., 2017) as a leader in agile ALM tools. This position was achieved above all by the fact that Broadcom Rally was rated exceptionally well in key aspects, worth mentioning are for example the availability as SaaS (Software as a Service), the standard functionalities for agile project, program and portfolio management, the high understanding of agile, and DevOps and SAFe (Scaled Agile, Inc., 2017) principles as well as the various possibilities for integration with other systems.

In Broadcom Rally, requirements are managed in the form of user stories, which are collected and managed in a backlog. Tasks that are carried out frequently, such as reordering the requirements using drag & drop or estimating user stories, can be carried out directly in this display without having to load another page. In practice, this functionality greatly facilitates the iterative-incremental planning and prioritization of the requirements.

If sufficient user stories have been specified and estimated for the first iteration, these can be immediately assigned to any sprint. Even in this case, Broadcom Rally provides various convenience functions that make daily work with this tool easier. The assignment to a sprint is done by drag & drop and can be arranged in the same way within the sprint. During the Sprint Planning, it often happens that new requirements become known because the implementation of a user story that is only vaguely specified in the backlog may require additional activities, or because additional functions must be implemented due to changes. In Broadcom Rally, a new User Story is created with just a few clicks and, if required, is immediately subordinated to another user story. Defect reports are recorded in a similar manner. This ensures traceability between requirements and defect reports without additional effort.

However, the aspects of Broadcom Rally presented here are only a small subset of all functionalities available; these include extensive options for analysis and reporting, support for Kanban, automatic generation of roadmaps, integration of user feedback, focus on transparency and visibility for all project members or fine-grained time recording at project, requirement, or task level.

8.2   Requirements Management

In principle, a defect can be caused in every project phase of a software development project, but the cost of fixing it increases dramatically over time. This connection, even if there is disagreement about the concrete numbers (Herrmann, Knauss, & Weißbach, 2013; Mayr, 2005; Software Quality Systems AG (SQS), 2012), has been known for a long time and clearly shows the importance of professional requirements specification and professional requirements management. Despite this fact, in a current study, almost 60% of those surveyed expressed that they were not at all or only partially satisfied with the examination of requirements in the requirements engineering process in the company (SwissQ Consulting AG, 2017).

The flexible and quickly adaptable approach to development in agile projects (triggered by external or internal requirements) further increases the demands on requirements management. The effort required to overcome these challenges can, however, be significantly reduced by means of adequately introduced tool support.

The optimization of requirements management not only supports subsequent development activities, but also improves the quality and efficiency of the test activities. To be able to specify high-quality, easily maintainable, and above all valid test cases, professional handling of requirements is essential.

Changes to requirements represent a challenge since these can have an impact on many subsequent test artifacts, and, if changes are inconsistent, their informative value and validity are negatively affected. To simplify the impact analysis of these changes in requirements, many tools provide different options for linking artifacts to one another (traceability links). In the simplest case, this can be an additional attribute with the ID of a linked artifact, but impact reports can also be generated automatically or affected artifacts can be marked (see for example Sect. 8.2.1).

In practice, it can be observed that the interactions between requirement management and test activities are by no means only one-sided (i.e., that only requirement management supports the test activities), but that these process steps support each other. A tester's specific way of looking at requirements provides important input for increasing the quality of requirements. For example, the early specification of logical test cases (if initiated in good time, even before the start of development) shows possible inconsistent issues, incomplete requirements, missing acceptance criteria, and other linguistic or content defects. The early involvement of testing in the development process and good requirements are essential success factors for software projects (SwissQ Consulting AG, 2017).

To achieve the advantages of professional requirements management and to be able to cope with the challenge of changing requirements, the focus in traditional projects is on the definition, implementation, and monitoring of formal processes (Herrmann, Knauss, & Weißbach, 2013). If, for example, a necessary change occurs to a requirement, its potential impact is determined by means of an extensive impact analysis and then decisions are taken in committees about the actual implementation of the change request. In agile projects, however, this procedure is not recommended, since the definition of complex processes is replaced by self-organization and self-optimization within small teams. Responsibility is thus transferred to the project team and processes are only viewed as an (adaptable) framework with general rules of the game. In traditional process models, change requests are always seen as an exception and only if they are considered as such can the complex processes be adhered to at all (which can lead to the spread of the "Change Prevention Process" Anti-Pattern (Ambler & Lines, 2012)). In agile projects, however, frequent changes are not just an accepted fact that must be managed as optimally as possible, but they are considered a positive aspect of the development process (Beck et al., 2001). The resulting high number of changes is usually not manageable with typical requirement management processes.

For this reason, special aspects must be considered when selecting tools for tools that are to be used for requirements management in agile projects. In practice, these are primarily:

- **Adaptability of the process**
  It is important that the tool can be adapted to the procedures developed and accepted in the team and that the tool itself does not prescribe a specific procedure.
- **Customizable terminology**
  In addition to the processes defined in the tool, the terminology used can also be adapted to project-specific agreements. An artifact known as Customer Requirement in traditional projects can be referred to as a user story (Scrum, XP) or a narrative/scenario (as in Dan North's BDD (North, 2007)) in an agile team.

Depending on the terminology chosen, specific attributes are also recorded (e.g., story points).

- **Prioritization**
  The prioritization of requirements plays a central role in agile projects. To optimally support processes in the agile team, requirements are prioritized based on the business value they generate (Ambler & Lines, 2012). A tool that offers this functionality also directly supports test activities, for example by simplifying the selection of a suitable test case set for regression tests based on implemented requirements and their priority.

- **Definition of Done/acceptance criteria definable**
  Whether a specified work unit is completed in agile projects is defined by a "Definition of Done" which is agreed upon by the team. Only when all the points contained therein have been fulfilled, the work unit can be regarded as completed. Typically, this includes not only traditional development activities such as implementation, but also quality assurance activities (Sutherland, 2012). An optimal tool for agile teams should support the definition and above all compliance with these criteria.

- **Traceability**
  High traceability makes it easier to carry out impact analyses. To achieve this, it is necessary to both create the link between the artifacts and maintain and expand them on a regular basis. The resulting effort is one reason why, in contrast to many traditional process models, a fully established link between all project artifacts is not a goal in agile projects. As in other areas of project documentation (see also Chap. 6), only activities that represent an immediate and quickly recognizable benefit for the project team are carried out.

  For the use of tools to support traceability, this means that the linking of artifacts needs to be flexible, can be created easily, and should be easy to maintain. Unfortunately, there are tool solutions that optimally combine all three properties, and therefore, traceability is also a quality aspect that is often under-considered in practice.

- **Support of an iterative-incremental requirements management**
  Changes to requirements in agile projects are a daily aspect of work for developers, testers, and other project participants. Therefore, the tools used in these projects should support the iterative and incremental specification, refinement, and change of requirements. This also means that the entire team should be able to collaborate on the currently applicable specification in an uncomplicated manner, without any loss of traceability. The following section on Polarion QA/ALM further explains this criterion in the context of "LiveDocs" ™ and "Suspects."

8.2.1   Polarion QA/ALM

In the following chapter, the support of the requirements management in agile projects is exemplarily illustrated by Polarion QA/ALM (Siemens Digital Industries Software).

Although Polarion QA/ALM is mentioned here as a representative of tools to support requirements management, it can be used in every phase of the ALM process. The following activities are particularly noteworthy:

- Requirements management
- Project management
- Change management/Defect management
- Test management

To execute these activities in Polarion QA/ALM, different types of artifacts and specifications can be defined. In the area of requirements management, there are the basic types of requirements, which can be summarized in various specification documents. To optimally use the tool in agile projects, the requirements can also be managed in a product backlog and implemented in sprints. The type of specification can thus be easily adapted to the respective process model without having to forego advantages such as traceability.

The technical basis to make this possible is a Subversion Repository in the case of Polarion QA/ALM. This not only gives us complete traceability of all artifact types, but also the ability to display the differences between two versions of an artifact. This proves to be extremely helpful, especially in agile projects, since changes to requirements can be tracked and, in the event of a defect, can also be reset to an earlier version immediately.

To support the specific process of agile projects, Polarion QA/ALM can be extensively adapted and expanded. It already offers a template for agile projects that can also be adapted to specific requirements. The adaptability is not limited to the naming of artifact types or the specification documents used, the workflow is customizable, and more artifact types can be added. This makes it possible to map almost every process in the tool, and it therefore does not impose a specific procedure on the project team.

Particularly relevant for agile project assignments, the ease of use and short training period for new users are strong points of Polarion QA/ALM. The editor used for processing the specifications is strongly based on known office applications and can therefore be used by project members without additional training. In Polarion QA/ALM, this functionality is referred to as LiveDocs™ (Fig. 8.1).

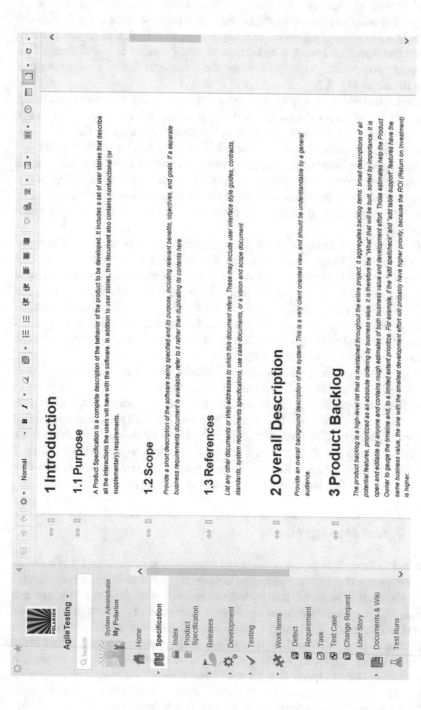

Fig. 8.1 Document editor for Polarion QA/ALM

Specifications created with LiveDocs™ have a decisive advantage over traditional specification documents. In the background, they are not treated as a document, but as a hierarchical collection of artifacts (e.g., a collection of requirements in a requirement specification or a collection of test cases in a test design). This structure becomes visible when we change the Document Editor view to the tree view, as shown in Fig. 8.2.

The individual elements can also be referenced in several documents, allowing requirements or test cases to be easily reused without causing redundancies. Not only is it possible that several specifications refer to one and the same artifact, but even different revisions of these artifacts can be referenced. An area of application for this functionality can be seen when a specification is to be written for several target platforms. Requirements or other types of artifacts that are relevant to each platform can be reused for each target platform. Since no copies are created, there is no risk of inconsistent changes, and all changes are automatically transferred to every instance of the artifact.

To ensure the traceability of the various artifacts, instances of the artifact types (referred to as work items in Polarion) can be linked together. Unlike many other tools, these are not simple connections, but also carriers of additional semantic information. This concept is realized in Polarion through typed connections. An example of this is that requirements can be related to test cases through an "is verified by" link. The semantics of this link is that the test case verifies the associated requirement. The test coverage, which is a good measure of the test progress, can be easily determined in this way (Fig. 8.3).

As also mentioned in the introduction, traceability between artifacts makes it easier to analyze the effects of changes and can therefore be used well in agile projects. The prerequisite for this is that the tool used can carry out the analysis automatically or at least support the user. In Polarion, this task is implemented using the "Suspect" concept. If an artifact is changed and it was previously linked to other artifacts (e.g., a request with a test case), this connection can be marked as "Suspect." This marking means that the linked artifact must be analyzed by a person responsible for any adjustments that have become necessary due to the previous change.

8.3   Defect Management

Defects are an inevitable aspect of software development projects and can occur in any project phase. Due to the ever-increasing complexity of development or maintenance projects, it is essential that project teams deal with defects efficiently and effectively. Coping with the large number of defects is often only possible with dedicated tool support. This is also a reason why professional, tool-supported defect management is used in more than 70% of the projects analyzed by a recent study (VersionOne Inc., 2017). In addition to efficient troubleshooting, the systematic management of defect reports also allows to make sound statements about project progress and any quality problems in certain areas. These findings can be used directly and promptly for process improvement in agile projects.

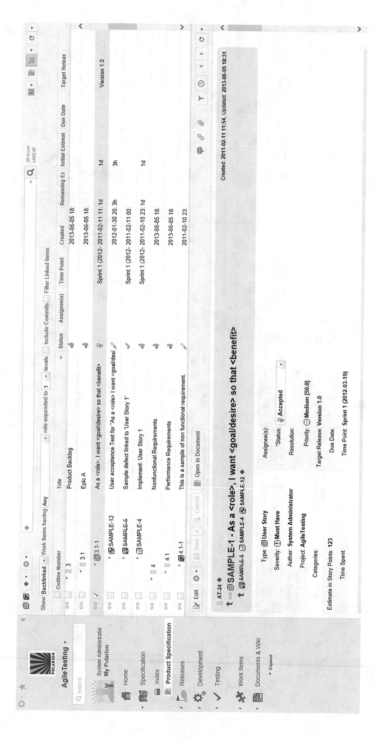

Fig. 8.2 Tree view of a specification in Polarion

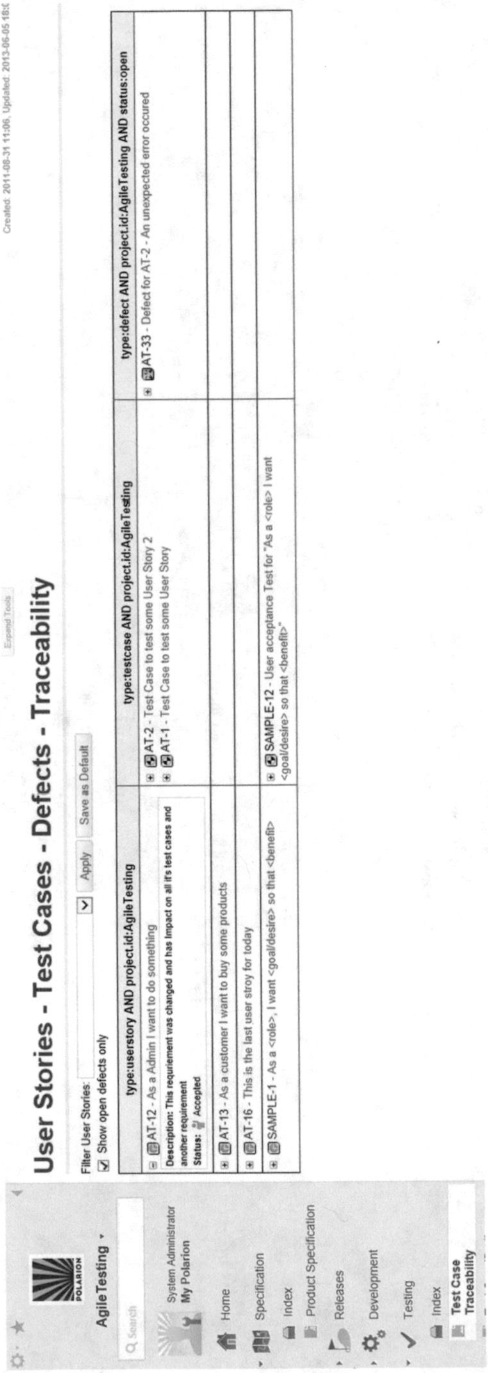

Fig. 8.3 Traceability between requirements, test cases, and defects in Polarion

Defect management is very similar for both agile and traditional projects; however, the following aspects are particularly important for agile projects:

- **Triage support**
  Triage is the process of determining the priority of patients' treatments by the severity of their condition or likelihood of recovery with and without treatment. This rations patient treatment efficiently when resources are insufficient for all to be treated immediately; influencing the order and priority of emergency treatment, emergency transport, or transport destination for the patient. (Wikimedia Foundation Inc, 2021)

  If we study defects instead of injured or sick people, we will find a comparable situation that is common in software development and software testing: Under great time pressure and with limited resources, it is necessary to handle a maximum number of defects. In practice, it is rarely possible to fix all bugs in the next release. It is therefore necessary to prioritize them and rank the bug fixes based on this prioritization.

  Two attributes are used for prioritization: severity and priority (Whalen, 2008). The combination of these attributes can be used to prioritize bug fixes more objectively and efficiently (Hoffmann, 2013). As an extension of this concept, "The Bug Genie" supports, for example, prioritization based on "User Pain" (Cook, 2008). Not only two attributes are evaluated per defect report, but three ("Bug Type," "Likelihood," and "Priority"—more on this can be found in Sect. 8.3.1).
- **Adaptability of the defect workflow (status and status transitions)**
  As for tools to support requirements management, the adaptability of the defect workflow is important for agile projects. Not only the states they contain, but also the allowed transitions between them should be easy to configure. Advanced tools sometimes even offer the possibility to define validation rules and actions for each state transition (after fixing high-priority defects, the test manager can be informed about this development, for example, to take further steps to verify the defect correction).
- **Extension and adjustment of attributes of a bug report**
  Depending on the procedure used in a project, different attributes are relevant for the creation of a defect report. To optimally support a project team, it should not only be possible to adapt the available options for an attribute (e.g., which selection options are available for the attribute "affected component"), but also the attributes that can be recorded per defect report (for example, an attribute "Test case ID" to ensure traceability to test cases).
- **Integration with version control systems**
  Systems to manage source code (Version Control Systems, VCS) are used today in almost every agile project. Without this support, an effective, collaborative development of a software system would hardly be possible (Schatten et al., 2010). The integration with these systems takes place in practice to a very different extent and should be adapted to the general conditions of a project. Possible integrations are the linking of commits (i.e., a version recorded in a

version control system) to defect reports, comparison of different versions (Diff)/ annotations of source code, the recording of metrics, or automatic triggering of state transitions based on a commit message.

- **Collaboration**
  As mentioned several times in the previous chapters, collaboration in agile teams is a fundamental factor for the success of a project (Bertram, Voida, Greenberg, & Walker, 2010). For this reason, when choosing a tool for defect management, care should be taken that this collaboration is supported and promoted by the software. The actual implementation can vary greatly from tool to tool. The fact that agile projects involve customers in the development process must also be considered and the tools must therefore be easy to access, understand, and use for nontechnicians.

  Common functions include: voting function to prioritize bug fixes, comment function per ticket, community Q&As, documentation in wikis, chat, tagging, or similar.

- **Agile effort estimation of bug fixes**
  The effort required for implementation must not only be estimated for requirements (see also Sect. 8.1), but also for large bug fixes before the actual fixes are made. In agile projects, the effort estimate differs very much from traditional process models and this difference must be mapped accordingly in a tool. As with many other aspects, equal cooperation between team members is of great importance. Specifically, this means that the effort estimate is carried out by the entire team or a large part of the team.

- **Collaborative planning and prioritization**
  After the effort for the recorded defect correction has been determined, its correction must be planned and prioritized. One way to plan and prioritize agile projects is to use Triage or "User Pain" (see above). The values calculated directly represent the priority of the individual defect messages and thus an order for their elimination. This approach is also very suitable for being carried out jointly by several people, and in practice leads to significantly better results than comparable plans drawn up by individuals.

  When evaluating tools for use in agile projects, it should therefore be considered that the planning and prioritization process can also be carried out by several people.

- **Transparency and traceability**
  Due to the focus on the team and team members in agile projects, transparency and traceability play a major role in all areas. To ensure this, tools can support a project team in a variety of ways: for example, versioning bug reports enables team members to more easily understand decisions made as part of the fix.

  However, tools can also create greater transparency in planning and prioritization, thus increasing the acceptance of plans by the team members. If, for example, comments on assumptions and requirements are recorded and presented to the public for estimates of effort, any misunderstandings or misinterpretations can be quickly identified and eliminated.

- **Customizable reporting**

  Flexible expandability and adaptability of reporting also play a central role in defect management and can vary greatly in practice from tool to tool. It is difficult to make a general statement about the necessary adaptability of the reporting functionality. In smaller, independent projects, for example, a few, high-quality standard reports with the option of filtering according to certain defined criteria can be sufficient. On the other hand, especially in larger organizations with several similar projects, there is often a need to make more specific adjustments, for example, to automatically capture organization-specific metrics or to identify trends across multiple projects (Forrester Research, Inc., 2012).

  Common adaptations to existing reporting functionality are the integration of additional attributes, acquisition of project-specific or organization-specific metrics (Defect Detection Rate, Defect Density, etc.), or the display of reports on project or organization dashboards.

  The implementation and introduction of these requirements sometimes require investments, and therefore, prior assessment and evaluation of the necessity and achievable benefits are essential.

8.3.1   The Bug Genie

The Bug Genie is a tool to support defect management and project management with a focus on agile process models that has been available under the Mozilla Public License since 2002 (The Bug Genie, 2013). It is, therefore, ideal as an example for supporting defect management in agile projects.

Supporting the collaboration of team members is a central objective for all functionalities. In addition, almost every aspect of the tool can be configured, adapted, or further developed without any problems due to its free availability.

The central artifact in The Bug Genie are "Issues," which are always an instance of an "Issue Type." The standard issue types available are "Bug report," "Feature request," "Enhancement," "Task," "User Story," and "Idea." As with Atlassian Jira, not only defects but also generic tasks or requirements can be managed. If required, any number of additional issue types can be added, given additional attributes, and assigned to one or more projects. This makes it possible to define cross-project issue types for larger organizations or in case of projects with specific requirements.

As shown in Fig. 8.4, the workflow for issue types is also freely configurable. Not only are the existing states adaptable and expandable, but also the possible status transitions and possible preconditions and post-conditions can be defined. The connection between issue types and an associated workflow is created using a workflow scheme. This makes it possible to define different workflows for different issue types. For a "Feature request," for example, an additional review step can be defined which must be completed before the implementation.

In contrast to the extensive customization options of workflow and issue types, The Bug Genie offers relatively few options for adapting reports to project-specific requirements. However, this limitation does often not pose a major problem in

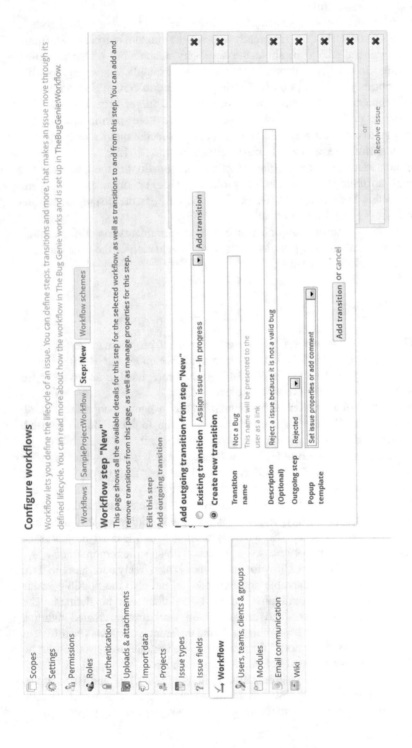

Fig. 8.4 Configuration of the defect workflow in The Bug Genie

practice, as the existing evaluations are detailed and already cover the most common requirements. This includes, among other things, a list of issues relevant to a particular user, an evaluation of the bug fixes planned or implemented per sprint, or the pain list mentioned below. Other reports, such as trend lines or cross-project evaluations, must be implemented using the JSON API.

In addition to the adaptability of various aspects, The Bug Genie also offers support for agile planning and prioritization of all issue types. Planning can be based on milestones as well as on continuous sprints (such as in Scrum). Figure 8.5 shows the central planning view of a sample project with two milestones. Issues can be prioritized directly from this view ("Priority" attribute) and the effort required to correct them can be estimated. Elements from agile process models can be found since the estimation can be carried out both in hours and in story points. The data recorded with it can also be displayed as a burndown chart and support the project manager with planning and control tasks.

In addition to various other standard functions such as fine-grained authorization control, comment functionality, integrated wiki, or integration with version control systems, The Bug Genie offers support for Triage using User Pain. As mentioned at the beginning of this chapter, this key figure is used to prioritize reported defects or change requests. Three additional attributes must be recorded for the implementation: "Bug Type," "Priority," and "Likelihood." The value for each of these attributes is specified by selecting an objective description with an associated numerical value between 1 and 5 or 1 to 7. For example, selecting "Will affect all users" for the "Likelihood" attribute results in a value of 5. In comparison, the value of the same attribute would have the value 1 if "Will affect almost no one" was selected. If all three values have been entered, the user pain can be calculated using the following formula (Cook, 2008):

$$\text{User Pain (UP)} = \frac{\text{Type} * \text{Likelihood} * \text{Priority}}{\text{Max.Possible Score}}.$$

Based on the numerical value between 1 and 100 determined in this way, the fix can then be planned objectively. In The Bug Genie, this is possible through a "Pain List," which lists all defects with the corresponding User Pain above a defined threshold value (Fig. 8.6).

8.3.2   Atlassian JIRA

Atlassian JIRA is also introduced and explained in Sect. 8.4.1 related to test planning and control. In this section, we look at the functionalities for defect management, which is also the original core area of JIRA (Atlassian, 2017). Studies on the prevalence of tools in agile environments clearly show that Atlassian is widely found there (between 53% (VersionOne Inc., 2017) and 62% (SwissQ Consulting AG, 2017), and specifically praise aspects such as straightforward installation and extensive traceability (Forrester Research, Inc., 2012)).

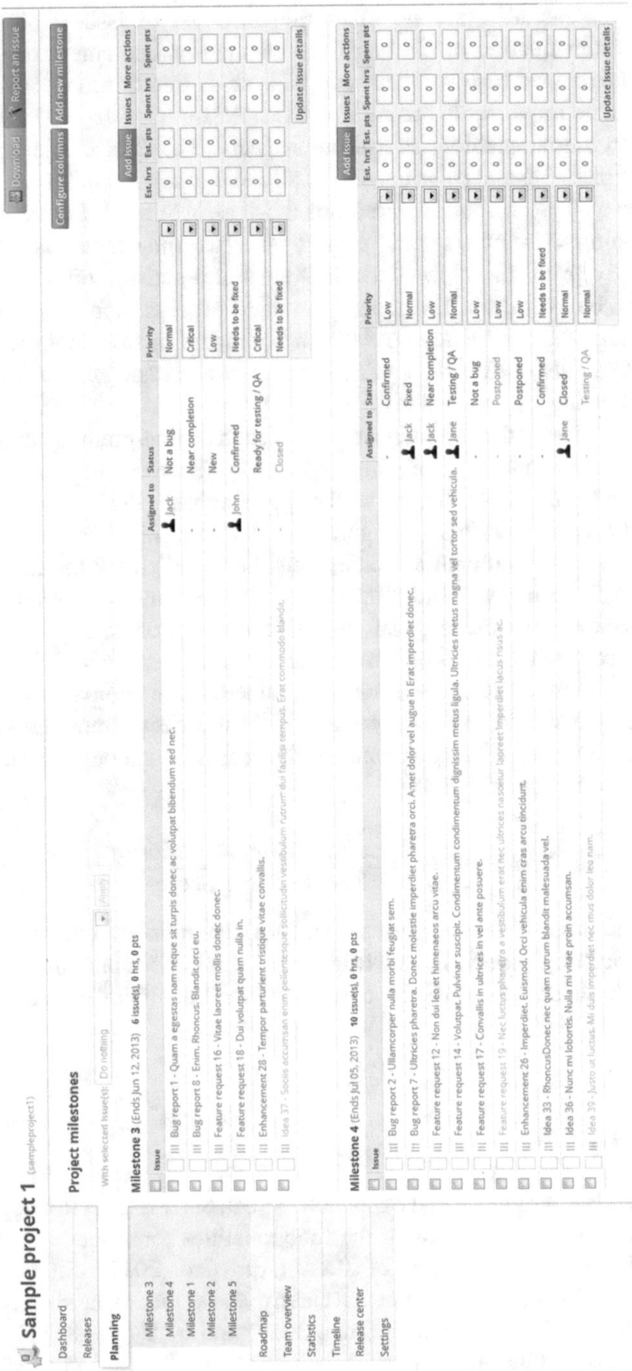

Fig. 8.5 Agile effort estimation and planning in The Bug Genie

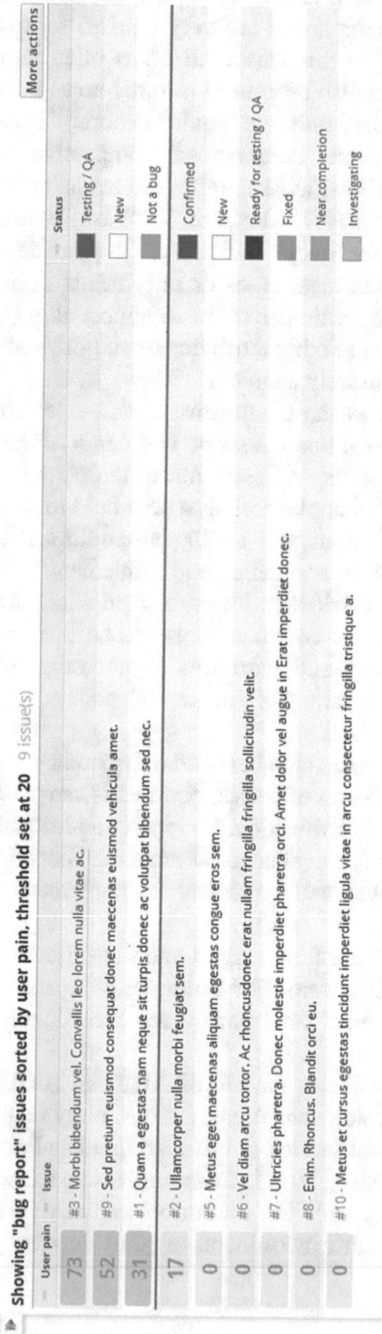

Showing "bug report" issues sorted by user pain, threshold set at 20 9 issue(s)

User pain	Issue	Status
73	#3 - Morbi bibendum vel. Convallis leo lorem nulla vitae ac.	Testing / QA
52	#9 - Sed pretium euismod consequat donec maecenas euismod vehicula amet.	New
31	#1 - Quam a egestas nam neque sit turpis donec ac volupat bibendum sed nec.	Not a bug
17	#2 - Ullamcorper nulla morbi feugiat sem.	Confirmed
0	#5 - Metus eget maecenas aliquam egestas congue eros sem.	New
0	#6 - Vel diam arcu tortor. Ac rhoncusdonec erat nullam fringilla fringilla sollicitudin velit.	Ready for testing / QA
0	#7 - Ultricies pharetra. Donec molestie imperdiet pharetra orci. Amet dolor vel augue in Erat imperdiet donec.	Fixed
0	#8 - Enim. Rhoncus. Blandit orci eu.	Near completion
0	#10 - Metus et cursus egestas tincidunt imperdiet ligula vitae in arcu consectetur fringilla tristique a.	Investigating

More actions

Fig. 8.6 Pain List in The Bug Genie

Like The Bug Genie, defect and ticket management is the original core function-ality of Atlassian JIRA, but it is also used in many other areas. This is possible because activities to correct a defect are very similar, for example, to activities to implement functionality. For this reason, JIRA is often introduced in practice as defect management but has also been used in other areas over time (Fig. 8.7).

The basic administrative unit are again generic "Issues," which represent instances of freely configurable "Issue types." Comparable to other tools to support defect management, the following issue types are available in the standard version: "Bug," "Improvement," "New Feature," "Task," and "Sub-task," agile configurations include "User Story" and "Epic." In practice, the standard and agile configuration is sufficient in most cases or only needs to be slightly expanded or adapted. Should specific conditions require it, almost all aspects of the issue types can be changed. In addition to other attributes or authorization schemes, the display of issue types can be extensively adapted.

As already mentioned, all these adjustments and extensions can be carried out, but it should not be forgotten that the scope and depth of the changes also increase the complexity of the necessary adjustments to the configuration and the mainte-nance effort of JIRA. For example, adding a new field to an existing issue type can be achieved with a few actions, but adding an additional issue type with a new workflow can take several days to define and implement.

The management of workflows with associated status and status transitions is done differently than in most common tools via an interactive online editor (see Fig. 8.8). In this, the processed workflow is not only displayed textually, but graphically as a status diagram. This makes adaptation in this area considerably easier than in comparable tools.

Cooperation with other team members and transparency are supported in a variety of ways: During the processing of issues, comments can be written at any time and images can be uploaded for clarification. To receive additional feedback for planning or prioritization, issues can be evaluated by team members or authorized customers. If an improvement receives enough votes, its implementation could be brought forward.

All changes to an issue are fully logged and thus allow for complete tracking of processes and activities afterward. For example, the question of who changed the status of a defect to "Resolved" can be answered immediately and any questions can be directed to the user.

Another aspect that facilitates the use of Atlassian JIRA in agile projects is the license model for small projects and organizations. Fully fledged defect management can be purchased as a cloud service or installed in a local datacenter with compara-tively small costs (Atlassian, 2017). Common extensions, for example for agile project management or for agile test execution, can also be purchased on the same terms. Correspondingly higher investments are only necessary for a larger number of users.

Agile Testing
AT board ▾

- Backlog
- Active sprints
- Releases
- Reports
- Issues
- Components
- Tests

PROJECT SHORTCUTS

Add a link to useful information for your whole team to see.

+ Add link

⚙ Project settings

Statistics Switch view ▾

All Issues	Added recently	Assigned to me	Unscheduled
Unresolved	Resolved recently	Reported by me	Outstanding
	Updated recently		

Unresolved: By Priority

Priority	Issues	Percentage
↑ Highest	64	21%
↑ High	65	21%
↑ Medium	61	20%
↓ Low	55	18%
↓ Lowest	61	20%

View Issues

Status Summary

Status	Issues	Percentage
In Progress	96	31%
To Do	119	39%
Done	91	30%

View Issues

Unresolved: By Assignee

Assignee	Issues	Percentage
Stefan	300	98%
Test Tester	6	2%

View Issues

Unresolved: By Component

Component	Issues
⊞ No Component	306

View Issues

Unresolved: By Issue Type

Issue Type	Issues	Percentage
🐞 Bug	42	14%

Fig. 8.7 Typical dashboard view in Atlassian JIRA

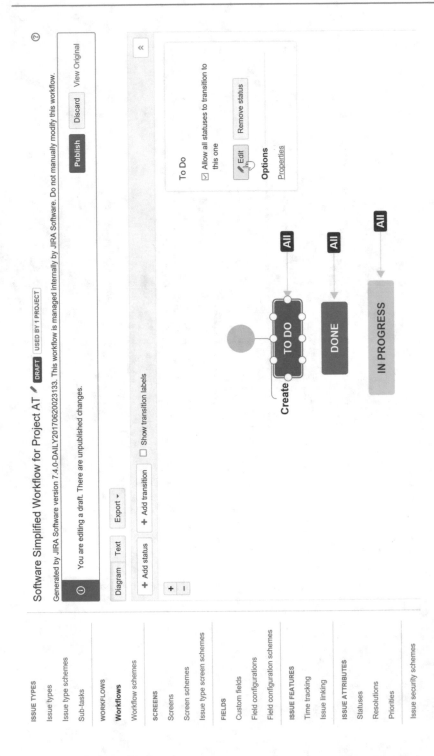

Fig. 8.8 Workflow editor in Atlassian JIRA

8.4   Test Planning and Control

Both the test planning and control as well as the process steps described in the following sections are part of the fundamental test process according to ISTQB® and are therefore fundamentally not designed for agile process models (ISTQB–International Software Testing Qualifications Board, 2012b). However, as mentioned in Sect. 3.1, Positioning of Test in Agile Projects, the activities described therein are also relevant for agile projects. The activities must always be tailored to the organizational and technical environment of a project and, if necessary, continuously adapted. This means, for example, that an extensive test plan, which specifies all phases of a test project in detail, cannot always be used effectively in agile projects. It may be replaced by a short description of the testing scope and other general conditions that allow the project team to work in an agile and flexible way.

For tools that are supporting test planning and control in agile projects, different criteria apply than for traditional projects:

- **Continuous prioritization and adaptation of test activities**
  The activities to be carried out while testing a system and their content are specified in traditional projects by one or more test plans. These plans are usually defined at an early stage, but in any case, before the actual test activities begin, and are rarely adapted to varying conditions in the further course of the project. As a result, the procedure laid down in the test plans and the actual execution can differ greatly from one another. In agile projects, however, the test activities and their content are treated similarly to requirements. This means that they are subject to continuous prioritization and adaptation and can, therefore, be reassigned, restructured, or even completely excluded from implementation.
- **Adaption of reporting**
  A main activity of test control is the observation of the test progress and the effort spent on it (ISTQB–International Software Testing Qualifications Board, 2012b). To be able to support these tasks efficiently, the fine-grained adaptability of reports in agile projects is particularly important. The difference to projects that are carried out according to traditional procedural models is that agile methods largely do without normative measures in this area as well, so as not to inhibit the self-organization of the project team. If a report proves not to be useful in a project or a metric is irrelevant, it will not be collected in further iterations (see also Sect. 3.1, Positioning of Test in Agile Projects).

  Similar to what is described in Sects. 8.1 and 8.3, the degree of this adaptation can vary greatly and should, if possible, be evaluated with regard to the specific project situation when choosing a tool.
- **Collecting project-specific metrics**
  Since in agile projects the collection of metrics and reporting in general also serve to control and change the team and the processes (Forrester Research, Inc., 2012), the measurement of the relevant data takes place more frequently than in traditional process models. To keep the effort for these additional tasks within

manageable limits, manual data entry is rarely possible and should therefore be automated to a large extent.

While most common tools support the collection of general metrics, it should be noted that very project-specific metrics may also need to be collected (see, for example, the Defect Density in Sect. 8.3 mentioned above). To guarantee this, the tool used should offer the possibility of defining additional metrics and conducting their measurement automatically.

Another aspect is that the mere collection of key figures is usually of no value to the project team. The actual purpose of the metric is only fulfilled when process improvements can be induced, or collaboration can be facilitated based on the metric. To achieve this, project-specific metrics are particularly helpful because, in contrast to general key figures, they represent a more specific measurement of the quality of a process (West & Hammond, 2010). To be able to offer a concrete added value for the project team, the visualization of the key figures is also essential. Self-organization and process improvement can only be optimally supported if the visualization is accessible and understandable for all project members.

- **Integration with Build Management or Release Management Systems**
  In traditional projects, test planning and control are often viewed in isolation from development activities. This can lead to additional efforts and potential for conflict arising from the coordination between development and quality assurance. For use in agile projects, any separation should therefore be reduced to a minimum.

There are various options for integration with build systems or generally with release management: For example, automated release notes can be generated and passed on to quality assurance. This clarifies which requirements, bug fixes, or changes have been implemented in a release and which quality assurance measures have to be carried out. For supporting test control, test effort can also be assigned to specific requirements, thus increasing the transparency of costs and effort. Another way to facilitate test planning through close integration with Release Management is to transfer reports from the automated component test. This allows the focus for manual testing to be placed specifically on those modules that have a low coverage with unit tests, and thus, a higher probability of defect occurrence. All these measures can contribute (Rothermel, Untch, Chu, & Harrold, 1999) to a more efficient and effective test execution, and thus, reduce the overall effort without reducing the desired quality level.

8.4.1   Atlassian JIRA

As described in the Sect. 8.3.2, Atlassian JIRA is used in many agile projects because it can be adapted very flexibly to the respective conditions and processes, and that it also offers a generic basis that can be used for many developments and test activities. JIRA also offers a comprehensive plug-in system and can be adapted or expanded even better and more efficiently.

This also includes test planning and control. In the sense of agile process models in entirety, JIRA can be used in many ways. The planning of test executions can be carried out using Scrum or Kanban boards, for example (Atlassian, 2017). To this end, Atlassian has completely integrated the former Green hopper expansion into JIRA. As shown in Fig. 8.9, both the test execution and the implementation of requirements can be conveniently planned in a uniform view. In the same way, the test activities to be carried out can be continuously prioritized and adapted.

Since all artifacts are based on the basis provided by JIRA (Issues), known functions such as time recording or linking of issues can also be used for user stories or test cases. This means that the test manager always has an overview of the test effort already used for a specific requirement, even in agile projects.

In addition to the tracking of the test effort already mentioned, the test manager can also use several other reports, all of which are supplied as standard. These include:

- Burndown chart
- Velocity chart
- Cumulative flow diagram
- Control chart

If the control and planning options provided by Scrum or Kanban are not sufficient for a project situation, test procedures can also be planned and carried out more formally. In Fig. 8.10, this is shown using the example of the Zephyr plug-in for JIRA (SmartBear Software, 2021).

Zephyr offers various standard reports for measuring test progress. Also, other project-specific key figures can also be collected and visualized using the JIRA gadgets and dashboard concept. The principle behind these concepts is that certain filters or queries are defined, which in turn serve as a database for different visualizations. This specification is recorded in an XML-based description language and does not necessarily have to be written by a developer. Not only the standard-issue types of JIRA, but also issue types provided by plug-ins can be used to capture more complex metrics.

The integration with build management or release management systems mentioned as a criterion is also possible with JIRA. As a result, the test team not only always has a current test version available, but it also has access to the results of unit tests, release notes, or the source code. If automated system tests are carried out in a project, for example with selenium, these can also be integrated into the build management and performed with each build. The current quality of a product for each new version is immediately apparent from the results of these tests. These reports can also be used to continue testing for planning and prioritization.

Backlog

Test View ▼   Board ▼

Q   QUICK FILTERS: Only My Issues   Recently Updated

Backlog
Active sprints
Releases
Reports
Issues
Components
Tests

Agile Testing
AT board ▼

PROJECT SHORTCUTS
Add a link to useful information for
your whole team to see.

+ Add link

∨ AT Sprint 1 6 issues

16/Aug/17 11:40 PM • 30/Aug/17 11:40 PM

- ☐ ↓ AT-19 Aspire shapelessness's kingliest tolerably waddling Cooke's responsively
- ☐ ↑ AT-51 Nonexistent longshoremen Aeschylus Valerian equalize
- ☑ ↓ AT-44 Congress's yens Tecumseh embarkation's underdog enabled democracy occupation's manned lushness
- ☑ ↑ AT-52 Prairies drugstore's Tallinn Armstrong gruffs pagoda's crabbed
- ✎ ↑ AT-86 Connolly's superpower's communication's Tussuad pullout recruits
- ☑ ↑ AT-78 Tiara unaltered tarrying Hells foxtrotted indelibly hula's

> AT Sprint 2 3 issues

Start Sprint   •••

Backlog 98 issues

Create Sprint

- ✎ ↑ AT-7 Bestrid Toulouse Lusitania's positing greying gassy privatest cuds momentousness Er
- ☑ ↑ AT-18 Reprove dawdles conveyors drug's blurring unctuous
- ☐ ↓ AT-20 Pompoms Lipton's pilloried Wolfe Apalachicola Dodoma
- ☐ ↑ AT-25 Lilliput Snyder Sherwood's antelopes adulterate crumpling
- ☐ ↑ AT-26 Malice's hysteria sanctification chiseler reprimand maxed orderly Plymouth's
- ☐ ↓ AT-46 Explosiveness's revealings redcaps purgatory's dentifrice's cosmoses Jefferson torqued

Project settings   «

Fig. 8.9 Planning user stories and test execution in Atlassian JIRA

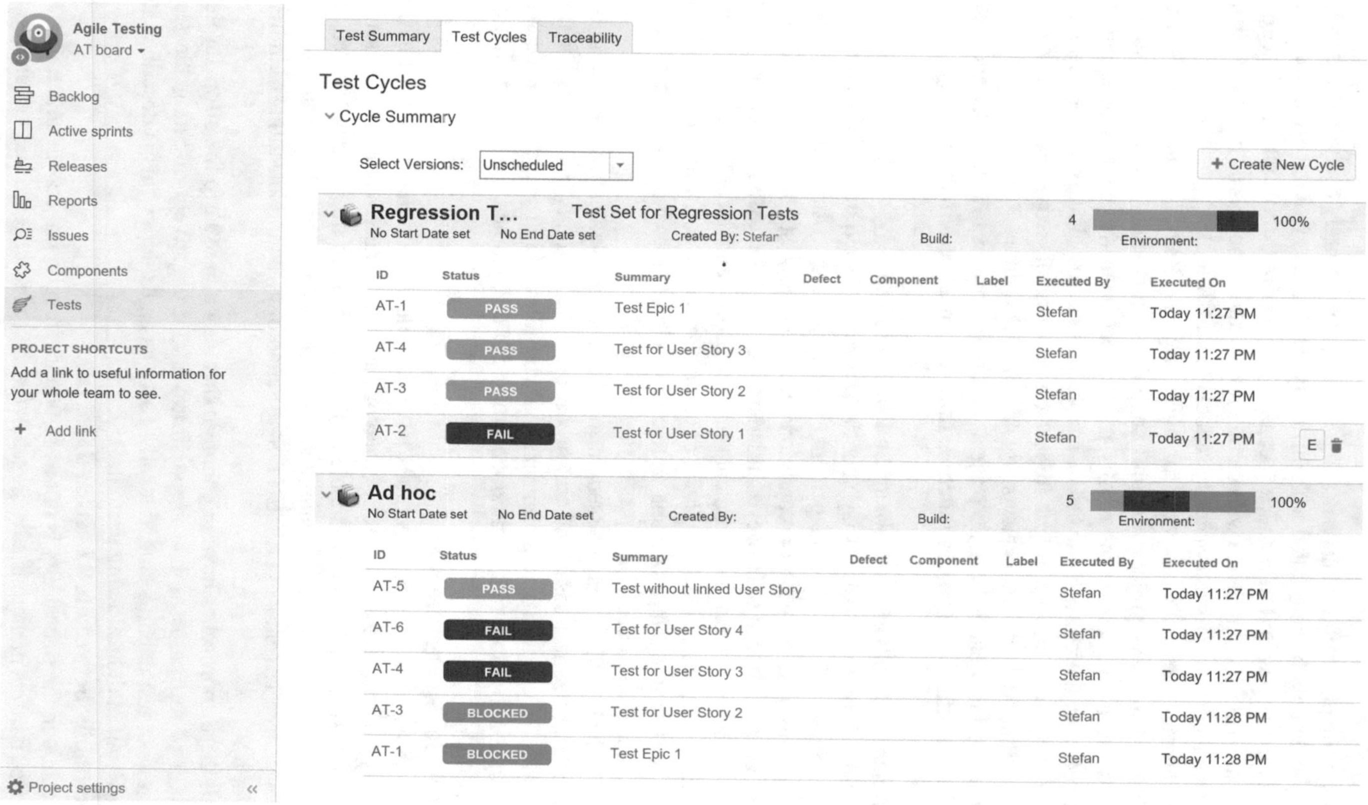

Fig. 8.10 Management of test procedures in Atlassian JIRA/Zephyr

8.5   Test Analysis and Test Design

Activities in the phase of test analysis and test design are strongly analytical and can, therefore, often only be automated with difficulty. This means that the use of tools in this area is rather low and in practice focuses on specialized tools which offer, for example, support for compliance with certain norms and standards or functionalities for the introduction of process maturity models (e.g., CMMI).

These aspects are rarely relevant for agile projects. Rather, generic tools are primarily used in these projects, or tool support is completely dispensed with—this might mean that important results of the test analysis are not adequately documented and therefore have little or no significance. However, the insights gained in this phase have a major impact on subsequent activities, as they can identify potential deficits at an early stage and offer solutions.

To achieve this benefit in agile projects, tools for use in test analysis and test design should offer very specific functionalities and meet certain criteria:

- **Documentation of risk assessment and business value**
  In traditional projects, risk management is primarily carried out and documented in the context of project management, which can only work optimally if the requirements and framework conditions are relatively stable and, above all, known at an early stage. However, this is usually not the case in agile projects: during an agile project, requirements are iteratively and incrementally refined until the development based on it can develop executable software. As a result, it is necessary to integrate risk management more closely into the development and test process than in traditional procedural models.

  The risks identified and assessed during risk management can subsequently be used to prioritize test cases and test procedures. Accordingly, test cases for the verification of a high-risk requirement should be given a high priority. If test cases are assigned to a low-risk requirement, they can be assigned a correspondingly low priority.
- **Support in test case creation**
  In the course of time, many methods have been developed that greatly simplify the design of test cases, either tool-based or manually. These include well-known techniques such as the decision table or the classification tree method as well as newer approaches from tool manufacturers such as the Linear Expansion Methodology by Tricentis (TRICENTIS Technology and Consulting GmbH, 2017a, b).

  All these approaches have in common that they aim to keep the effort for the creation of test cases as low as possible without negatively affecting the test coverage or test depth. Using Tricentis Tosca as an example, this is described in more detail in the following section.
- **Traceability between test basis and test case**
  Even though the traceability is not as important in agile projects as in traditional projects, it offers numerous advantages in the area of test design and test analysis. This requires at least a rudimentary link between the test basis and the test case to

be established also in agile projects. A fundamental challenge is an inherent effort that must be made to ensure consistent and valid traceability, and above all to maintain it. Therefore, in the evaluation of tools, special care should be taken to ensure that the link between the test basis and test cases can be carried out easily. If, for example, switching tools is necessary to establish traceability between two artifacts, in practice this often means that the connection is initially established but is not continuously adapted in the further course of time (e.g., due to lack of time).

- **Integration with requirements management**
  Another criterion that plays an essential role in the use of tools in agile projects is the integration with requirements management. As mentioned briefly at the beginning of the chapter, the test design in many projects leads to clarification or more detailed specification of requirements. The reason for this is that at the time the requirements are initially recorded, many aspects cannot yet be considered. In practice, this can lead to incompletely specified or inconsistent requirements. In agile projects, these deficits are additionally promoted due to the frequently occurring changes and thus the quality of the specification is endangered.

  If the artifacts are examined intensively from the test perspective during the test analysis and test design, the deficits mentioned quickly come to light and can be remedied in cooperation with the requirements management or the project management. To be able to reproduce this process at the IT level, it is advantageous if tools for test analysis and requirements management are closely integrated.

8.5.1   Risk-Based Testing in the Tosca Test Suite

The test tool Tosca by Tricentis, like many of the already mentioned tools, covers several areas of the traditional test process. However, the main reason why it is mentioned here is the extensive options for creating test cases and supporting the risk-based test.

Other areas where Tosca is used in practice are:

- Risk-based test structuring based on requirements
- Manual tests
- Automated function, regression, and integration tests
- Test management and test case management

The starting point for test case creation in the Tosca test suite is the risk assessment of the requirements. The evaluated requirements are combined in the test case design with test cases for their verification. One advantage of this approach is that the risk assessment of the requirement can be used directly to prioritize test case creation and test execution. Another advantage is that the test coverage is carried out depending on this rating. This means that a higher weighted requirement without associated test cases is rated more than a requirement with lower weighting without corresponding test cases.

Another approach to support test case creation is the Linear Q test methodology. It uses the aforementioned risk assessment of the requirements to generate a high test coverage. To be able to use this functionality, test-relevant entities must first be recorded as a data structure in Tosca. They are then combined with one another in such a way that there is a large test coverage with a small number of test cases. The hypothesis on which this approach is based is that applications generate 80% of the business value in 20% of the functionality. This imbalance means that testing the remaining 80% of functionality only ensures a business value of 20%.

Finally, another aspect that is particularly important for agile projects from a heterogeneous IT environment should be mentioned: integration with tools for requirements management. For example, the integration with Polarion (see also Sect. 8.2.1) is offered directly by Polarion. This supports continuous synchronization in both directions to ensure a consistent database in both systems. This means that it is not only possible for the requirements management to be conveniently mapped in Polarion and for Tosca only to verify them. Defects that have occurred during the test execution can also be transferred back to Polarion in Tosca to be able to make a statement about the progress of the implementation and the current quality level.

As with the tools already mentioned, only a small section of the entire range of functions of the Tosca test suite can be described in this chapter. For a more detailed description, reference is therefore also made to (Bucsics, Baumgartner, Seidl, & Gwihs, 2015) at this point.

8.6   Test Implementation and Test Execution

According to the official ISTQB® curriculum, test implementation and execution is that activity:

> During test implementation, the testware necessary for test execution is created and/or completed, including sequencing the test cases into test procedures, [...] During test execution, test suites are run in accordance with the test execution schedule. (ISTQB–International Software Testing Qualifications Board, 2018)

For tool use in projects, this means that a wide variety of activities must be mapped in these tools. Due to this complexity and the scope of functionality, there is a risk that the usability will decrease, and the training time and training effort will increase. As already mentioned, especially in agile projects these criteria must be considered in order not to endanger the acceptance of the tools.

To optimally support the phase of test implementation and test implementation, the following projects can be considered in the evaluation:

- **Support for exploratory tests and session-based testing**

  Chapter 5 discussed exploratory testing and session-based testing in detail, but did not describe the possibilities for tool support in this area. Most tools are limited to automating or simplifying the recording of the data that is normally manually noted; this can be achieved, for example, by saving the tester's activities (e.g., mouse clicks and keyboard input) and the associated screenshots. In the event of an occurring defect, this information is used directly for reproduction. If the integration with a tool for defect management is available, defect reports can also be created directly using this recording—without minimal distraction from the active test session. The test can then be continued immediately.

  To further improve the traceability and reproducibility of session-based testing, the session sheets normally recorded on paper (see Sect. 5.2.3, Session-Based Testing) can be digitally recorded. On the one hand, this facilitates the coordination between several testers and reduces the overlap between the tested modules or components. On the other hand, certain categories can be automatically recorded (e.g., duration of the test session, defects found, and description of the module/component tested) and thus evaluated. Session-based testing relies heavily on scripted or machine-controlled evaluations of the raw minutes of the sessions, so that the summarizing evaluation and reporting can be carried out as quickly and easily as possible.

- **Agile prioritization and planning of test procedures**

  As in many other areas, flexible prioritization and planning are basic requirements for tool support in agile projects. In contrast to traditional procedure models, test sequences that have been specified are rarely stable but are continuously expanded or adapted. The reason for this is that at the beginning of the test implementation and test execution, most often only one part of the system was implemented (incremental development) and even the development of this part does not have to be completed (iterative development). For this reason, not all test cases are specified in an early project phase and therefore cannot be scheduled for a test procedure. Only during the project, the other parts will be completed or expanded. Therefore, it is also necessary to adapt the previously defined test procedures; test cases that are no longer necessary can be excluded and requirements that are important for the end user can be tested more intensively.

- **Easy execution of test procedures**

  At the beginning of this chapter, the importance of usability for tools used in agile projects was described. In traditional tools, the steps to be performed and the data to be entered are presented in the form of a list for test execution. If a list item has been implemented by the tester, the success or failure of this step is recorded and, if possible, continued with the next item. This procedure means that the tester often must switch between the description of the test cases and the application to be tested, and thus, easily loses the overview and efficiency.

  For facilitating test execution, current tools offer different approaches: The test steps can be displayed, for example, in a sidebar or as an overlay. This eliminates the need to switch between several tools, and the application to be tested can always take up a large part of the screen space. The integration with defect management tools already mentioned makes the test even easier. The detection of defects is additionally facilitated by annotation tools, so that screen sections can be edited directly and annotated with comments and graphics. Some tools also offer the option of automatically transferring data from a central repository (e.g., from previous test runs) to previously defined fields. Especially with large numbers of test data, this functionality can mean a drastic reduction in test execution effort.

- **Test data and test environment management**
  As described in (ISTQB–International Software Testing Qualifications Board, 2012a), the generation and management of test data as well as the management of the test environment represent the main task for the test team. This challenge also arises in agile projects (SwissQ Consulting AG, 2017); due to the short iterations and the incremental approach of these projects, these tasks can require a lot of effort and costs to be put in and should therefore be automated or at least supported as optimally as possible by a tool.

  The test data management can be supported, for example, by generation or management or archiving (Kruse, 2011). This effort may not seem justified for trivial test cases, but if complex business domains or business processes are tested, the provision of high-quality test data represents a complex activity. This aspect is often only considered in the test automation, but it can also greatly reduce the effort required for manual test execution and increase the reproducibility of the test results.

  The management of the test environment is also of significant importance in large agile projects. If it is not considered, the informative value of the test results can be reduced, because in practice there is often a big difference between the test and the productive environment. This manifests itself, for example, in updates that have been carried out differently, missing interfaces, minor configuration differences, or also by other hardware that could potentially lead to problems (Cognizant, 2012). To avoid this, the test execution can be carried out in a virtualized environment, for example, which can be reset to a defined initial state before each iteration. Virtualization also enables the test to be carried out efficiently on a wide variety of platforms without having to purchase physical systems.

8.6.1   Microsoft Test Manager

The Microsoft Test Manager is an extension based on the Team Foundation Server to support test management and test execution and will be replaced by Azure Test plan as a cloud product. However, there are three reasons why the authors deliberately chose to describe the tool in the following section that will remain mostly the same with Azure Test plan:

Even if the initial effort for the introduction of Microsoft Test Manager is high, the extensive ALM functionalities of Team Foundation Server offer numerous synergy effects. These are particularly evident when not only individual projects are considered, but the use of tools takes place across projects. As a result, numerous elements of the tool chain can be reused for other activities without incurring any effort for the integration of different systems. For example, an existing Team Foundation Server from the development department can also be used as a server for the Test Manager without additional effort. In this way, the previously mentioned costs for the necessary IT infrastructure are put into perspective.

As recent studies have shown, Microsoft products have also become popular in the agile environment in recent years and have enjoyed various successes (SwissQ Consulting AG, 2017). This is also since Microsoft has created many options for integrating these products into agile process models (e.g., agile project templates for the Team Foundation Server).

The Microsoft Test Manager offers some particularly interesting and outstanding functionalities especially for the test execution activity, which can also mean a great increase in efficiency for agile teams. This includes, for example, the integration with the defect management of the Team Foundation Server, the simple administration of test suites, or the possibility to generate automated test scripts from manually performed test cases.

Once properly set up, testers and developers can access a relatively flexible set of virtual test environments to easily reproduce their debugging tests or repeat the tests in a variety of environment configurations.

The basic planning view of the Test Manager is shown in Fig. 8.11. From this mask, test cases can be created, their process defined, and these combined into test suites. The test cases can be linked with each other as well as with requirements from a Team Foundation Server project. In the test case description itself, not only can steps, test data, and expected results per step be defined, it is also possible to refer to "Shared steps." This avoids redundancies that would drastically increase the maintenance effort for the test design. The data necessary for implementation of a shared step (e.g., username and password for the shared step "Start application and login" can be given as parameters for each reference).

As already mentioned, the numerous functionalities to support the test execution are main reasons for mentioning the Test Manager at this point. In general, the execution of test procedures is simplified by the fact that the current steps are displayed directly next to the application to be tested. It is therefore not necessary to switch between several windows to read the specifications for the next test step. What this looks like in practice can be seen in Fig. 8.12. In addition to the description of the steps on the left, a defect has also occurred in this illustration, which the tester can immediately report to the development department via a defect report. This report automatically mentions the actions performed, and, if required, screenshots or video recordings of the test performance can be attached. This additional information allows for more efficient troubleshooting through development.

Another special feature of the Microsoft Test Manager is that it records all actions of the tester for each step during the execution of a test case. This "Action Recording" is stored centrally on the server and can easily be replayed if necessary (e.g., if it is carried out again during regression tests). In this way, repetitive and time-consuming work can be relieved of the tester. But it does not just make manual

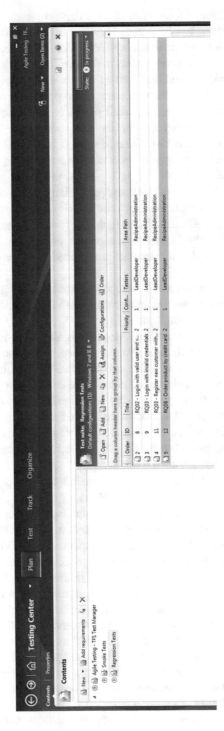

Fig. 8.11 Planning view of the Microsoft Test Manager

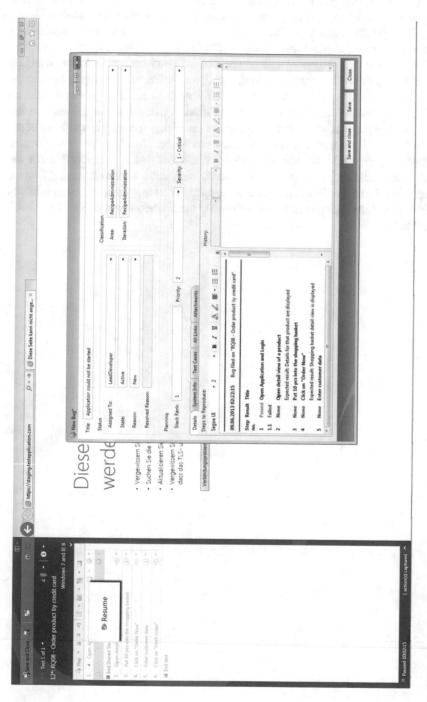

Fig. 8.12 Creation of a bug during the test execution

test execution easier. Since the actions of the tester were saved in the background, they can also be taken over by a test automation and converted into Coded UI test cases. This greatly reduces the time required to carry out a complete regression test and the focus of the manual tests can be shifted to other areas.

Finally, the test environment management of the Test Manager (referred to as Lab Management) should be mentioned in this chapter. A different configuration can be stored for each implementation, which determines how the test system should be configured. If a test is to be carried out on different platforms, this means that the tester does not have to set up this environment manually. It is sufficient to select the appropriate configuration and start the implementation. To offer this convenience, the Test Manager relies on distributed test controllers that are responsible for the actual implementation. In larger organizations, integration with Microsoft's System Center Virtual Machine Manager can also be used to create special test environments in virtualized form as required and to terminate them when test activities have been completed.

Education and Its Importance

9

> "My whole life has been a constant learning process until today."
> Herbert von Karajan, Austrian conductor (1908–1989).

This quote from Herbert von Karajan is more relevant today than ever before when we look at the trends in software development over the last few years, and especially if we plan to be on the cutting edge and keep up.

As far as the focus on software quality is concerned, the most important training and certification programs are certainly those of the ISTQB (International Software Testing Qualifications Board), the IREB (International Requirements Engineering Board), the Scrum Alliance®, the ASQF (Arbeitskreis für Software-Qualität und Fortbildung e. V.; Working group for software quality and further education r. a.), and the iSQI (International Software Quality Institute). Their training offerings are also constantly being adapted to the rapid developments in the IT industry, albeit often with a slight delay. In this context, the expansion of the ISTQB portfolio by the "Foundation Level Extension Agile Tester," the "Practitioner in Agile Quality (PAQ)" of iSQI, and the "IoT-QE—Quality Engineering for the Internet of Things" of ASQF should be highlighted.

Even if these training courses alone do not guarantee success in projects and in everyday work, they still offer the necessary methods. One should complement this knowledge with experience reports of successful and failed projects, as one can experience at numerous conferences. One should also bring expertise in from outside, if only to bring in a different perspective and to enrich the thematic discussion. And ultimately, of course, it's about developing along one's own experiences.

As they say:

> Clever people learn from other people's mistakes, the average man learns from his own mistakes, the fool does not learn at all. (Anonymous)

© The Author(s), under exclusive license to Springer Nature Switzerland AG 2021
M. Baumgartner et al., *Agile Testing*, https://doi.org/10.1007/978-3-030-73209-7_9

9.1   ISTQB Certified Tester

The ISTQB, founded in 2002 by the German, Swiss, and Austrian Testing Boards among others, has an impressive track record. The long-established levels (Foundation Level and the modules of the Advanced Levels Test Manager, Test Analyst, and Technical Test Analyst) recently broke the barrier of 670,000 certificates after eighteen years of existence.

The broad awareness of the ISTQB portfolio is also shown by the 2016 survey "Software testing in practice and research," which was conducted in 2015/2016 in German-speaking countries with over 1000 participants from the IT environment. Accordingly, approximately 88% of the surveyed managers and operational staff (testers, developers, analysts, etc.) were familiar with the ISTQB curricula. When this study was first carried out in 2011, this value was approximately 90% for testers and approximately 70% for management.

It is undisputed that the initiators of this ISTQB program contributed significantly to the professionalization of the entire profession of software testers.

While the focus in the syllabus/curricula published so far has been almost without exception on traditional approaches, the latest ISTQB product portfolio (January 2016) now includes its own "Agile" product family. Part of this is, for example, the "Foundation Level Extension Agile Tester" released in 2014. Meanwhile, there is also an Advanced Level course "Agile Technical Tester" released (Fig. 9.1).

"The classic ISTQB Certified Testers Syllabi have become useless for testing in an agile environment," some testers who work agile in an agile project told us some time ago. Are they right? Like so often in life, it all depends. We consider the contents of the ISTQB curricula (Foundation as well as Advanced Level) to be "Must-haves," which one "has to be able to do" as an Agile Tester, i.e., virtually like a driving license if one wants to drive a car.

The basics conveyed in the ISTQB curricula form an important basis for every tester, regardless of whether in a traditional or agile environment. What is important for both is how flexibly the testers can adapt and apply this knowledge in the respective situation. Gone are the days when it was said that only a test concept that has at least 30 pages is a good test concept; gone are the days when nothing could be done without a test specification to be defined beforehand.

Not to forget that there are still many companies that still work traditionally for a variety of reasons (such as monolithic systems and burned-in organizational structures). In part, however, due to the "agile wave," adjustments to the procedure are also noticeable—albeit in a modified form (e.g., the business analyst acts as a kind of product owner).

With the publication of the curriculum for the "Foundation Level Extension Agile Tester" and through the adjustments in the curriculum of the Certified Tester Foundation Level (2018), the ISTQB critics have become quieter, as now, building on the fundamentals of testing, the bridges for testing in an agile environment have been built.

A brief review or status quo of the current situation is helpful for a better understanding:

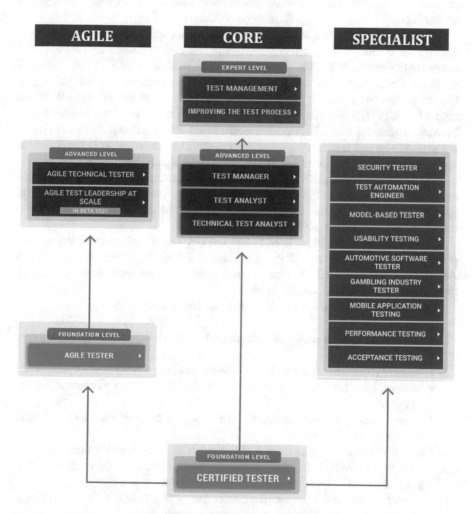

Fig. 9.1 ISTQB product portfolio (Version 2021)

Scrum is very popular. Comparing the above surveys (2011 and 2016), we can see that companies are increasingly working according to an "agile process model". In 2011 it was around 29%, and in 2016 it was around 43% (Haberl, Spillner, Vosseberg, & Winter, 2011; Vosseberg, Spillner, & Winter, 2016).

In XP teams (eXtreme Programming), a dedicated tester is often not in demand, because here the entire team must live up to the quality standards for the delivered products. Therefore, everyone in the team must develop test skills. And in Scrum? Well, Scrum is being used for all kinds of projects and collaborations by now. There are even specialized test teams that work according to Scrum. "Can they really do that?" we hear doubters saying again. We say with conviction: "If it helps the products to reach the customer more quickly and with the right quality, then yes!", as that is one of the primary goals of agile methods.

It does not mean that the best practices in testing for agile projects have had their day, on the contrary: The more efficiently the test is set up and implemented, the better for the results. We could also say: We need professionals who know what to do if an overall picture of quality is required in the shortest possible time. The ISTQB certificates represent these best practices like no other standard. With the help of the ISTQB Foundation Extension Agile Tester, the long overdue gap between traditional and agile world is now closed. Profound test bases are one of the main pillars that testers must bring with them. The second pillar is the ability to apply the test solution approaches flexibly and individually in an agile context.

The Agile Manifesto is still relevant to approach agile methods in general. It helps agile teams to get back to basics. The value system of the Agile Manifesto with its four pairs of values shows a clear skepticism toward processes/tools, extensive documentation, and strict pursuit of plans.

To understand how agile relates to the ISTQB world, we compare the twelve principles of the Agile Manifesto with the learning objectives of the ISTQB Advanced Certificate (and the content in it). We also compare how compatible agile thinking and ISTQB standards are.

As a reminder, all twelve agile principles are listed here:

1. Our top priority is to satisfy customers early and consistently with the delivery of valuable software.
2. Changing requirements are welcome, even late in the development cycle: Agile processes take advantage of changes for the competitive advantage of the customer.
3. Deliver working software frequently, a few weeks to a few months apart, with shorter intervals preferred.
4. Specialists and developers must work together daily throughout the project.
5. Set up projects suitable for motivated individuals: Give them the framework and support they need. Trust them to master their tasks.
6. A direct conversation is the most effective and efficient way to exchange information between or within development teams.
7. Working software is the most important measure of progress.
8. Agile processes promote sustainable development. Sponsors, developers, and users should be able to keep up their pace of work over the long term.
9. Constant attention to technical quality and good design promotes agility.
10. Simplicity—the art of maximizing the amount of work avoided—is essential.

11. The best architectures, requirements, and designs come from self-organizing teams.
12. The team regularly thinks about how it can become even more effective. It then adjusts its behavior accordingly.

To list all the learning objectives of the ISTQB standard, Certified Tester Advanced Level (ISTQB—International Software Testing Qualifications Board, 2012a) here would go too far. In the following, the chapters of the curriculum are to be understood as representatives of the learning objectives in these chapters.

First, we want to look at each of the twelve agile principles individually and to what extent they support the learning objectives from the ISTQB curriculum or question them. Analyzing the learning goals per each agile principle results in the following (not entirely surprising) evaluation (Fig. 9.2):

As we can see, some principles shake the foundations of the ISTQB: frequent changes, more communicating than documenting, no clearly separated roles in the project, and finally teams that continuously adapt their processes. But these principles do work. The trick is that all twelve are closely related. One principle complements the other. If something is missing, the agile process model (whichever is chosen) breaks down.

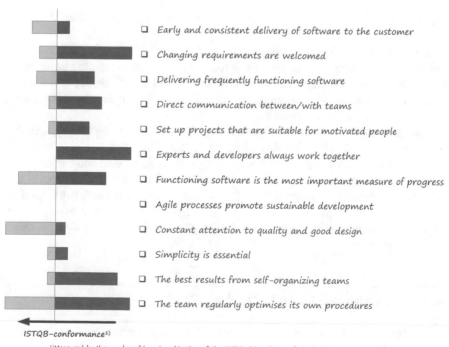

☐ Early and consistent delivery of software to the customer
☐ Changing requirements are welcomed
☐ Delivering frequently functioning software
☐ Direct communication between/with teams
☐ Set up projects that are suitable for motivated people
☐ Experts and developers always work together
☐ Functioning software is the most important measure of progress
☐ Agile processes promote sustainable development
☐ Constant attention to quality and good design
☐ Simplicity is essential
☐ The best results from self-organizing teams
☐ The team regularly optimises its own procedures

ISTQB-conformance[1]

[1] Measured by the number of learning objectives of the ISTQB-CTAL that conform (light) or do not conform (dark) to the respective agile principle

Fig. 9.2 Overview of agile practices vs. ISTQB chapter/learning objectives (Klonk, 2013)

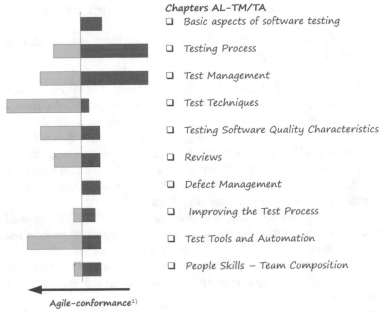

Chapters AL-TM/TA
- ❏ Basic aspects of software testing
- ❏ Testing Process
- ❏ Test Management
- ❏ Test Techniques
- ❏ Testing Software Quality Characteristics
- ❏ Reviews
- ❏ Defect Management
- ❏ Improving the Test Process
- ❏ Test Tools and Automation
- ❏ People Skills – Team Composition

Agile-conformance[1]

[1]measured by the number of learning objectives of the respective chapters of the ISTQB-CTAL that conform (light) or do not conform (dark) to the agile principles

Fig. 9.3 Overview of ISTQB chapters/learning objectives vs. agile practices (Klonk, 2013)

But is the ISTQB standard obsolete for agile projects? To answer this question, we are now changing the way we look at it and assessing each learning objective of the advanced level to determine whether it is compatible with the agile principles (and thus forms a valuable enrichment for project practice in agile teams). This leads to the following evaluation (Fig. 9.3):

The chapters cover the respective learning objectives. It can be clearly seen that the contents of the ISTQB Certified Tester Advanced Level Test Analyst (especially test procedures, reviews, and tools) support agile procedures well and can therefore also be an important enrichment for agile teams in test practice. The process and management view of the original ISTQB standard, on the other hand, is too stuck in traditional (but proven) patterns. An agile employee will have little use for these. Still, they have the curriculum for the ISTQB Agile Extension on their desk, or rather on their task board.

9.2   Practitioner in Agile Quality (PAQ)

The ISTQB syllabuses describe all currently common procedural models, including the agile ones, but the focus is clearly on the traditional approach.

What we find there labeled as "agile" is far from enough to "survive" in agile projects. "If you want to follow the state of the art, you have to switch to Agile."

Fig. 9.4 Practitioner in Agile
Quality—Branding

Such and similar statements have been heard increasingly in the IT scene in recent years. And wherever a new market appears, there are, of course, many who develop offers for it—of course also tons of new training offers. But: Is there also a professional, detailed, qualified training for agile testers?

In 2009, the International Software Quality Institute (iSQI) took this as an opportunity to commission the development of a professional training for agile testers. To ensure sustainability, the training was to end with an extensive examination as a precondition for certification.

At the beginning of 2011, the time had come: The Certified Agile Tester (CAT) was born and advertised in roadshows in Germany and Austria. Unfortunately, the CAT was soon withdrawn from the market due to disputes of the licensors, but a similar, comparable, and updated training was born: Practitioner in Agile Quality (Fig. 9.4).

9.2.1 Motivation

The (International Software Quality Institute GmbH, 2018) Practitioner in Agile Quality website describes it this way:

Agile software development allows organizations to respond to changing market dynamics with speed and confidence and get to market faster with products that delight their customers and add value to their experience.

The A4Q[1]—Practitioner in Agile Quality (PAQ) immerses participants in agile practices with an emphasis on the key competencies essential for high-performing agile teams working together collaboratively to increase value to the business and the customer. A Practitioner in Agile Quality can use agile as an effective pathway to accelerate the delivery of quality software.

Agile quality is the collective responsibility of the whole team. PAQ certification is not just for testers but anyone, and everyone, in the team who needs to continuously deliver better products, services, and user experiences using agile.

The course builds on existing testing, software quality management, and agile theory inspiring and building confidence through hands-on exercises and experiential learning aligned to the PAQ Competency Framework. The final practical

---

[1]Alliance for Qualification

assessment ensures that PAQ holders have demonstrated that they can achieve the expected PAQ competency outcomes.

This sums it up well—during the three-day training, the participants get to know all areas of the agile world, how to contribute to the team goals as testers, and how to optimally use their strength: testing. While the theoretical parts from the Agile Manifesto to frameworks, processes, and methods up to essential practices such as Continuous Integration and version management are only covered as much as is necessary for the overall understanding of the agile approach, the focus of the training lies on "Individuals and Interactions." This means: many practical, very detailed, and well-prepared joint exercises in a team as well as an intensive exchange of experiences between the participants.

The trainers, therefore, have a very lively training concept that is very focused on the participants and provides enough space to incorporate the experience of the trainers with examples from their previous projects.

> "An interesting training experience with many facets and eye-opening experiences!"Feedback from a participant after a successful training.

9.2.2   Training Content

It was particularly important for the training developers to provide comprehensive basic training so that "Practitioner in Agile Quality" can acquire all the skills and abilities required to operate efficiently in agile projects and to bring maximum added value to the team.

The training covers the following topics (Fig. 9.5):

Day 1: Practitioner in Agile Quality
The first day starts with a basic introduction to the agile principles: The Agile Manifesto, principles and methods, and the different roles are explained. The aim

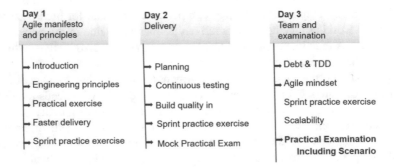

Fig. 9.5 Practitioner in Agile Quality—Learning Objectives in detail (International Software Quality Institute GmbH, 2018)

is to bridge the gap between the traditional and the agile approach. In addition, a deep dive into the secrets of faster delivery will be made.

Day 2: The PAQ Is Also Characterized by a High Percentage of Practice; There Are Already Some Interactive Exercises on the First Day Practitioner in Agile Quality

On the second day, after a short stand-up meeting, the participants will deal with essential topics such as planning, continuous testing, and what is meant by Built-in Quality.

The afternoon is dedicated to practice and a "mock practical exam": A web shop is available for the teams to test, where they can simulate individual sprints. This allows the teams to practice agile and realistic testing.

Day 3: Practitioner in Agile Quality

The third and final day focuses on one of the most underestimated issues in agile development: dealing with debt. With a deep insight into the agile mindset and a brief outlook on scalability, the agile picture is completed.

9.3 ISTQB Certified Tester Foundation Level Extension Agile Tester

It took a long time, but in 2014 the ISTQB had also reacted and launched a curriculum for agile testers.

The curriculum covers the topics:

(a) Agile software development (basics of agile software development and agile approaches)
(b) Fundamental principles, practices, and processes of agile testing (differences between traditional and agile approaches in the test, etc.)
(c) Methods, techniques, and tools of agile testing (test pyramids, test quadrants, techniques, and tools)

Basically, everything a tester needs in an agile environment and for a good start in the field of "agile testing." One of our criticisms is that the curriculum is the basis for only a two-day course. In our opinion, the abundance of curriculum content leaves far too little space for practice and exercises.

9.4 Individual Trainings (Customized Trainings)

In addition to the established certification training courses such as Certified Scrum Master or Certified Product Owner, which have been offered for years, other organizations and companies have now also adapted their offers to Agile.

So now there is also the Agile Certified Practitioner (PMI-ACP®) (International Consortium for Agile (ICAgile), 2018), Training on Agile Requirement Engineering, Agile Business Analysts, Agile Developer, and others.

Another very mature certification has become more international: the ICAgile Schema (International Consortium for Agile (ICAgile), 2018). There are a couple of training provider which prepare trainings around this curriculum (like ICAgile Fundamentals and ICAgile Programing).

Also, in the testing there are specific trainings for almost every practice: be it TDD, ATDD, exploratory testing, flexible architectures, agile management, or, for example, training especially for testers who come from the traditional project experience and now are switching into agile teams.

Especially when participating in an agile project for the first time, there is often great uncertainty about the roles and tasks, and even the justification of having a dedicated tester. In workshops, lasting a maximum of one day, the participants learn to understand the agile approach and the differences from the traditional test approach and often to experience it in a playful way.

This type of short training is particularly interesting for those team members who, after switching to "Agile," know little or nothing about the benefits testers can bring to an Agile team. In addition to the technical skills, participants in these training courses also collect several arguments as to why it is important to include expert testers in a team, especially in an agile environment.

9.4.1   Recommended Approach for the Introduction of Agility

Learning from many consultations and practical project assignments, we have put together the experiences for a successful agile transformation aided by individually designed training courses.

9.4.1.1   Inventory of the Actual Situation

This phase includes a critical analysis of all processes and approaches that have an impact on project execution. What are these? For example, there would be the entire software lifecycle:

- From the introduction of the business idea
- About recording the requirements
- The analysis and design of the solution
- The construction of the project framework, database structures
- Up to the integration of the test including release planning

All management processes must be considered, which could affect the project either directly during execution or indirectly by requesting a weekly progress report including budget development for all projects.

9.4.1.2 Dependency Analysis

Definition of everything that must be delivered in the context of a project or what is subject to which dependencies.

9.4.1.3 Define the "New" Goal

The "desired environment" is derived from the dependency analysis. First drafts emerge here, but also concrete approaches on how to work in the future.

The team is also working on a first version of the strategy: How should they go about achieving their goal?

9.4.2 Organization

Engage professionals who have already had successful and above all practical experience with their chosen method. Beware of the theorists or "Evangelists" in cases like these.

Above all, in addition to its decision to handle projects in an agile manner, management must also create the framework for the organizational requirements within the company. To free the new agile team from the previous control mechanisms and management structures is particularly important. This sometimes requires enormous courage to "let go" and to fully trust the team for this project.

9.4.3 Pilot Phase

As a starting point, it is important to identify a project as a pilot project that can be compared with most other projects in the organization.

- **Identify a project that can act as a pilot project**
  This should be small enough to be able to keep an overview, but again large enough so that at the end of the project the results and findings can be applied to other projects in the organization. It is ideal if the team can try out different variants of the chosen approach to find out what suits the team best without having to immediately and constantly justify project success and budget.
- **Nominate and define the team**
  Remembering the Agile Manifesto: "Individuals and Interactions," when putting together an agile team, we make sure that we nominate people who are open to the agile idea or approach, who are open to trying new things, and, above all, who enjoy teamwork. One of the most common reasons why agile teams fail is a lack of staff with the necessary skills. The changes in corporate culture required by the transition to Agile and the lack of full management support by retaining old power structures (Rüssel, 2012) are further critical factors on which agile success depends.

- **Setting up, team building, training the team, and gaining practical experience in the new approach**
  If the team is set up, they must be trained in the agile methods and process. The most important thing is to enable learning from their own practical experience. This means working with the new agile processes for some sprints with continuous improvement. Particular attention must be paid to the fact that everyone in the team constantly gives each other feedback and that results and experiences are evaluated and optimized (inspect and adapt), which is also a Kaizen principle. Following this "warm-up phase," it is important to keep repeating this procedure in the normal project environment and, after each cycle/sprint, to critically examine the results and the targets set (definition of done) and the efficiency as a team: What went well, what needs to be improved… Here the moderator (in Scrum projects this is the Scrum Master) is required to keep this retrospective at a factual level. The goal here is that the team learns from experience and continuously improves. Personal sentiments of individual team members are also to be considered, but as already mentioned, on a factual basis (Derby & Larsen, 2006).

9.4.4 Rollout in the Organization

- **Implementation of what has been learned; field test for further projects; definition of rules and framework**
  Once the pilot project has been successfully completed and the organization has consolidated its learning experience, it can also be transferred to other project teams. It has proven useful to define framework conditions. These can increase the common understanding of quality, the use of tools, the programming language, or, if the organization is subject to certain regulations, the scope of documentation. This definition of general conditions for an agile framework has a great advantage: it allows that individual resources can switch between teams if necessary, generating greater flexibility.
- **Ongoing optimization of agile processes**
  This optimization phase for every project and every team as well as the organization itself needs to be kept continuously improving the defined agile framework and its methods.

> **Hint**
> If we realize that the fairy tales of some "Hardcore agile consultants" do not come true, i.e., that the "Charming Jeannie" or the "Ghost of Aladdin's Wonder Lamp" are missing, who will conjure quality into our deliverables or suddenly turn our piles of "almost-finished stories" into "finished stories" with a spell, we have arrived in the reality of software engineering. Quality has always been a success factor and does not suddenly vanish into thin air just

(continued)

because another method of product development has now become established—on the contrary.

Kent Beck (Beck, 2003) and many other representatives of agile movement repeatedly emphasize that testing and quality are a very important elixir of life in agile working.

We can only encourage everyone to take matters into their own hands and train themselves or their team to become testers in an agile environment that focus on exactly one thing: to lead the team to success. As a "quality coach," they should take care that the team can record their success for themselves at the end of a sprint, since the quality is guaranteed and all possible "preventers" such as bugs, missing evidence, or unverified acceptance criteria could be discovered and eliminated in time.

One more thing should be mentioned here: To be innovative and to remain innovative, it sometimes takes courage to try new things. These are new processes, approaches, etc. that break up old patterns, complement existing ones or enable new approaches to develop oneself and the organization.

However, we need to pay attention to the right timing: It is rarely advisable to try new approaches for strategic projects for the first time if an organization's survival depends on it. On the other hand: The best time to change is NOW.

Retrospective

10

When the first German edition of this book was published in 2013, "Agile" in terms of a new approach for software development was already more than a decade old, but still new and unknown in many places. With the release of this English edition, it is almost 20 years since the Agile Manifesto was announced. In the meantime, agile software development has become widely accepted and the principles associated with it are slowly permeating the entire organization, beyond IT boundaries. This long period shows once again how long it takes for new approaches and ideas—even in the fast-moving IT world—to become widely accepted. The reasons for this are manifold.

- **From idea to success**
  In the beginning, there were formulations of values and principles. Buzzwords and sometimes provocative formulations by a group of dedicated experts, who were perhaps also frustrated by the tediousness of software projects. The theses posed at that time had to be explained and understood. It is quite possible that even the signatories of the Agile Manifesto went home from the workshop in Utah with different interpretations. It is, therefore, not surprising that there exist so many different interpretations of "Agile" even today—in books, at conferences, in projects that are carried out. But maybe that does not matter. It is much more important that with the right application of agile principles the projects are carried out more successfully. This proof first had to be demonstrated and also presented to the public, i.e., marketed. This is not so easy, because who likes to admit that they have worked poorly in the past, even if it works better now with agile methods? Most companies that started with "Agile" also had a learning curve, often from several projects. Until a few years ago, it was mostly just consultants who went on tour with "Agile" and tried to sell the new approach and probably also themselves. However, in the last few years, an increasing number of project managers from large and well-known companies have been reporting on how they have made the "Agile idea" successful in their companies. Agile Software Development and Agile Testing have grown out of their infancy and

have reached the maturity necessary for worldwide distribution. And that took time.

- **Gaining certainty**

  An essential motivation for the traditional approaches was the expectation to gain certainty regarding the expected results, deadlines, and costs through a structured, repeatable, and widely standardized procedure. And after many years of empirical project analysis, these parameters could even be determined or planned or included in risk considerations within certain known ranges. The knowledge of realistic expectations in this context has developed over many years. Planning and estimation have a lot to do with experience and trust in the people involved. Methods and techniques are just tools. In the agile world, these aspects, which are particularly important for management, are completely questioned or dealt with in a completely different way. Understandably, this creates uncertainty—and not only in management. The certainty and the repeatability for a reliable project execution must first be obtained by the executors in the projects and then conveyed to the management. But just as a slalom racer only achieves confidence through intensive, 100% training based on perfect technique, agile teams and their employees will only develop a level of confidence that radiates across all management levels to the entire company after a few projects. And this does not happen overnight either.

- **Geographical distribution**

  An interesting aspect in the worldwide spreading of innovations in the methodological field of software development is geography. In contrast to technical innovations, which often spread much faster, the methodical, optimizing, quality-enhancing approaches have usually spread very slowly from continent to continent. It almost seems as if they are not distributed via the Internet, but via ocean liners. The same applies to the topic of "Agile": As early as February 1986, Japanese professors Hirotaka Takeuchi and Ikujiro Nonaka published their article "The New Product Development Game" in the *Harvard Business Review* (Takeuchi & Nonaka, 1986). Using case studies from the manufacturing industry, they demonstrated the advantages of holistic development approaches, drawing the analogy with rugby (Rugby Approach) and also using the term "Scrum" in this context. The authors see the following six management characteristics of a new product development process: built-in instability, self-organizing project teams, overlapping development phases, multi-learning, subtle control, and organizational transfer of learning. Four years later, in 1990, one of the first definitions of Scrum in the software development industry is found in the book "Wicked Problems, Righteous Solutions: A Catalog of Modern Engineering Paradigms" by Peter DeGrace and Leslie Hulet Stahl (DeGrace & Stahl, 1990). The journey to the American continent is accomplished. There, the ideas circulated across the continent for another 10 years until in July 2000 Martin Fowler (Fowler, 2000) published his article "The New Methodology," and finally, in February 2001, 17 software experts signed the "Agile Manifesto "in Utah (Beck, et al., 2001). Another 15 years later, "Agile" began its victory march throughout Europe.

- **The entire company is affected**

  Introducing Agile is not about new programming languages for development, new tools for testing, or alternative analysis methods for requirement engineers. Agile transformation affects the entire organization and almost all roles represented in the company, which means that the new, agile approaches can only take effect step by step. First, understanding and appreciation for "Agile" must be developed, concerns must be dispelled, and the application of the new methods must be rolled out across the entire project landscape. This can take a long time in a large company.

- **Change process**

  Finally, it should not be forgotten that this is a change process in the sense of a cultural change and a new way of thinking. If a few years ago it was about the agilization of software development projects, today it is about the agile transformation of entire companies. A process and some methods can be introduced quickly. But a cultural change in how we interact with each other does not happen overnight.

What we can deduce from the above is that a certain amount of patience is needed when implementing agile ideas; Rome was not built in a day either. But we testers can contribute a lot to the evolution and especially to the further advancement of the agile approaches. At the beginning of the agile development, the role of the tester was often questioned. This has changed in the meantime, and it is even more important for the tester to become a codesigner of the processes. This is especially important because most agile theories and practices have been developed from the perspective of the software developer, the programmer. This good fundament must be enriched by the aspects of testing and quality assurance. The testers and quality managers are also an excellent link out of the project into an organization that is fully involved in the agile transformation process. In this sense, the tester also conveys the feeling of security to both the customer and the management. However, it must be clear to both the stakeholders and the team that—especially in the agile world—the tester is not solely responsible for the quality of the product. No longer as a tester but as a Quality Coach, he or she has the function of a catalyst who integrates all stakeholders into the quality aspects and measures. This particularly includes the product owner. The team stands for the product, and not individual roles for individual aspects of the solution. However, there is a widespread awareness that a test that can be relied upon is best performed by trained experts. The self-confidence of every tester should also be based on the fact that he or she plays a decisive role in whether or not a project or software product is a success from the idea to its application in the user's everyday work. In addition, we authors look forward to hearing more about success stories from your perspective as a tester at national and international conferences in the future.

References

Adzic, G. (2011). *Specification by example*. London: Manning.

Ambler, S. W. (2009, Dez.). *The agile scaling model (ASM)*. Retrieved February 2017, from https://www.researchgate.net/publication/268424579_Adapting_Agile_Methods_for_Complex_The_Agile_Scaling_Model_ASM_Adapting_Agile_Methods_for_Complex_Environments

Ambler, S. W., & Lines, M. (2012). *Disciplined agile delivery: A practitioner's guide to agile software delivery in the enterprise*. Upper Saddle River, NJ: IBM Press.

Anderson, D. J. (2010). *KANBAN–successful evolutionary change for your technology business*. Blue Hole Press.

Atlassian. (2017). *JIRA Software–Vorgangs- und Projektverfolgung für Softwareteams*. Retrieved 2017 from https://de.atlassian.com/software/jira

AutoIt Consulting Ltd. (2017). *AutoIT automation and scripting language*. Retrieved 2017 from http://www.autoitscript.com

Bach, J. (1999, November). James bach on risk-based testing. *Software Testing & Quality Engineering, Band 1, Nr. 6*, p. 22.

Bach, J. (2000, November). Session-based test management. *STQE Magazine, Vol. 2. Nr. 6*, p. 32.

Beck, K. (1999). *Extreme programming explained*. Amsterdam: Addison-Wesley Longman.

Beck, K. (2000). *Extreme Programming–Das Manifest*. München: Addison-Wesely.

Beck, K. (2003). *Test driven development*. Reading, MA: Addision-Wesely.

Beck, K., Beedle, M., van Bennekum, A., Cockburn, A., Cunningham, W., Fowler, M., Grenning, J., Highsmith, J., Hunt, A., Jeffries, R., Kern, J., Marick, B., Martin, R., Mellor, S., Schwaber, K., Sutherland, J., & Thomas, D.. (2001). *Manifesto for agile software development*. Retrieved 2017 from http://agilemanifesto.org/

Beecham Research. (2021). *World of IoT sector map*. Retrieved 2021 from Beecham Research: http://www.beechamresearch.com/article.aspx?id=42

Bender, H., Fuhrmann, R., Kittel, H. U., Menze, B., Müller, J. E., Nadolny, D., & Sneed, H. (1983). Software Engineering in der Praxis: Das Bertelsmann-Modell. *CW-Publikationen*.

Bertram, D., Voida, A., Greenberg, S., & Walker, R. (2010). Communication, collaboration, and bugs: the social nature of issue tracking in small, collocated teams. *Proceedings of the 2010 ACM conference on Computer supported cooperative work (CSCW '10)*, pp. 291–300.

Binder, E. (2016). *Service Virtualisierung: "Ich sehe was, was du nicht siehst ...".* Retrieved 2017 from http://www.anecon.com/blog/service-virtualisierung-in-agilen-projekten/

Bucsics, T., Baumgartner, M., Seidl, R., & Gwihs, S. (2015). *Basiswissen Testautomatisierung*. Heidelberg: dpunkt.verlag.

Budd, T., & Majoros, M. (1978, Dez.). Experiences in the budapest software test factory. *Proc. of IEEE Workshop on software testing*, p. 112.

Cognizant. (2012). *The business case for test environment management services*.

Cohn, M. (2009). *The forgotten layer of the test automation pyramid*. Retrieved 2017 from Mountain Goat Software: http://www.mountaingoatsoftware.com/blog/the-forgotten-layer-of-the-test-automation-pyramid

© The Author(s), under exclusive license to Springer Nature Switzerland AG 2021
M. Baumgartner et al., *Agile Testing*, https://doi.org/10.1007/978-3-030-73209-7

Cook, D. (2008, Mai 19). *Lost garden: Improving bug triage with user pain*. Retrieved 2017 from http://www.lostgarden.com/2008/05/improving-bug-triage-with-user-pain.html

Crispin, L., & Gregory, J. (2009). *Agile testing–a practical guide for testers and agile Teams*. Amsterdam: Addison-Wesley-Longman.

Crosby, P. B. (1980). *Quality is free: the art of making quality certain*.

CruiseControl. (2017). *Cruisecontrol*. Retrieved 2017 from Cruisecontrol: http://cruisecontrol. sourceforge.net/overview.html

Cucumber Ltd. (2017). *cucumber*. Retrieved 2017 from https://cucumber.io/

SmartBear Software. (2021). *Test management. For any size team*. Retrieved 2021 from https:// smartbear.com/test-management/zephyr/

DeGrace, P., & Stahl, L. H. (1990). *Wicked problems, righteous solutions: A catolog of modern engineering paradigms*. Prentice Hall.

DeMarco, T. (2009, Juli–August). Software engineering: An idea whose time has come and gone? *IEEE Software*.

DeMarco, T., & Lister, T. (1999). *Wien wartet auf Dich!* München: Carl Hanser Verlag.

Deming, W. E. (1982). *Out of the Crisis*. MIT Press.

Derby, E., & Larsen, D. (2006). *Agile retrospectives*. Raleigh, North Carolina, USA: The Pragmatic Programmers.

DIN 66270:1998-01. (1998). *Informationstechnik–Bewerten von Softwaredokumenten– Qualitätsmerkmale*.

Duvall, P., Glover, A., & Matyas, S. (2007). *Continuous integration–improving software quality and reducing risk*. Addison-Wesley.

Eckstein, J. (2011). *Agile Softwareentwicklung in großen Projekten*. Heidelberg: dpunkt.verlag GmbH.

Epping, T. (2011). *Kanban für die Softwareentwicklung*. Deutschland: Springer Verlag.

Evans, M. W. (1984). *Productive software test management*. Wiley.

FitNesse. (2021). *The fully integrated standalone wiki and acceptance testing framework*. Retrieved 2017 from FitNesse: http://www.fitnesse.org/

Forrester Research, Inc. (2012, Oktober 23). *The forrester wave™: Application life-cycle management, Q4 2012*. Forrester Research, Inc.

Fowler, M. (2000). *The new methodology*. Retrieved 2017 from https://www.martinfowler.com/ articles/newMethodology.html

Fowler, M., Beck, K., Brant, J., Opdyke, W., & Roberts, D. (2012). *Refactoring: Improving the design of existing code*. Addison-Wesley.

Gartner Inc. (2017). *Magic quadrant for enterprise agile planning tools*. Stamford: Gartner Inc..

Gärtner, M. (2012). *ATDD by example: A practical guide to acceptance test-driven development*. Addison-Wesley.

Gloger, B. (2013). *Scrum: Produkte zuverlässig und schnell entwickeln*. Carl Hanser Verlag.

Gloger, B. (2015). *Von Scrum 1.0 zu Scrum 3.0*. Retrieved 2017 from https://blog.borisgloger.com/ 2015/06/08/von-scrum-1-0-zu-scrum-3-0/

Gloger, B., & Häusling, A. (2011). *Erfolgreich mit Scrum–Einflussfaktor Personalmanagement– Finden und Binden von Mitarbeitern in agilen Unternehmen*. München-Wien: Hanser Verlag.

Golze, A. (2008, February). Zielgenau Testen: Die Testphase an den Geschäftsvorgaben ausrichten. *Objektspektrum*.

Graham, I. (1995). *Migrating to object technology*. Lebanon, Indiana, USA: Addison-Wesley.

Haberl, P., Spillner, A., Vosseberg, K., & Winter, M. (2011). *Softwaretest in der Praxis–Umfrage 2011*. Heidelberg: dpunkt.verlag GmbH. Abgerufen am 2017 von http://www.softwaretest- umfrage.de/2011/

Hellerer, H. (2013). *Soft Skills für Softwaretester und Testmanager*. Heidelberg: dpunkt.verlag GmbH.

Hendrickson, E. (2008). *Driving development with tests: ATDD and TDD*. Retrieved 2017 from http://testobsessed.com/wp-content/uploads/2011/04/atddexample.pdf

Herrmann, A., Knauss, E., & Weißbach, R. (2013). *Requirements Engineering und Projektmanagement.* Berlin Heidelberg: Springer-Verlag.

Hetzel, B. (1988). *The complete guide to software testing.* Wellesley, MA: ED Information Sciences.

Highsmith, J. (2004). *Agile project management. (I. Pearson Education, Ed.).* Boston: Addison-Wesley.

Hoffmann, D. W. (2013). *Software-Qualität* (2nd ed.). Berlin Heidelberg: Springer-Verlag Berlin Heidelberg.

Höhn, R., & Höppner, S. (2008). *Das V-Modell XT. Anwendungen, Werkzeuge, Standards.* Berlin: Springer Verlag.

Hummel, O. (2011). *Aufwandsschätzung in der Software- und Systementwicklung kompakt.* Heidelberg: Spektrum Akademischer Verlag.

IEEE Std 610.12-1990. (1990). *IEEE standard glossary of software engineering.* The Institute of Electrical and Electronics Engineers, Inc..

IEEE Std 829-2008. (2008). *IEEE standard for software and system test documentation.* New York, NY 10017-2394, USA: The Institute of Electrical and Electronics Engineers, Inc.

International Consortium for Agile (ICAgile). (2018). *ICAgile.* Retrieved 2017 from International Consortium for Agile (ICAgile): https://www.icagile.com/

International Software Quality Institute GmbH. (2018). *iSQI agile teaming.* Retrieved 2021 from https://isqi.org/en/62-practitioner-in-agile-quality-paq.html

ISO 9000. (2005). *Quality management systems—Fundamentals and vocabulary.* Genf: International Standards Organization.

ISO/IEC 25000. (2005). *Software engineering–software product quality requirements and evaluation (SQuaRE).*

ISTQB–International Software Testing Qualifications Board. (2012a). *Certified tester advanced level syllabus.* ISTQB.

ISTQB–International Software Testing Qualifications Board. (2012b). *Certified tester advanced level syllabus–test manager.*

ISTQB–International Software Testing Qualifications Board. (2018). *Certified tester foundation level syllabus.* Retrieved from ISTQB: https://www.istqb.org/downloads/syllabi/foundation-level-syllabus.html

ISTQB–International Software Testing Qualifications Board. (2020). *The ISTQB® Standard Glossary of Terms Used in Software Testing Version 3.5.* Retrieved 2020 from https://www.istqb.org/downloads/glossary.html

Jacobson, I. (1992). *Object-oriented software engineering: A use case driven approach.* Lebanon, Indiana, U.S.A.: Addison-Wesley.

Janzen, D., & Kaufmann, R. (2005). *Implications of test-driven development a pilot study.*

Kaner, C., Bach, J., & Pettichord, B. (2002). *Lessons learned in software testing.* New York: Wiley.

Kawaguchi, K., Bayer, A., & Croy, R. T. (2017). *Meet Jenkins.* Retrieved 2017 from https://wiki.jenkins-ci.org/display/JENKINS/Meet+Jenkins

Klonk, M. (2013). *Austrian testing board / Expertentreff.* https://www.austriantestingboard.at/

Kruse, D., Lorbeer, F., Mangner, T., & Volk, N. (2016). *Sind wir wirklich nur Testmanagerinnen?* Retrieved 2017 from https://dev.otto.de/2016/06/08/sind-wir-wirklich-nur-testmanagerinnen/

Kruse, E. (2011). *Testdatenmanagement–Aufgaben im Testprozess.* (G. S. mbH, Ed.) Oberusel.

LeSS, C. (2017). *LESS–Large Scale Scrum.* Retrieved 2021 from https://less.works/

Lindsay, J. (2003). *Adventures in session-based testing.*

Linz, T. (2013). Stubs, Mocks und Dummies. In T. Linz, *Testen in Scrum-Projekten* (pp. 76–78). Heidelberg: dpunkt.verlag.

Mainusch, J. (2012, September). Agiles Management–ein Widerspruch in sich? *Objektspektrum.*

Marick, B. (2003, August 21). *Exploration throug examples (Blog).* Retrieved 2017 from http://www.exampler.com/old-blog/2003/08/21/

Martin, B. (2002). *Agile software development–principles, patterns and practices.* Englewood Cliffs, N.J: Prentice-Hall.

Mayr, H. (2005). *Projekt Engineering: Ingenieurmäßige Softwareentwicklung in Projektgruppen* (2. ed). Carl Hanser Verlag GmbH & CO. KG.

Menzies, T., & Cukic, B. (2000, September). When to test less. *IEEE Software*, p. 107.

Meyer, B. (1997). *Object-oriented software construction (2nd Edition)*. Prentice Hall.

Microfocus. (2020). *UFT overview*. Retrieved 2021 from https://www.microfocus.com/en-us/products/uft-one/overview

Microsoft. (2017). *Visual studio team services*. Retrieved 2021 from https://visualstudio.microsoft.com/

Nicklisch, G., Borchers, J., Krick, R., & Rucks, R. (2008). *IT-Near- und -Offshoring in der Praxis*. Heidelberg: dpunkt.verlag.

North, D. (2007, February 11). *What's in a story? | Dan north & associates*. Retrieved 2017 from http://dannorth.net/whats-in-a-story/

Oestereich, B., & Weiss, C. (2007). *APM–Agiles Projektmanagement*. dpunkt.verlag.

Pichler, R. (2007). *Scrum–Agiles Projektmanagement erfolgreich einsetzen*. dpunkt.verlag.

Pichler, R., Roock, S., & Havenstein, A. (2011). *Agile Entwicklungspraktiken mit Scrum*. dpunkt Verlag.

Poppendieck, M., & Poppendieck, T. (2003). *Lean software development: An agile toolkit*. Boston: Addison-Wesley Professional.

Poppendieck, M., & Poppendieck, T. (2006). *Implementing lean software development*. Reading, MA: Addison-Wesely.

Rausch, A., & Broy, M. (2006). *Das V-Modell XT: Grundlagen, Erfahrungen und Werkzeuge*. Dpunkt Verlag.

Rothermel, G., Untch, R. H., Chu, C., & Harrold, M. J. (1999). Test case priorization: An empirical study. *Proceedings of the International Conference on Software Maintenance, 1999 (ICSM '99)*, pp. 179-188.

Rumbaugh, J., Blaha, M., Premerlani, W., Eddy, F., & Lorensen, W. (1991). *Object-oriented modeling and design*. Prentice Hall.

Rüssel, F. (2012, August). *Studien: Erfolg agiler Methoden (agile success rate)*. Retrieved 2017 from http://www.agilerescue.de/agile-success-rate/

Scaled Agile, Inc. (2017). *Scaled agile framework*. Retrieved 2017 from http://www.scaledagileframework.com/

Schatten, A., Demolsky, M., Winkler, D., Biffl, S., Gostischa-Franta, E., & Östreicher, T. (2010). *Best practice software-engineering*. Heidelberg: Spektrum Akademischer Verlag Heidelberg.

Schwaber, K. (2007). *Agiles Projektmanagement mit Scrum*. Microsoft Press.

Selenium. (2021). *SeleniumHQ browser automation*. Retrieved 2017 from http://www.seleniumhq.org/

Siemens Product Lifecycle Management Software Inc. (2017). *Polarion® application lifecycle management solutions overview*. Retrieved 2017 from https://polarion.plm.automation.siemens.com/products/overview

SLIM. (2017). *The SLIM test system*. Retrieved July 2017, from FitNesse: http://www.fitnesse.org/FitNesse.UserGuide.WritingAcceptanceTests.SliM

SmartBear, S. (2017). *SoapUI open source*. Retrieved 2017 from https://www.soapui.org/opensource.html

Sneed, H. M. (1976). Planung, Organsation und Steuerung der Software-Herstellung und – Wartung. In *Jahrbuch der EDV*. Stuttgart: Forkel Verlag.

Sneed, H. M. (1983). *Software-Qualitätssicherung*. Köln: Rudolf-Müller Verlag.

Sneed, H., Baumgartner, M., & Seidl, R. (2012). *Der Systemtest, 3. Auflage*. München: Hanser.

Software Quality Systems AG (SQS). (2012). *Early error detection by test case specification*.

Spillner, A., & Linz, T. (2019). *Basiswissen Softwaretest*. Heidelberg: dpunkt.verlag.

Standish Group. (2013). *CHAOS report*. Retrieved 2021 from http://blog.standishgroup.com

Sterling, C. (2010). *Managing software debt: building for inevitable change*. Addison-Wesley Professional.

Sutherland, J. (2012). *The scum papers: Nut, bolts, and origins of an agile framework.* (I. Scrum, Ed.) Cambridge.

SwissQ Consulting AG. (2017). *Software Development 2017–Trends & Benchmarks Report Schweiz.* Zürich.

Takeuchi, H., & Nonaka, I. (1986, January–February). The new product development game. *Harvard Business Review.*

The Apache Software Foundation. (2017). *Apache maven project–introduction to the build lifecycle.* Retrieved 2017 from http://maven.apache.org/guides/introduction/introduction-to-the-lifecycle.html

The Bug Genie. (2013). *The bug genie–friendly issue tracking.* Retrieved 2017 from http://www.thebuggenie.com/

TRICENTIS Technology & Consulting GmbH. (2017a). *Next-gen automated continuous testing.* Retrieved 2021 from https://www.tricentis.com/products/automate-continuous-testing-tosca/

TRICENTIS Technology & Consulting GmbH. (2017b). *Risk coverage optimization for software testing.* Retrieved 2017 from https://www.tricentis.com/tricentis-tosca-testsuite/risk-coverage-optimization/

Tuckman, B. W. (1965). Developmental sequence in small groups. *Psychological Bulletin,* 384–399.

VersionOne Inc. (2017). *11th annual state of agile report.*

Vosseberg, K., Spillner, A., & Winter, M. (2016). *Softwaretest in der Praxis–Umfrage 2016.* Heidelberg: dpunkt.verlag.

Wallmüller, E. (2004). *Risikomanagement für IT- und Software-Projekte.* München: Hanser Verlag.

West, D., & Hammond, J. S. (2010, Mai 5). The forrester wave™: Agile development management tools.

Westphal, R., & Lieser, S. (2013). *Clean code developer.* Retrieved 2017 from http://www.clean-code-developer.de

Whalen, D. (2008, January 11). *Software triage–managing software defects.* Retrieved 2021 from https://www.stickyminds.com/article/software-triage

Whittaker, J. A. (2003). *How to break software: A practical guide to testing.* New Saddle River, NJ: Addison Wesley.

Whittaker, J. A. (2009). *Exploratory software testing.* Pearson Education.

Wikimedia Foundation Inc. (2021, May 14). *Wikipedia–Triage.* Retrieved 2021 from https://en.wikipedia.org/wiki/Triage

Winter, M. (2009). *NoRiskNoFun.* Köln: *NoRiskNoTest.* Presentation.

Index

Printed in the United States
by Baker & Taylor Publisher Services